ESSAYING
BIOGRAPHY

ESSAYING BIOGRAPHY

A Celebration for Leon Edel

EDITED BY
Gloria G. Fromm

A Biography Monograph
Published for the Biographical Research Center by
University of Hawaii Press
General Editor: George Simson

Library of Congress Cataloging in Publication Data

Essaying biography.

(A Biography monograph)

Bibliography: p.
Includes index.
1. Biography (as a literary form) 2. Edel,
Leon, 1907– . I. Fromm, Gloria G., 1931– .
II. Edel, Leon, 1907– . III. Series.
CT21.E79 1986   808'.06692   86-19280
ISBN 0-8248-1035-X (pbk.)

CONTENTS

I. PREFACES

II. FORMULATIONS

III. AMERICANA

IV. EXEMPLA

V. OPERA VITAE

I
PREFACES

EDITOR'S FOREWORD

THIS book celebrates a major literary form and a master practitioner. Reflecting Leon Edel's achievement over more than half a century, it bears witness to the range of his biographical writings and to the span of his influence on contemporary letters. Indeed, few modern biographers can match his versatility; none has worked so tirelessly to refine the image of twentieth-century literary biography, or argued so eloquently and humanely for the truth of art as well as of scholarship.

Some years ago, in an essay-dialogue, "The Poetics of Biography," Leon Edel described "the recreation in words of a life [as] one of the most beautiful and most difficult tasks a literary artist can set himself." He has taken on this challenge, time and again, with his own "new biography," which "accepts the idea that there is a providence in every word a poet chooses, but also knows it cannot always discover that providence." As paradigms he offers on the one hand the large-scale magisterial life of Henry James, on the other the canny essay-portrait of Thoreau, and as a model of the art of narrative synthesis the more recent group-portrait of Bloomsbury.

Most recently, after bringing together his essays on literary psychology in *Stuff of Sleep and Dreams,* he has set forth anew, in *Writing Lives,* the principles of literary biography that have governed all his work in the genre. And he has called once again for a criticism worthy of the biographer's art, one that recognizes the inseparability of biography and criticism. Certain that a critic is not only involved "in his own process . . . but in a biographical process as well," conscious as biographers have rarely been of both ends and means, Leon Edel has already secured a place for himself in literary history. This book, dedicated to him and providing a chronological list of his published writings since 1929, seeks to demonstrate more than anything else the elasticity of the Edelian model of biography, one of whose chief requirements—the fitting of form to subject—has been met, it is hoped, by all the essays included here, from Sir Rupert Hart-Davis's "open letter" to Gavan Daws's excursion "beyond the laboratory brain."

The prefaces, including one by Leon Edel himself, are followed by three essays which attempt formulations: Adeline Tintner's study of the James biography both as text and as source material for the critic; Muriel Shine's exploration of James's own work for educational theory; and Harvena Richter's investigation of Virginia Woolf's biographical premises and practices. The next group of essays illustrates certain aspects of American biography: Gay Wilson Allen sums up the issues involved in the writing of his life of Emerson and John Tytell provides the background for his biographical study of the Beat Generation, while Viola Hopkins Winner examines the letters of Henry Adams as a special kind of biographical problem. In the final group are three examples of the biographical essay, one of Leon Edel's favorite modes: Jean Strouse's "partial portrait" of a tantalizingly obscure member of the James family; and two reconstructions: my own of the extraordinary life of a healer and Gavan Daws's of a remarkable episode in Hawaii.

All the authors represented here (as well as two financial supporters who wish to remain anonymous) are Leon Edel's former students, colleagues, and fellow biographers—celebrants together of his ripe years and mindful, every one, of the Jamesian epigraph he chose for *The Master*: "Art *makes* life, makes interest, makes importance."

GLORIA G. FROMM
North Barrington, Illinois

AN OPEN LETTER FROM AN OLD ADMIRER

Sir Rupert Hart-Davis

Dearest Leon

Fearing that your *Festschrift* might be overweighted by "the new biography," I rashly volunteered to contribute an irreverent scrap of old biography, yours and mine.

When I started my own publishing business in 1946, I wrote to Theodora Bosanquet, who had been Henry James's secretary, to ask whether I might reprint (if possible in an expanded form) her excellent pamphlet *Henry James at Work,* which had been published by Leonard and Virginia Woolf in 1924. She pleaded her age, her busyness, her disinclination to tinker with something written so long ago, and advised me instead to get in touch with a brilliant young American who had published a thesis in French on Henry James's "dramatic years."

Clutching at this straw I dispatched a letter to Lt. J. L. Edel 02026430, Information Control Div., H.Q. U.S.F.E.T., A.P.O 757, c/o U.S. Army, little guessing that this would lead to one of the most rewarding and delightful friendships of my life.

Needless to say no immediate answer arrived, but in a couple of months I received a cordial letter from 58 West 83rd Street, New York, and thus began a correspondence that still flourishes after forty years. Its first fruits were my publication of *The Other House,* with your introduction, in 1948, your edition of *The Complete Plays of Henry James* in 1949, and a stream of similar volumes, culminating in the five volumes of your great biography of the Master.

Do you remember the fun we had planning the twelve volumes of *The Complete Tales?* My schoolboy son Adam, who was good at maths, counted the words, which came to two million, and the tales had to be divided, chronologically, into twelve parts, each of roughly the same length. We tried two different ways of deciding what was a tale and what a novel: first a maximum length of, I think, 15 thousand words; secondly anything that had been originally published by itself in one volume (such as *In the Cage*) counted as a novel. To our delight both systems produced the same result.

Meanwhile came our meeting, on my first postwar visit to New York in January 1950. You invited me to an excellent French restaurant, where we had a first-rate lunch, and delightedly discovered that we were almost exactly the same age (but never forget that I am twelve days your senior), and on the same wavelength concerning Henry James and other literary matters.

On another day you gave me lunch at your miniscule apartment at 309 East 23rd Street, within rifle-shot of the huge headquarters of the United Nations, whose endless discussions you were faithfully reporting in the ill-fated evening paper *PM*. Your apartment was indeed one of the smallest I have ever seen: the sort in which you can't stand up in the bathroom without taking the key out of the door.

Your friendship transformed my visit from a chore into a pleasure, and you repeated your benefactions on all my subsequent visits, entertaining me first at 150-67 Village Road, Jamaica, then at your fine apartment at 336 Central Park West, and finally in the splendors of the Century Club, where you gave a men's dinner party in my honour.

When you began to come to London you sometimes stayed with me in the flat above my office in Soho Square, and we went out and about together. In particular I remember our running into Tommy Lascelles and Siegfried Sassoon watching a cricket match on the roof of the pavilion at Lord's, and a party at Rosamond Lehmann's in Eaton Square, where you scored a left and right with T. S. Eliot and the American Ambassador.

Sometimes you spent a weekend with me and my family at Bromsden Farm, near Henley-on-Thames. At the end of one such visit we had our Most Terrible Day. Nowadays you are an intrepid air traveller, quick as the light from Pole to Pole, but in those days you were as terrified of flying as I still am. After breakfast I drove you to Heathrow to catch a plane to New York, only to learn that the flight was delayed for some five hours. Naturally, this increased your apprehension.

I suggested that we should visit my son Adam at Eton, and on arrival at the boys' entrance to his house we were met by an insensible boy (happily not mine) being carried out on a stretcher. You were continually anxious to discover the latest departure time of your flight, and we several times had to replenish our stock of pennies for the telephone.

After a good lunch at Monkey Island in the Thames we toured the secondhand bookshops of Eton and Windsor, each buying a few books. When yet another telephone call brought the news that your flight was still further postponed, you couldn't bear it any longer and begged me to take you back to Heathrow, where I left you apprehensively waiting. It's funny that, while details of our many happy times together are blurred together in memory, everything about that disastrous day is still with me.

Then came your translation from journalist into teacher, editor, biographer, bibliographer, man of letters, and as your fame steadily grew I was proud and happy to be your publisher and your friend.

Now you are a happy Professor Emeritus, laden with honours, basking in the sunshine of Honolulu with your dear Marjorie beside you, and I am a happy recluse in North Yorkshire with my beloved June. Across the miles and the years I greet you on this happy occasion with love, admiration, and gratitude.

Ever your devoted

RUPERT

LEONARD WOOLF AND
THE WISE VIRGINS

Leon Edel

Introduction

Howard Fertig

Written by Leon Edel in 1978 to accompany an edition of Leonard Woolf's novel, *The Wise Virgins,* planned by Howard Fertig, Inc., this introduction appears in print here for the first time—the projected edition having been put aside at the last moment.

As had happened many times before over the years, Leon had mentioned the novel, among several other titles, in the course of a conversation as one that had, curiously, disappeared from sight and yet for one reason or another seemed clearly to warrant publication.

A former student of Leon Edel's, later an editor and then a publisher, I had come to look forward to those talks (and, no question about it, I suppose, to take advantage of them). From one or another of these had come, years before, the first American edition of Henry James's *French Poets and Novelists,* and more recently, a facsimile of the manuscript of *The Europeans,* and the idea for a new edition of *The Outcry,* James's last published novel, long out of print. For all of these Leon had generously written introductions.

Now, I decided that I wanted to do *The Wise Virgins.* There had never been an American edition, and no English edition since the initial publication in 1914. As established in correspondence with the Copyright Office, *The Wise Virgins* had never been copyrighted in the United States; it seemed that no one else had wanted to do the book or was planning to do it now. We proceeded therefore directly to preparing a new edition: Leon Edel to write the introduction and I to locate one of the few existing copies in the United States, to be used for photographing the text.

Some time later, however, I learned that a new English edition was, after all, in the works; had been, coincidentally, proceeding parallel to our own efforts and moreover was already planned for joint publication with an American publisher. Though all parties were equally free to proceed given the copyright situation, the idea of such a crowded field was unattractive at best, but more to the point it seemed, on thinking about it, a matter of simple courtesy to step back, for the English firm had long been associated with Leonard Woolf's own publishing house, Hogarth Press, and with Woolf himself. Given this situation I decided against continuing work on our own edition and Leon Edel, when I discussed it with him, understood, and agreed.

LEONARD WOOLF AND
THE WISE VIRGINS

LEON EDEL

LEONARD WOOLF wrote *The Wise Virgins* when he was thirty. He had recently returned to England after spending seven years as a colonial administrator in Ceylon where he had gone, precociously, at twenty-four. It had been a hard return—to his mother's house in Putney with its old associations. In Ceylon he had lived in a large official residence (at Hambantota) and in effect ruled over a hundred thousand natives in an area of a thousand square miles. He would speak in his old age of the unending jungle, the great lagoons, the enormous sea pounding on the shore below his bungalow, the large open windowless rooms. The contrast was almost frightening. "I felt the walls of the Putney dining-room pressing upon me, the low ceiling pressing down on me, the past twenty years closing in on me." (He meant the twenty years that preceded his exile.) In a word he felt trapped. One couldn't go home again. During the ensuing months he took three important steps. Falling in love with Virginia Stephen, daughter of the eminent Victorian Sir Leslie Stephen, he resigned from the colonial service; after a strenuous wooing, he married her; and during the courtship he wrote a significant novel. He began another during the honeymoon.

The novel written during the courtship has become a classic. It is called *The Village in the Jungle,* and Asians speak of it as the most "knowing" work written about them. In it Woolf depicted the battle for survival of earlier societies seeking to wrest a bit of arable land from the periphery of jungles. He caught the tragic destiny of a village-farmer caste—its will-to-life in spite of endless defeat. The novel was a kind of parable of man's universal condition, a splendid "existential" statement. The second novel begun during his honeymoon, when he was with Virginia in Spain, was less universal, indeed highly personal. Leonard Woolf's bride has recorded the moment he began it. He was sitting on a red plush chair in their room a few feet from her and she wrote (in a letter to a friend) he was working on "the first chapter of his great new work, which is to be about the suburbs." Suburbs, of course, are created on the periphery of urban jungles; but Leonard Woolf's *The Wise Virgins* was a drama not of struggle for survival but of struggle into awareness. His suburb resembled Putney and the novel told of an unfinished young Jew like himself who seeks to escape from his middle-class horizons and to marry a woman like Virginia Stephen. Instead he is more or less entrapped by a romantic suburban girl; when their brief affair becomes known he does the respectable and noble thing—marries into the kind of claustrophobic life from which he himself escaped. The "wise virgins" of the story are this girl, who may have actually existed in Putney, Virginia Stephen, whom he names Camilla, and turns into a painter instead of a writer, and her sister Vanessa, named Katharine, who was really a painter.

The Wise Virgins was published by Edward Arnold in October 1914, a moment in history when light novels had little chance of survival. "The war killed it dead," Leonard Woolf said many years later. One suspects he shed no tears over its corpse. In later years he destroyed copies of the book if he encountered them. There were very few extant in any case. The printing had been small. Today they exist only in a few libraries and hardly ever turn up in antiquarian bookshops. Woolf had good reasons for his attempts to push this novel out of sight. It was an indiscretion of his early maturity. He had exhibited too much impatience with his Bloomsbury friends; he had not disguised Virginia's emotional difficulties; he had satirized his brother-in-law, Clive Bell; and in general had shown himself highly irritable—as Quentin Bell remarks—with "a certain amount of brittle talk" in Bloomsbury. The Bloomsbury we know had come into being while he was away—social gatherings of a group of friends who lived in that part of London. Leonard was a belated initiate; and to find himself in the drawing-room of Gordon Square, where a certain kind of civilized sophistication and superior tone existed, infused with art-world talk, distinctly rubbed the newly arrived man from the colonies the wrong way. He had been concerned with matters of life and death in Ceylon, and here sat these people talking of "the Good," "the

Beautiful," and a merry-go-round of copulations and personal relations. "You talk and you talk and you talk," exclaims Harry
Davis, the young unformed hero of *The Wise Virgins*—"no blood
in you! You never *do* anything!" Bloomsbury of course did a great
deal, but the friends were not "activists" in Leonard's sense.

It would take time to divest himself of his imperative need to sit
in judgment; to appraise; to want to change people and the world
into the kind of ordered government he had created around him
in Ceylon. He had acquired the habit of trusting his self-searched
logic; he had had to know always among the Sinhalese that he was
right. And if Clive Bell sometimes said silly things, and was a bit
raucous, and discovered things obvious to Leonard, as if they had
just come into existence, then he could be described as "a fat round
little body" and he must have "a little round fat mind." The truth
at all costs, Leonard believed then (he would always be impatient
with the fibs of civilization), and he apparently gave little thought
to being charitable. And then Leonard was touchy: he was Bloomsbury's only Jew. He had left his tribe and married a Gentile. In later
years, the question of his Jewish roots would take its proper place
in his life, but at the moment of his writing *The Wise Virgins* he
still possessed the *Weltanschauung* of his "caste." And he put it in
his novel, "One can't be born again; once and for all one has one's
father and mother in one, in every cell of one's body, so they say. I
am a good Jew; I obey the fifth commandment, and honour my
father and my mother—at any rate in myself."

It may be seen from this that *The Wise Virgins* was an attempt to
put to rights certain disturbed emotions within Leonard Woolf.
The subtitle he gave to his novel described it more accurately than
its title: "A Story of Words, Opinions and a Few Emotions."

There is good reason for reprinting *The Wise Virgins* which has
been hidden from us for the past sixty-five years. The new interest
in Bloomsbury and the abundant documentation we now have
about its personalities provide an interlinear for Woolf's obsolete
work and give it the status of a document—outside its modest literary values. We observe nascent Bloomsbury through the eyes of
a newcomer to its meetings and parties. We also discern Leonard
Woolf's problems and are made to understand that he did not step
into that charmed circle with ease; that he possessed a certain
amount of residual guilt at marrying outside his tribe; and that he
had—though one feels he was concealing this from himself—misgivings during his honeymoon about his marriage to Virginia,

whom he loved passionately; she was proving not only "cold," but showing signs of mental instability.

There is always, in any novel, a hidden center of personal fantasy which belongs to the author and is distributed among his characters: it resides in the choices, the patterns, the solutions the author finds for the drama he projects. We may therefore ask legitimately why Woolf, seeking to spin a drawing-room comedy and a lighthearted piece of fiction "about the suburbs" chose to give us the disagreeable young Harry Davis involved with his Gentile girl in suburbia at the same time that he is in love with the dazzling young woman from the world of art to which he aspires. In life, this problem has been settled for Woolf; yet he lives it over in the novel and provides a solution which is the opposite of what happened. We might say he simply wrote the story because it seemed to him to have dramatic meaning: but we still ask ourselves the psychological question: why entrap his hero, when escape is open to him? What this suggests is that Woolf remained troubled: and indeed the greatest intensities in his story are to be found in the young man's assertion of his Jewishness and his sense of entrapment. The confined feeling Woolf had had in Putney after Ceylon seems to have been present to him in a new form—in Virginia Woolf's "distance" from him physically, and her mental condition which ultimately made him her doctor, nurse, guardian—and surrogate parent. The question of "race" is strongly insisted upon in relation to the Clive character (renamed Arthur Woodhouse) and the Strachey character (named "Lion" Wilton—it almost sounds like Lytton). And then we are given also his deep feelings for the goddesslike Vanessa, whom Leonard Woolf had originally loved, but who had married Clive while he was abroad. Put in clearest terms the two unresolved problems in his own life which are transferred into *The Wise Virgins* are the question of "caste" and the claustrophobia of entrapment.

His relation to Virginia is brought out in discussions between the suburban Jew and the Clive character. Clive Bell had had a prolonged flirtation with his sister-in-law and he found that she was always virginal. "They simply don't know what desire is. What they want is to be desired;" an accurate description—as Spater and Parsons have shown us in their history of the Woolf marriage—of Virginia Woolf's feelings. Camilla-Virginia is described as having "a mind, an imagination; they intoxicate me." But in her need to be desired, she is also described as wanting something else as well. Her future feminism is adumbrated. "What she really wants, although she doesn't know it, is to be a man; and—damn,

damn, damn—she never will be." Then, as during their wooing, Camilla-Virginia tells the young Harry Davis "I can't give myself; passion leaves me cold." One wonders whether Leonard's wife, reading this, accepted it as simply the truth, for it is a record of things said between them during courtship. At any rate, she gracefully rewrote the story in her novel *Night and Day* a few years later, keeping for her sister Vanessa the name Leonard Woolf had given her, Katharine.

If in our interlinear we read the misgivings Woolf had about his marriage, and the writing out of his need to find answers, we require no gloss to the "Jewish question," as it affected him. He had been fortunate during his college days—amid the tensions and shock of the Dreyfus *affaire*—to have been little exposed to the kind of antisemitism that prevailed in other parts of the world. In general, among the upper-class intellectuals who were Woolf's friends, his being of Jewish descent mattered not at all. Virginia Woolf, however, during their engagement, had made something of their differences. She had never known any Jews in her sheltered Kensington, save as they appeared in Shakespeare, Marlowe, Dickens. When she announced to her friends she was going to marry "a penniless Jew" from Putney, she was saying nothing more than she might have said if she were marrying some "wild" Irishman from Dublin. To find herself in love with a Jew, and about to be married to him, caused her to speak in ways that sounded snobbish and, to some, condescending. But there was no suggestion of bigotry. She had after all, like Portia, chosen Leonard Woolf out of a field of suitors. One can understand that to some it did sound—and still does—as if she were speaking *de haut en bas,* even though it was a fact that Leonard was a Jew, that he was penniless, and that he came from Putney. Woolf, however, was just as conscious of these differences, and of the step he was taking. The passages in the novel in which Harry Davis explains himself as Jew contain considerable vehemence: "We aren't as pleasant or as beautiful as you are. We're hard and grasping, we're out after definite things, different things, which we think worth while. We don't drift, we watch and wait, wait and watch."

Camilla-Virginia replies that it is this desire for things that are "worth while" that makes him "different" and also appealing to her. His response is a piece of dramatic declamation:

> That's because I'm a Jew. Oh yes, you see what I mean, of course.
> We wait hunched up, always ready and alert, for the moment to

spring on what is worth while, then we let ourselves go. You don't like it? I see you don't; it makes you shrink from me—us, I mean. It isn't pleasant; it's hard, unbeautiful. There isn't sensibility, they call it, in us. We want to *get,* to feel our hands upon, what's worth while. Is it worth while? Is it worth *getting?* That's the first and only question to buzz in our brains.

Camilla-Virginia then wants to know exactly what *is* worthwhile. The young Jew continues his declamation:

Money, money, of course. That's the first article of our creed— money, and out of money, power. That's elementary. Then knowledge, intelligence, taste. We're always pouncing on them because they give power, power to *do* things, influence people. That's what really we want, to feel ourselves working on people in any way, it doesn't matter. It's a sort of artistic feeling, a desire to create. To feel people moving under your hands or your brain, just as you want them to move! Admiration, appreciation, those are the outward signs.

Other Jews, reading these lines in 1914—or even today—might differ strongly. They might argue that not all Jews are money-hungry or power-hungry. Whole segments of the Jewish population, in many countries, were (when not confined to ghettos) simply middle class; artisans or tailors or professionals, in quest of an honest living and quite prepared to live-and-let-live. And when given a chance they also could be good farmers, as the Israelis have shown. The apostrophes of Leonard Woolf's hero are in reality describing not Leonard's Jewishness, but his recent taste of power in Ceylon. He had learned—it had been a heady experience—how to "work on people."

We judge that Leonard Woolf's autobiographical reflections within this novel derive from his life-dilemma at thirty. Spater and Parsons are of the opinion that what Woolf pondered was "not the difference between Reformed Jew and Agnostic Christian, but that between the professional middle class and the cultured upper class intellectual." The substance of *The Wise Virgins* suggests that behind the class distinctions, and intermingled with them, there lingered inevitably questions of "race." This can be supported by Leonard Woolf's allusions to interracial marriage in a later tale called "Three Jews." It was published in *Two Stories* "written and printed by Virginia Woolf and L. S. Woolf" as companion piece to Virginia's "The Mark on the Wall," first publication of their newly founded Hogarth Press in 1917. The story of the "Three Jews" describes the shame of a Jewish father whose son has married a Gentile servant girl. The father considers this a disgrace and says "our women are as good, better, than Christian women." Leonard Woolf has said as much in *The Wise Virgins*. "Your women are cold and leave one cold—no dark hair, no blood in them. Pale hair, pale souls, you know." There is no doubt that Woolf, a man of powerful and powerfully controlled passions, worshipping Virginia Stephen's ethereal "purity," found her at times "pale"—that is, "cold."

In sum, we may regard this well-shaped but trivial novel (it seems frivolous beside *The Village in the Jungle*) as representing the fever-chart of Leonard Woolf, the repatriated Jew, at the time of his marriage. It had been a crucial step, and it left its problems. What emerged was an ill-shaped fictional version of his doubts and misgivings, his self-assertion and his undersurface struggle, un-pleasing to his friends who knew his iron strength and will and hu-manity. "A most unpleasant young man," remarked the *Times* re-viewer. Woolf, caught up in his deep and abiding love for Virginia, seems to be saying between the lines that he would have to pay a price for this kind of love. How he resolved his problems and sur-mounted them, the world knows. He made of his marriage a shel-ter for Virginia Woolf's creativity; he gave her a large measure of devotion; and within the shelter she had the security to exercise her art, that is her literary genius. *The Wise Virgins'* claim upon us now, as document, is clear. Its claim to literature is less certain. E. M. Forster called it "a remarkable book" although he was quick to say also that it was "very bad in parts, first rate in others." The writing is terse and lucid; there is considerable wit, and the story has its appeal in spite of its hackneyed frame of the virgin, the in-different suburban lover, the lost virginity, and the forced mar-riage. The deflowering of the conventional young girl who is a "foolish" virgin emphasizes the irony of the book's title, the jux-taposition of Bloomsbury and Putney. The book belongs, if we want to find the right shelf for it, among those English fictions which are called *romans à clef*—novels in which real life is scarcely dissimulated and in which we recognize the fictional creatures as disguises for those we have known in life or can recognize from history.

Half a century after the novel came out, the old Leonard Woolf— of the haunting eyes and the lined face, and the same high moral integrity—wrote in his autobiography that "nearly all Jews are

both proud and ashamed of being Jews." The turbulent feeling of
his early quest for selfhood belonged to the past. He described the
ambivalences and bitternesses in the many loyalties a Jew forms.
"The attitude of a person to the institutions, collectivities, groups,
herds, or packs with which he is or has been associated, throws
considerable light upon his character and upon hidden parts of it.
Biographers and autobiographers, as a rule, say little about it and
many people are reticent about their 'loyalties.'" Woolf was not reticent about his. He went on to summarize them. "I detect feelings
of loyalty to my family; 'race' (Jews); my country, England in
particular, and the British Empire generally; places with which I
have been connected, such as Kensington and London (born and
bred); counties, Middlesex and Sussex, where I have lived, Ceylon,
Greece; school [St. Paul's]; Trinity and Cambridge." His probing
mind then examines the qualities of loyalty—loyalties to landscapes of the material world and of the mind. He concludes: "My
loyalty to Trinity and Cambridge is different from all my other loyalties. It is more intimate, profound, unalloyed. It is compounded
of the spiritual, intellectual and physical, inextricably mixed." He
quotes a letter Desmond MacCarthy wrote to him in Ceylon saying that Cambridge "made a claim on one's feelings, as standing
for something." MacCarthy asked Woolf: "Do these words mean
much to you?" This was a logical question for a young sahib distanced by miles of ocean from his native, his familiar, scenes. In his
autobiography Woolf gives his answer. These things meant everything to him—"spiritual qualities, memories, traditions, history."
There is perhaps a continuity between this dialogue and *The Wise
Virgins;* for we note that Woolf dedicated the novel to Desmond
MacCarthy.

In his own way, Leonard Woolf, in this old novel which now
takes on new meanings, speculated on his confusions of feeling
about his loyalties. To read *The Wise Virgins* as a stage in Woolf's
journey is to gain direct insight into the consistency and depth of
his self-probing which would culminate in the supreme pages of his
autobiography—his unusual journey from Cambridge to Ceylon,
from Ceylon to familiar London and Bloomsbury, and his ultimate
years of dedication to his wife and to humane "activist" causes—a
behind-the-scenes figure in British labor and a maker of blueprints
for world organization.

II
FORMULATIONS

BIOGRAPHY AND THE SCHOLAR: *THE LIFE OF HENRY JAMES*

Adeline R. Tintner

The Fertile Fact

As the Sam Johnson who dominates the imagination of the English-speaking world is Boswell's Johnson, so, too, it is Leon Edel's Henry James who represents the American author. In 1980, for instance, the international novel invented and perfected by Henry James suddenly appeared in a dazzling, gilt, popular version as the number one, best-selling novel, *Princess Daisy,* by Judith Krantz. Throughout Krantz's novel are evocations of "Daisy Miller" and *The Princess Casamassima,* of "The Jolly Corner" and *Roderick Hudson*—all in the service of a twentieth-century sensation story filled with alter egos and doubles. This substantial debt to Henry James was concealed by the author until the end of the novel, when, as HJ would say, she "gives herself away." One of her characters, a business tycoon, finding it impossible to sleep in spite of pills, "read a few more pages of Leon Edel's five-volume biography of Henry James. This great scholarly work, detailed, leisurely and undoubtedly good for him," occupied him "until about five in the morning." Afterwards, "trying hard to think only about James churning out books in London, books [he] had never read, he ventured back to bed."

Here is the evidence that not only Hilly Bijur, the cosmetic king, but also perhaps his creator, Judith Krantz, has gone to James via Edel, a path symptomatic of the way the great novelist has gradually been absorbed by the audience he courted all his life to little avail. For it is in Edel's biography rather than in James's fiction that the American public has come to know the great novelist (and we make allowance for the movies and television plays which have circulated the plots of his stories). The reason Edel's has taken the place of James's own work, books "they had never read," for a large proportion of our reading public, is that he has made the "figure" of James assimilable. The quintet of volumes becomes a five-act play in which the hero is James and the characters his novels and tales. Each volume has its own climax, its shock of discovery, and its personal problems and solutions. Each volume, moreover, has been affected by Edel's own maturity, for the twenty-year period covered by the publication of the biography has allowed for his own growth as a scholar and writer.

The reprinting of the quintet as a boxed set of Avon paperbacks at a greatly reduced price has further helped create a new audience which will never read James himself, but which is fed and informed by the brilliant re-creation of the author's life, by the succinct review of the novels and stories, and by the consistently balanced estimate of them. In our age of living vicariously through the great, the James family provides models which satisfy the popular thirst for identification with troubled persons who overcame their troubles and with successful celebrities who suffered from incurable wounds. The recent biography of Alice James is a case in point; both feminist interests and curiosity about one of our most gifted families are satisfied, in spite of the fact that Alice left no creative records outside her diary.

The serious literature of our time, like Philip Roth's novels, often depends heavily on James's fiction for both technical and moral support; in an analogous way, to a certain segment of our reading population, Leon Edel *is* Henry James. An Amanda Cross mystery recently published also brings in the *Life* and comments on how wise the James family was to entrust James's life to Leon Edel. Although this comes from the pseudonymous pen of an English professor, and from the lips of the book's criminal, it is still Edel who is evoked, not James, providing us with an example, comparable to Boswell's *Life of Johnson,* of the personality of the subject towering over the work because of the biographer.

The quintet is like the great mother earth from which the scholar can feed, and like the good earth it seems to move and swell with facts. To use a favorite image of Henry James, it is like a plum pudding, from which the plums are never exhausted by the greedy eater. The quintet has two readerships—the popular one for which it stands for all of James, and the scholarly one which uses it as an index to James. The volumes are not only a mine of information and a stimulus to further findings of one's own, but also a check on

those findings. It becomes therefore all things to all those interested in Henry James. Edel is James's Baedecker, and in the several
years since the *Life* was completed very little has turned up to
modify his factual account of James. However, certain attitudes to
the society in which he moved have been newly influenced by data
involving many members of the subterranean homosexual group
containing a number of James's friends. How our notion of his personal life may be modified in the future, we cannot tell, although
Edel himself has prepared us for changes with his suggestions
about James's homoeroticism and with his account of James's extreme view of personal privacy, which led to a bonfire of personal
papers in 1910. As time goes on, however, letters from friends of
James may well turn up to reveal secrets kept from us so far.

Edel has recognized James's sibling rivalry, his homoeroticism,
and his "relation" with a woman, Constance Fenimore Woolson. In
paying attention to these deeper elements, he leads the way to future developments, both in interpretation of what existed and in
relation to possible "new facts" about his case, if case there be—
and there well might. Testimony to James's kindness, to his help-
fulness as an artist, and his openness to friends is countered by re-
ports of his snobbishness, his dislike of women (in spite of his close
and warm friendships with many women), his fuddy-duddyness,
his foppishness, and the corpulence of his later years, bearing witness to those massive Edwardian banquets of his London dinings-
out. Yet a life like his is ultimately interesting only so long as it
bears witness to—and further explicates—his subtle, complex,
and rigorous art. The scholar uses the facts of James's life to help
him unravel some of the artistic secrets. Present attitudes to the
gradually revealed secrets of the life- and love-styles of James's
group may soon become reflected in the criticism of his work, and
there is nothing in Edel's *Life* which denies such a possibility. Indeed, his one-volume version of the *Life* takes into account our
changing notions of the human body and speaks of the physical
more directly.

How much, after all, do we really know of Henry James? Is there
a hidden side to his life? Why should Rebecca West have said that
he was a supreme artist but that he was also a horrid old man and
his brother equally horrid? Does this reflect H. G. Wells's attitude
to James and the atmosphere of the *Boon* incident and James's reaction to it? What relation does his personality have to his work? The
genteel tradition of reading James ignored his sexual problems.

The later charge was that he had omitted in his work not only sex but violence as well and the hidden side of human personality. But if one examines his work one sees that these are unsafe generalizations. Take, for instance, "The Turn of the Screw," "The Figure in the Carpet," and *The Sacred Fount*. Here is murder; here is adultery; and here (in "Maud Evelyn") is unconventional morbid sexuality, with "The Figure in the Carpet" containing figures of speech decidedly onanistic. But the handling is from a civilized level, not from the simplistic level of the sensational or the salacious. He understood the corrupting effect of money (*The Ivory Tower*) and the "black things behind the great fortunes," and he did not skim over the unpleasant aspects of life. His personal peculiarities were noted by Edith Wharton, without giving him away, in a story such as "The Eyes," where his domination of a group of acolytes is mirrored. The salutary point about Maxwell Geismar's attempt to define a James "cult" and attack it was that he rescued James from the Jamesians of the genteel tradition. Edel recognizes these things and opens the way for future Freudian or other psychological interpretations, those that are bound to come when more is published about life habits at the turn of the century. *The Spoils of Poynton*, however, has always been perceived as a reverse "oedipal" situation—the struggle for the son in this case on the part of the mother; and there are many other examples.

The *Life* has great uses for creative scholarship because it is a creative biography in which the author has not seen fit to "divorce the literary work from its creator," to quote Edel's revolutionary *Literary Biography*. This book was written over twenty-five years ago, when the New Critics were isolating the text, but times have changed, and the entertaining part is that people now read Edel's *Life* in lieu of James himself. There are few of Edel's critiques of James's twenty novels and one hundred and twelve stories that have been faulted, but modern readings have become more complex and detailed. In general, Edel seems to have a more balanced edge on interpretation over the garrulous and tail-biting critics. And he gives us, in Virginia Woolf's words, "the creative fact; the fertile fact." *

With such a biography, is there any room left for the scholar? Of

---

* As far as I know, nothing has been discovered to disprove Edel's facts; and recent biographical studies of the family (by Jean Strouse and Howard Feinstein) have extended rather than counterbalanced Edel's interpretations. Although Barzun and Trilling attempted to refute Edel's data about the sibling rivalry between William and Henry, their evidence was not convincing.

course there is, because Edel has not even pretended to do a complete job of textual explication. Every careful scrutinizer of the land which is the text has to go to the *Life* to see what we know concerning the events in James's life which might account for or be correlated with what he has written. To dissect the fiction, to analyze it, requires as much biographical information as pertains to the problem at hand. To illustrate this, I shall cite a few instances from my own attempts to explain certain opaque figures of speech or references in the stories. Their solutions in many cases depend on how James's experience in life could make my explanations of his work plausible, and the *Life* is currently the only comprehensive source for that experience.

The Uses of Biography

There are two aspects of the *Life* that are essential for the scholar to heed. One is the actual material of the life of James which is required to situate the text one has under scrutiny. The other is the form and structure of the *Life,* the way the materials have been digested and assembled, the rhythm of the writing, and the grouping of events that have a similarity, events which in turn clarify the production of the novels and tales. For Edel's aim has been to make as clear as possible the conditions under which James's fiction came into being. He has taken a quiet uneventful life—no tempests, no "scenes," no mistresses, no love struggles—and step-by-step fascinates us by unfolding the exciting life of a great imagination.

In addition to being *the* fascinating life of a writer by a master biographer, it can serve as a major tool for the Jamesian scholar. What, the skeptical reader might ask, is left for scholarship after Edel's *Life?* What I call scholarship, or rather my form of scholarship, is an unrelenting analysis of the text for all its possible meanings and contexts—justifiable in tackling a difficult writer who urged repeatedly that the reader reread, cooperate, and join in a reciprocal relation with him. This kind of scholar simply does what James asked of the reader. Given that a hundred years have passed since much of James's fiction was written, with the century's changes in mores, language, and standards, today's scholar must revive dead meanings so that the stories may regain some of their original significance.

One of the more general aids to such a scholar consists in Edel's technique, his way of presenting some illuminating connection between the facts of James's life and the facts of his fiction. In book 5 of volume I, in the subchapter, "Jacob and Esau," Edel begins by retelling the biblical story of the active brother beloved by the father and the slightly younger twin, who "took away my birthright, and now . . . my blessing," an analogue for Henry and William's relation to one other. Then he cuts back to the James brothers' relations in 1866. He tells how Henry's back aches when William is on the family scene, and how he recovers when William leaves; nor does William do well physically when he is near Henry. This is the first analysis in the book of their sibling rivalry, of which much will be made. Henry's continued staying at home makes Edel ask, "Was he really a fledgling who took longer than most to try his wings? Or was he a Jacob quite satisfied to dwell in tents?" He answers by citing from three tales written at this time, and in each case "the usurper pays with his life or with defeat." The neat analogy ends with the culminating quotation from a guilty William who is enjoying Europe. "'I somehow feel as if I were cheating Henry of his birthright,'" followed by Edel's conclusion: "Thus the two brothers played out their Jacob and Esau drama. The curious thing was that they both cast themselves in the role of Jacob." This is a fine example of the way in which a gifted writer can formally manage his scholarly findings so that the revelation of his discovery is exciting reading, yet the cause of it is kept for the end. The form is dramatic.

The prologue or thematic chapters which open volume I are a triumph of concision and wit. In these opening chapters Edel has struck all the themes of his work—from the pictures of the parents to the ultimate Napoleonic hints which will surface in *The Master* four volumes later.

What is suggestive in the facts of Henry James's life which can elucidate his writing? The ignited balloon that was responsible for his father's burnt leg and amputation must have had some effect on his son's recurrent use of the figure of the balloon as the symbol for romanticism. Byron, the great romantic poet, limped, but James's father limped more. Therefore, his father was perhaps the most burned by the romantic urge, even more than Byron. Another chink for the scholar to widen for himself occurs in "The Sense of Glory," in those pages concerned with the effect of the Galerie d'Apollon in the Louvre. When I read that chapter long ago I thought it behooved the scholar to *see* those Delacroix and Le Brun pictures and to find out whether their imagery was present in James's work.

I can only begin to describe the hints, suggestions, and "fertile facts" that have set me on my way pursuing the trails of James's creative imagination in his novels and stories—Edel's use of significant phrases from James's letters, his way of providing comments by observers, his tracking down inscriptions in books—those "silent witnesses," as he says, of moments of literary history. Edel knows the value of the "imaginative leap"—which does not exhaust the material, but enables others to have that leap for themselves: he leaves much out since he must stick to a "story line," and as he says, "a biographer who tries to tell everything ends by telling nothing."

One has to take each volume at a time because each has its own rhythm and density. The sheer number of fascinating and back-grounded personalities James meets in Edel's second volume, *The Conquest of London,* allows the interested Jamesian to select sources for the tales and novels. Rereading volume II I found, for example, corroboration for a thesis of my own in Edel's quoting a passage from HJ's life of Hawthorne. It had a striking echo of a passage in James Fenimore Cooper. This suggested that James had been re-reading Cooper when he wrote his Centennial story ("An International Episode"), and that Cooper's *Home as Found,* a July Fourth celebration, may have been a source for Bessie Alden's declaration of independence in the James tale. The pulling together of James's meetings and friendship with the Andrew Langs (from the first dinner early in his English residency) gave a fillip to my discovery that Lang was the very reviewer in the *Pall Mall Gazette* who made slighting remarks about the "International Episode" which resulted in the friendship between Stevenson and James.

So much we take for granted originates in the *Life,* such as the identification made by Edel (and others) of the Palazzo Barbaro and the Palazzo Leporelli in *The Wings of the Dove,* or the identification of the palace in "The Aspern Papers." For the scholar who attacks James's fiction from every side, from the underbelly as well as the carapace, all facts may be helpful or useful.

The only place in which we follow the careful chronology of James's and Constance Fenimore Woolson's period together in Italy during 1886 is in book 4 of Edel's *The Middle Years.* We read that in "the absence of documents" about "the life these two writers led on their Florentine hilltop," only "certain books which Henry gave to Fenimore have survived; nearly all of them bear the date of this time." After Fenimore died James "was invited to take such books of Fenimore's as he wished." He took a number of books itemized in *The Middle Years*. "Clare Benedict [her niece] kept the books which Henry had given to her aunt, silent witnesses of their various meetings." Two such volumes have ended up in my possession and it is from the facts sifted by Edel that the two-volume (third) edition of *Anna Karénine* by Tolstoy, in the French translation of 1886, bound in half morocco, becomes an eloquent testimonial to the friendship of the two writers. On the flyleaf of volume one Henry James wrote his signature, and we read "C. F. Woolson" on the title page. The second volume has her name again on the title page, but on the first leaf of the binding paper "C. F. Woolson, Florence, 1886" is written in ink. We can figure out from what Edel tells us that they eventually entered the collection of books given by Clare Benedict to James after Miss Woolson died. They are indeed silent but still concrete witnesses of a relationship. James's signature, a late one, was placed on the flyleaf of volume one probably years later. The facts we have learned from the *Life* about Fenimore's suicide and about the suicides in her fiction made the death of Anna Karenina, also a suicide, trigger our imagination, especially since the book entered into James's possession.

In book 3 of volume IV of the *Life,* in a paragraph beginning "Between 1895 and 1898 the twentieth century began to knock loudly at Henry James's door," we learn that the writer in 1898 "went to one of the earliest movies, the 'cinematograph—or whatever they call it' to see pictures of the Fitzsimmons-Corbett prize fight." This was the important fact I needed to show that James had written a "movie" story, "Crapy Cornelia," with prizefight images as well as movie close-ups serving as metaphors in a tale written in 1909 after James's visit to the United States in 1904–1905. Here the event is accompanied by James's own account of his pleasure in the experience.

One can also make one's own connections between social encounters and fictional characters from Edel's material. On 15 September 1878 James meets a "Sidney Holland, one of those manly, candid, good-looking young Englishmen who only need a touch of genius, or of something they haven't got, to make one think that they are the flower of the human race. As it is, they come near being it." In December 1878, "An International Episode" appeared with just such a young aristocrat in it, Lord Lambeth, whose "need of a touch of genius" makes it easy for Bessie Alden to throw him over. Edel allows us to see the character *en herbe*.

Since this scholar gets her clues from the text, she checks on supporting evidence in Edel. In his section introducing Isabella Gardner, Edel quotes from a letter to her from James in 1881 that declares that someday "I will immortalize you." Mrs. Mesh in "A New England Winter," a story written a few years later when he was seeing a lot of Mrs. Gardner in Washington, is a recognizable portrait of Mrs. Jack herself, someone who drew a "mesh" over young men.

Edel's report in *The Treacherous Years* that James had served on a jury involving a divorce hearing in the summer of 1897 provided the key to understanding one of James's most difficult stories of 1898, "The Given Case." The *Life* continues to be a tissue of evidence for the imaginative scholar.

From Edel's account of James's entertaining Sargent in 1884 with introductions to Millais, Leighton, and Burne-Jones, it was useful to learn that the latter painter showed the two Americans "his new painting 'King Cophetua and the Beggar Maid,'" for certain unmistakable traces of this painting appear in *The Bostonians* where James's Cophetua, Basil Ransom, takes on the poor, red-haired Verena, who like the "beggar-maid" goes into trances.

The scholar then can use the *Life* as an encyclopedia (and its uses are unending in this role); but in doing so he not only necessarily deforms the book's organic structure but he must not miss information which neither comes under the rubric of "facts" nor can be found in the index.

One does not always agree with Edel's conclusions. For instance, he says James changed the form of death from poison to drowning in *The Other House,* that is, to "the form of death he himself had described . . . when he had spoken of having been under water," after the failure of his play. On the contrary, I think that the change took place because in between James had read Ibsen's *Little Eyolf,* where the child is drowned. (His calling his little girl "Little Effie" surely suggests the influence of "Little Eyolf.") Also, the child Effie is merely a pawn, not a character, as Maisie and Nanda are, although Edel's thesis in general, that these stories in sequence reveal themselves as a "productive disguise of his early years," by which "James performed imaginative self-therapy," is a heuristic notion, dependent on a Freudian concept of the return to "the stuff of childhood." However, one must remember that while James was writing these novels and stories he was also writing tales about adults, and possible adulteries ("The Given Case," 1898, "The Great Condition," 1889, "Paste," 1899, "The Real Right Thing,"

1899). Moreover, in the late eighties and nineties Stevenson and Kipling were writing stories of children and their consciousnesses, and were popular because of it.

What the scholar can learn from this arrangement of the stories is how to arrange his own material in hand. The very little girls are there, at least in two stories, and what one does with them depends on one's training and interests as well as the curve of our subject's life and work. It is a technique—the "sequence analysis"—which demonstrates how the position of a story *in a series* can tell us something very important. Edel also demonstrates that the number 23 in relation to the number of volumes James wanted for his New York edition links up in a very meaningful way with the number of volumes in James's own set of Balzac, a writer about whom he was thinking more from the years 1902 until 1913 than he had even in 1875–76. The dramatic handling of data is a technique few of us can manage as Edel does, but if we keep his model before us we may learn. It is this dramatic handling—this "showing" of the material instead of telling it, as Joseph Warren Beach said of Edel— that saves his biography from the dullness of "quiet lives."

There are places for more work even where Edel has seemed to control all the elements that go into a story, as in his masterly chapter on "The Beast in the Jungle," which he calls "The Impenetrable Sphinx." He points out here Maupassant's story "Promenade," which James had read, as well as personal sources from James's relation with Miss Woolson, yet the way is left open for other as yet untapped sources, not only in the fin de siècle French Symbolist art of Moreau, who painted *Oedipus and the Sphinx* and pictures "powdered with silver" (as James says in the tale), but also in the fin de siècle English interest in the Greek plays.

Literary Biography as Art

Determining the value of Leon Edel's *Life of Henry James* is like assessing the value of virtue, for no one writing today in the field of Henry James's fiction is capable of standing outside of that *Life*. Edel has opened the door by the publication not only of the complete life but also of its revised definitive edition, the Penguin two-volume (but not reduced) version, not available in the United States for copyright reasons. It is hard to know whether the Penguin edition (preferred by the author) will be read by American readers who now have the five-volume paperback Avon reprint.

The one major difference is that in the Penguin version the references and notes have been eliminated. By so doing Edel has placed his volumes into that class of biography where they stand by themselves as works of literature. In fact, Edel has excluded the scholar in this sense from his preferred band of readers. However, to make up for the omitted apparatus, Edel has incorporated new findings since 1972, revised opinions, used more elegant language and more condensed and clarified passages. The preferred version is itself, then, a notable work of art.

The revised *Life of Henry James* is in some ways what the revised *Roderick Hudson* is to the early *Roderick Hudson*—a more totally organized affair now viewed by a writer who rereads an old text at maturity. So too Edel's style and genius for synthesizing and organizing have matured. He has not changed his text; what he has changed is the syntax of his language. For example, in the part of the revised book which corresponds to volume V, *The Master,* in the section called *Theatricals; Second Series* he alters the sentence, "He had had enough of the treacheries of the theatre" to "he had had enough of the treacherous stage," using the form of the word which gave the name *The Treacherous Years* to the penultimate volume of the quintet. This change is typical of certain other changes we notice throughout the revision.

Since Edel is a literary scholar and critic as well as a biographer, he has found lost stories, and re-created basic and hidden personal relations. He has clarified and exposed the interfraternal drama, and has validated his evidence by such discoveries as William James's letter to the American Academy calling his brother "frivolous." He has also been a translator of sorts, for he has translated into lucid statements those complex books, the *Autobiography* and *The American Scene,* written in a style difficult for contemporary readers. His dedication to summarizing more than one hundred pages of each of them in his first two volumes has proved an inestimable service to those of us who are too tired or lazy to cope with those highly individualized and perhaps monstrous examples of James's genius. This power of autobiographic reconstruction is conveyed in persuasive yet unpretentious and easily assimilable prose that has extended the reading public of his *Life* during the past ten years. In their rainbow variety and holdable format, the Avon paperbacks are themselves a kind of New York edition. If the "Master" could see it, it might reconcile him to his having been so pried open and anatomized, even though the prying has been of the transcendental variety. Edel himself has made an *apologia* for it in due deference, one supposes, to the posthumous feelings of his subject.

Certain placements of paragraphs to dramatize points and a generous allotment of quotations from James are secondary to the remarkable effect the disposition of the parts and the characters has created. Edel has had as his model James himself, who in many cases, especially in his later works such as *The Wings* and *The Bowl*, made changes that consisted of renumberings of sections and chapter sequences. In France it was Balzac whose organization of material for the *Comédie Humaine* into special categories was a fluid thing; his rearrangement of their places and their definitions, such as *Scènes de la vie privée*, depended on how the contours of his work changed as he added story to story. James's New York edition is an emulation of the Balzacian scheme which Edel has described in his chapters on the architecture of this edition.

The reader is thus confronted by the two Edel editions of the biography. The first is in five parts, each part designed as if a novel, with artfully planned climaxes. The first volume has an extraordinary shape, with James's late autobiographical résumés ushering in his extraordinary family life, with Edel's feeling for the brotherly rivalry and an artist's feeling for the entire family drama. This exposition leads to "the banquet of initiation," the solo trip made by Henry James to Europe and his baptism in the waters of civilization. The climax is marvelously hewn from the life material. The second volume also shows this cooperation between the facts and the framework of the story around them. We go from Rome and back to America, and then to Paris and London and its "conquest," a natural voyage; it is the picaresque view of the novelist who lived in his perceptions and in his art, winding up with the creation of his first great masterpiece, *The Portrait of a Lady*, and the growth of a hitherto concealed private relationship with a lady writer, apparently of a nonsexual kind, as in "The Beast in the Jungle."

On the other hand, the form and shape of the biography's definitive edition seem to have a lot in common with Edel's recent *Bloomsbury: A House of Lions*, the group biography he published in 1977 and on which he was working during the period in which he revised his five volumes. The style of *A House of Lions* is more sonorous and the language more resonant, yet more economical than that of the earlier books. It is Edel's late style, and we may judge it as resulting from his aging, his authority, and his heightened vision of essences. For it is the elegant, yet penetrating voice of the author of *A House of Lions* which has put its mark on the revised James life—as if the older Edel, like the older James, were looking back at his earlier work and deciding it needed improvement, saying, in effect, as in the Max Beerbohm cartoon, "how badly you wrote."

The preface to the first volume of the definitive edition might be considered an equivalent of James's prefaces. It is a kind of *apologia pro sua labore* in which Edel explains himself as a kind of "story teller." As a modern biographer he must "melt down his materials" or be "smothered" himself. He has produced a quintet "presented as if played at a single concert." To me it seems to correspond more to Proust's *A la Recherche du Temps Perdu* than to Durrell's *Alexandria Quartet,* which Edel uses as analogy. It was composed under time sequences and interruptions, like Proust's novel, but the latter never had the benefit of the author's viewing the whole at once and making the proper refinements and emphases. "The quintet never revealed its plans to me in advance. . . . The quintet had a mysterious organic growth about a living person whose sense of humour was as boundless as his egotism, whose mannerisms could irritate as well as amuse." Reading Percy Lubbock's *The Region Cloud* we recognize the main character as a thinly disguised Henry James, but we might never have done so without Edel's directing us to it, in spite of such hints in the novel as "the real right thing," "the Master," "the dear man" and other locutions we have met only in James's fiction.

Edel's interest in form is shown in the preface to the fifth volume of the quintet. "I claim for this work a specific form and a high selectivity, [covering as it does] half a century of writing and [representing] a synthesis of many thousands of letters. . . ." He tells us that he has used the "retrospective method," scenic where permitted. Questions of form, composition, and structure follow Strachey's "selection, detachment, design." He has incorporated the "flashback" into biography—a distinct innovation.

Edel assumes that the tightness of his biographical form depends on "selection." This we see, although it operates differently as between the first and the definitive editions, for Edel is preeminently skilled in scholarly procedure. His management of material is masterly, since he combines scholarly acuteness in nosing out significant relationships among facts with a finesse in presenting those relationships. In the definitive edition we cannot see Edel growing up with James, as we had in the quintet, in itself an exciting experience, nor do we see his own style acquiring the characteristics of a later manner like his subject's (without, however, acquiring his subject's orotundity). These are the dynamic attributes of two organically meshed personalities, the biographer and his subject, which animate the surface of the original quintet. We miss the five climaxes, the five groups of evocative pictures as well as the five prefaces which are biographical manifestos and which clearly summarize what we have read before and what we are about to read. Above all we miss the scholarly notes which invite us to refer ourselves to Edel's sources and to pursue further any aspect of the *Life* Edel merely touched on for the purposes of his book's design.

If this is what we miss, what do we gain in the unabridged Penguin two-volume edition? In it Edel, like Sophocles, saw his *Life* "steadily and saw it whole" and *as* a whole. Edel is like a tour leader in the Alps who had previously taken his fellow travelers and tourists by train, making a number of stops, but who now travels by plane, giving his tourists a view of a whole range of mountains without leaving the vehicle. The point of view, in addition to being higher up and loftier, becomes more panoramic. The rhythm of the biography is now more continuous, and to agree with this totalizing grasp of James's life Edel has changed the position of some chapters and paragraphs, and some of their titles. This rearrangement alone dramatizes James's life as a whole, now not cut up into five sections, like railway cars that are detachable. So the definitive edition presents a more organically accurate representation of a life that is continuous and not artificially segmented by its division into five books spread over a number of periods, like a "Masterpiece Theatre" serial on television.

The growth of the quintet is that of the subject, James, maturing while Edel himself was growing up as a scholar and a person. Each volume reveals a development in Edel's perception, in the control of his technique, and in the plenitude of his materials. The last volume is indeed a symphony while the earlier ones are concerti. The harmony has expanded with the growing number of instruments, those instruments to which the personalities who became friends of the Master in his last decade are equivalent. The figure of Wagner as the composer comes to mind as a comparison from a reading of the entire work, which I prefer to think of as a symphony rather than a quintet, for the involvement is richer than in a piece of chamber music.

The reader too grows up as he reads the complete life. He is not what he was when he first read about the James family's ancestor arriving in the United States right after the Revolution. One also feels this way when one reads the novels of James in their original editions. On the New York edition the late James has put his imprint, and the revised *Roderick Hudson* and the revised *Portrait of a Lady* have enough changes to make the reader know he is now meeting the mature personality and talent of James. That is what the definitive edition of Edel's *Life* does to us, but if we read each volume as it originally appeared (as we read them now in the Avon paperbacks), we have the advantage of seeing the biographer, and his subject, grow up.

With the aid of an editor Edel has just carved from the Penguin revised edition a seven-hundred-page one-volume biography. It is typical of his unflagging commitment to Henry James that in his later years he has produced the only one-volume full-length biography for a new generation of readers. Dupee's life was merely a biographical sketch of fewer than two hundred pages, with none of the material we find in any of Edel's editions of his *Life*. In the new truncated version, moreover, Edel tries to answer some of the criticism that has been made of his fudging of the issue of James's homosexuality. Today's generation is very anxious to get as close as possible to the definitions of the bodily functions and activities of its literary heroes, even when it is impossible to do so. For instance, the omission of a letter about James's constipation from a volume of Edel's recent edition of the *Letters* has seemed to one reader an omission symptomatic of a planned withholding of certain information.

To avoid such misunderstandings Edel addresses himself, in his preface, to the generation of the "sexual" revolution, even though, as he writes, "my data remains the same. What I have been able to do is to discard certain former reticences; to take less advantage of certain 'proprieties' I practiced out of respect for surviving members of the James family, the children of William James."

However one feels about reticence and plain-speaking, Edel's *Life* is not an overblown hypertrophied one, nor is it the pasted-together communal work of assistants. It does not share the impersonality of Ellmann's life of Joyce nor the breathlessness of Painter's life of Proust. No matter what revolutions occur in the taste for James or the judgmental attitudes to his work, it is unlikely that any new biographical material will significantly alter the shape of Henry James's life as we know it from Leon Edel.

IN SEARCH OF HENRY JAMES'S EDUCATIONAL THEORY: THE NEW BIOGRAPHY AS METHOD*

MURIEL G. SHINE

HENRY JAMES'S fictional children are of singular interest to the literary scholar for good reason. Not only do many of his major novels and tales have young people as focal characters, but his remarkably sentient rendering of such children as Miles and Flora, in "The Turn of the Screw," Morgan Moreen, in "The Pupil," and Maisie Farange, in *What Maisie Knew,* reveals a sensibility keenly attuned to the emotional and intellectual world of the child—an awareness of complexities rarely, if at all, found in the literature of his contemporaries. There are, as well, recurrent, if scattered, statements of philosophical principle on children, child-rearing, and the maturing process in his travel sketches, book reviews, and autobiography. Such preoccupation with children and themes of childhood suggests that James might have something important to say about young people and how they grow, something which might give us a new, a fresh perspective on the novelist's view of the human condition.

The Jamesian scholar intuitively senses a consistent pattern in the novelist's treatment of children which, despite its varied literary expression, produces a coherent, if unstated, theory of education. In the tales of the 1870s and 1880s, he repeatedly demonstrates a concern with the quality of the child's experience and the implica-

*Portions of this essay have been adapted from my book, *The Fictional Children of Henry James* (Chapel Hill: University of North Carolina Press, 1969).

tions of that experience for its future development. It becomes clear that for James the "helpless plasticity" of the young demands a sense of responsibility on the part of those who guide them. In the 1890s three significant tales and two novels specifically address the problem of how young people learn to cope with a hostile adult world; how they contrive to transcend the evil which surrounds them constitutes the dramatic action. Slowly but surely a uniquely Jamesian child takes form, one easily "spoiled" by permissive, uncaring, selfishly motivated adults, a child abused, manipulated, and sacrificed by unscrupulous, heartless parents but who, in James's later fiction, triumphs through awareness and the development of a strong moral sense.

Such are the intuitions of the Jamesian scholar who perceives in the author's fiction and autobiographical sketches recurrent variations on a theme which is never stated. The formulation of this theme as doctrine promises rewards. Such a project, however, requires us to extract from both fictional and biographical sources a premise never articulated by James himself, a formulation which, quite possibly, the novelist never consciously entertained. It becomes the business of the scholar to look behind the obvious statement or the manifest behavior in search of what Leon Edel calls "the figure under the carpet."[1]

Edel's approach to biography presupposes an understanding and acceptance of the concept of unconscious human needs which find expression—often in strangely contradictory ways—in conscious utterance and behavior. The biographer attempts to discern patterns of feeling and thought which manifest themselves in consistent, if unconscious, ways—anger behind a witticism, terror behind acts of bravado, aggressive gestures accompanying conciliatory moves.

A concrete example of Edel's approach is apparent in his way of looking at the dream-nightmare of the Galerie d'Apollon recorded by James in his autobiography, *A Small Boy and Others*. Jamesian scholars have been struck by the intensity and diversity of feeling expressed in the dream—feelings of fear and terror coexisting with feelings of triumph and transcendence; many critics have remarked upon the tenacity of the memory of the dream but not quite in the searching manner of Edel. F. W. Dupee, in his introduction to Henry James's *Autobiography*, discusses the dream in terms of circumstances in the novelist's early life which conspired both to favor and to threaten his development: his family's wealth and position, the doomed lives of so many of his relatives, his father's impractical mind, his childhood wanderings, the experimental nature of his education, and the impact of Europe as well as that of the Civil War on young Henry. All these, Dupee feels, engendered the conflict in James which found expression in this nightmare dreamed in adulthood and recalled so vividly in old age:

> Such things make up a dream of life which is always on the point of turning into a nightmare. And it is a certain dream or nightmare, long remembered by James and carefully recounted by him, which forms the climax and clarifies the meaning of *A Small Boy and Others*. With its setting in the Galerie d'Apollon of the Louvre, the dream or nightmare shows James suddenly turning on and violently routing a spectral pursuer who threatens to destroy him. The experience ends in triumph, but it also makes clear how great was James's estimate of his peril.[2]

Dupee's reading of the dream is based upon the manifest facts of James's life, the experiences we all know about and which, no doubt, deeply affected him in the ways suggested by this critic. Edel, on the other hand, looks behind the surface meaning of the dream and sees it as a manifestation of James's life-myth in which his brother, by the novelist's own admission, played such a significant role.

James tells us that his first perceptions were those of his "brother's occupying a place in the world to which [he] couldn't at all aspire . . . [he] never for all the time of childhood and youth in the least caught up with William or overtook him."[3] For all his "affection, admiration and sympathy" for his brother, James felt himself "too close a participant" in the beginnings of his older brother's life. It is a fact that in early youth and in adulthood, as devoted to and admiring of William as he was, Henry could not be with him for any length of time without developing a backache, a malady often associated with tension and stress. It is generally accepted that we carry into adulthood unresolved childhood feelings of anger and frustration which we may or may not be aware of, and that these unresolved tensions often find expression in physical symptoms. By carefully reading the psychological signs, by asking himself the right questions about the relationship between Henry and William, Edel arrived at a reading of the dream of the Galerie d'Apollon which is, like Dupee's, rooted in James's childhood experience but which, unlike Dupee's, reaches into the author's unconscious fantasy about his older brother. William, the source of

Henry's feelings of inadequacy and helplessness, is triumphantly conquered in "the palace of art." Dupee gives us the figure *in* the carpet; Edel has found the figure *under* the carpet. His portrait reveals a more complex Henry James, one who struggled with and successfully mastered his ambivalent feelings for his brother by transforming his nightmare into creative expression.

Similarly, Edel's analysis of James's fiction becomes more than a discussion of the use of symbol and metaphor or the identification of literary influences. Viewed as a rewriting of his life-myth, the novelist's fiction takes on a texture, a hermeneutic dimension that gives it a resonance not found in traditional approaches to literary analysis. A case in point is Edel's discussion of Milly Theale, the illusive heroine of James's complex late novel, *The Wings of the Dove*.

It is commonly held that the portrait of Milly Theale is commemorative of James's cousin, Minnie Temple, of whom he wrote with great intensity of feeling in *Notes of a Son and Brother*. Oscar Cargill remarks upon the "curious resentment some critics have felt for James's supposed solicitude for his heroines and for Milly Theale especially."[4] While Cargill disagrees with the view that Milly is not fully realized, his defense of James's rendering of her rests on the suggestion that critics have "an unwillingness today to accept a convention older than the *Divine Comedy* or the *Canzoniere* . . . we insist on dismissing Milly as 'other-worldly,' 'aethereal' and 'unreal.'"[5] In order to respond to Milly Theale, argues Cargill, we must accept her as the modern equivalent of Laura or Beatrice—in short, as a literary convention. Like the critics he takes to task, Cargill sees Milly in terms of James's technique.

Edel, on the other hand, views her as an integral part of a larger design within the novel which expresses the author's deepest feelings about life—and death. There is ample evidence that James associated sexual love and marriage with the death of creativity, if not with actual physical extinction. He could only sustain a relationship with a nonthreatening woman to whom he could be kind and attentive but who would demand nothing of him in return, thereby protecting him from a commitment he was afraid to make:

> The notes for *The Wings of the Dove* were written in the autumn of 1894 in James's notebooks, in the year of the death of Constance Fenimore Woolson, in Venice. She had been the most important of his "protective" ladies in all the years he had known her; only after her death had it occurred to him that she might have loved him more than he had been ready to admit.[6]

Minnie Temple had been another "safe" woman; she had figured
prominently in James's youth as his ideal heroine—a "luminary of
the mind." The death of Miss Woolson, "a woman with womanly
demands," stirred up long-buried, complex feelings for Minnie;
these, in turn, activated emotions associated with another earlier
and significant experience—the effect upon him of the relationship
between his father, mother, and his mother's sister, Kate, who
lived with the James family:

> The real-life Mary [James's mother] and Kate, the omnipresent
> older female figure of Henry James's childhood, may be regarded as
> the figure behind his cousin Minnie Temple and the Milly and Kate
> of fiction, the idealized mother and the down-to-earth aunt . . .
> Kate Croy and Milly—the strong and the weak, the bad and the
> good heroines . . . the representation of flesh and spirit. They were
> an outgrowth in the novelist's mind of elements in his buried life,
> the everlasting vision of a mother outwardly compliant and an aunt
> assertive and manipulative.[7]

Seen in conjunction with Kate Croy as a projection of the author's
basic conflict—"the myth of the fleshly, of spirit and body"—
Milly takes on a mythopoeic dimension; we respond to her because the duality of flesh and spirit is universal and timeless. It is
true that "in such complex equations [reside] the personalized form
of Henry James's women;" it is equally true that his is a widely
shared myth. Edel's approach leads us to the archetypal aspects of
his art and ultimately to a more profound appreciation of it.

   This methodology, then, can yield rich insights for biographer
and literary critic alike. We must, however, be mindful of the risks.
Biographer and critic must avoid pitfalls inherent in this way of
ordering material—unsubstantiated speculation, a tendency to
lapse into the language of psychotherapy, and the possibility of
losing sight of the work of art in the search for its psychological
underpinnings. The methodology of Edel's "new biography" requires a degree of self-awareness on the part of the scholar in order
to distinguish between personal fantasies and those of his subject;
it requires selectivity—the ability to identify significant patterns of
thought and behavior, and, having discerned them, the ability to
synthesize them so they do, in fact, coalesce to reveal the essential
thought of the author as reflected in his fiction.

   Henry James's attitudes toward child-rearing, then, are to be
found in the assumptions that lie behind his fictional representa-

tion of children as well as in his observations on the manners and mores of other cultures; most important, they are closely related to his feelings about himself as a child. "It is true," remarks Graham Greene, "that the moral anarchy of the age gave [James] his material, but he would not have treated it with such intensity if it had not corresponded with his private fantasy."[8] An educational theory truly representative of James's thought and feeling must grow out of an analysis and synthesis of his fictional children, his non-fictional statements about them, and his private fantasy or hidden personal myth about childhood and maturation.

In 1895, James Sully, the British psychologist, pointed out that "the child not only observes but begins to reflect on what he observes, and does his best to understand the puzzling scene which meets his eye."[9] Sully might well have been describing Maisie of *What Maisie Knew:* "It was the fate of this patient little girl to see much more than, at first, she understood, but also, even at first, to understand much more than any little girl, however patient, had perhaps ever understood before."[10]

In 1904, G. Stanley Hall, the American psychologist, noted:

> The adult finds it hard to recall the emotional and instinctive life of the teens which is banished without trace . . . the best observers see but very little of what goes on in the youthful soul, the development of which is largely subterranean . . . few writers have given true pictures of the chief traits of this developmental period.[11]

As early as 1891, in Morgan Moreen of "The Pupil," James dramatized with extraordinary sensitivity the characteristics of this period in a young boy's life:

> He . . . looked with intelligent, innocent eyes at Pemberton, who had already had time to notice that from one moment to the other his small satiric face seemed to change its time of life. At this moment it was infantine; yet it appeared also to be under the influence of curious intuitions and knowledges.[12]

James became increasingly preoccupied with the quality of the child's experience and the implications of that experience for its future development. He suggests in the tales of the 1870s and 1880s that adult dereliction—social as well as parental—could very well produce a generation of youngsters who would threaten the very fabric of society. These tales reflect a fresh view of the child–parent relationship. During the Victorian period, little, if any, thought had been given to interaction between adult and child; if children did not behave as their elders thought they should, they were considered inherently deficient in moral worth. The mature individual sought salvation through piety and virtuous deeds. Children, as diminutive adults, would be expected to exhibit the same tendencies. This attitude, which strongly affected English and American authors of the period, accounts, in part, for the numerous fictional representations of precocious infants performing acts of piety and charity for the good of their souls.

Henry James took a view of the child–adult relationship which was at variance with the dominant trend of his time. His fictional children of this period are not inherently good or evil. They respond to, are, in fact, to a significant degree, formed by the attitudes, feelings, and behavior of the important adults in their lives. If this attitude was foreign to the temper of his time, it is curiously familiar to that of ours. We find that in most instances the novelist's views on child-rearing are forward-looking and parallel attitudes we have come to associate with the twentieth-century habit of mind.

In "Master Eustace," 1871,[13] James explores a mother's misguided, compensatory love which is rooted in guilt and corruption. She envelopes her son with affection, anticipates his every wish, denies him nothing; inevitably he grows into a selfish, arrogant young man who breaks his mother's heart and tries to destroy himself. Eustace's mother comes to understand that "love" is not enough for a child, that guidance, firmness, and a sense of values are indispensable. She learns, as well, that her love was fed by guilt, for it turns out that Eustace is an illegitimate child, the fruit of a love affair in her youth. Love born of guilt, the poor woman realizes, is no love at all. In later, more complex tales such as "The Author of 'Beltraffio'," 1884, and "The Turn of the Screw," 1889, this theme of the twin evils of possessiveness and permissiveness is given full dramatic play.

If Eustace is a warning to parents of the danger of misguided love, Randolph Miller, Daisy's precocious little brother, in *Daisy Miller*, 1878, stands as a rebuke to parents who are guilty of neglect. The theme of the failure of many American parents to provide their children with precepts that would serve as guideposts in the conduct of their lives is fully developed in this novella. Daisy's unhappy little brother is armed against life with nothing but his alpenstock, "the sharp point of which he thrust[s] into everything that he approach[es]—the flower-beds, the garden benches, the trains of the ladies' dresses."[14] Randolph is a "pale" and lonely little nine-year-year who has "a voice immature, and yet, some-how, not young," a child who "does not sleep very much," and whose teeth are falling out from overindulgence in sweets. He is living a joyless, aimless childhood and faces an equally unhappy and purposeless adulthood. Never disciplined by his mother or older sister, without benefit of his father's presence, he is a child adrift. What he is pleading for, what his irritative behavior masks, is the need for someone to care enough about him to give stability and direction to his little life. In a review of a book by Louisa M. Alcott written in that same year, James says, "What children want is the objective, as the philosophers say; it is good for them to feel that people and things around them that appeal to their respect are beautiful and powerful specimens of what they seem to be."[15] In his own childhood James missed clearly defined expectations on the part of his own parents as evidence of their concern for him. He tells us that as a child he "breathed inconsistency and ate and drank contradiction."[16] The permissive nature of the environment in which he spent his formative years was to have a profound effect on his attitude toward child-rearing. Thematically significant through-out James's treatment of children is the notion that young people without guidance, standards and objects of authority they can re-spect, are lost little souls.

Between 1884 and 1886, James produced five tales specifically concerned with the mother–child relationship. These stories differ in tone and treatment, but essentially they dramatize a precept of conduct that James felt parents were obliged to follow—they must not manipulate their children in order to satisfy their own needs. Whether the impulse to dominate a child hides behind the genteel façade of Maria Temperly in "Mrs. Temperly," whether it is mani-fest in the foolish diplomatic maneuvering of Mrs. Daintry of "A New England Summer," or whether it reveals itself in the "ex-piatory" act of Mrs. Pallant in "Louisa Pallant," meddling in the life of a young person is usually indicative of parental aggressiveness and hostility toward the child. These mothers are "hard" women. Georgina Gressie of "Georgina's Reasons" is cruel; this woman's need to make her will prevail drives her to commit bigamy and abandon her child to his death. Latent or manifest, presented in the form of social comedy or bitter ironic comment, perversion of what James (in his tribute to his own mother) called the "divine commission" of motherhood is denounced in these tales of mater-nal manipulation of children.

Little Geordie and Ferdy Berrington, children of British aris-

tocracy in "A London Life," 1888, exemplify a kind of parental neglect which produces insensitive, unresponsive adults. In reaction
against a father who, when he does occasionally appear in the nursery, is drunk and a mother too busy with social activities and
lovers to appear at all, these little boys have developed a protective
passivity; they have shut off all feeling and thought. "Geordie
would grow up to be a master-hand at polo and care more for that
pastime than for anything in life, and Ferdy perhaps would develop into 'the best shot in England' . . . at any rate they would
never reflect upon anything in the world."[17] In this tale the children
serve as a gloss on James's commentary on the disparity between
the gracious decorum of the public life and the chaotic immorality
of the private existence among the upper classes. This tale is of singular interest since it prefigures his fullest and most complex indictment of parental hypocrisy, *The Awkward Age,* 1899.

Yet another "spoiler" is the mother in "Greville Fane," 1892.
Mrs. Stormer (who writes superficial, artistically worthless but
highly popular novels under the pen-name of Greville Fane) decides that since the life of a popular novelist is pleasant and lu-
crative, she will educate her son to be a writer like herself. The
artistic imperfections of the deluded lady-novelist become emblematic of her deficiencies as a mother. Mrs. Stormer's project is,
of course, doomed to failure and her son, Leolin, becomes a ne'er-
do-well; he is paid by his mother to give her "ideas" for her own
novels. "In addition to his salary he was paid by the piece: he got so
much for a striking character, so much for a pretty name . . . and
so much promised him if he would invent a new crime." "He *has*
invented one," the narrator tells her, "and he's paid every day of his
life."[18] Mrs. Stormer does not appear to understand that the crime
Leolin invented (and which she helped him perpetrate) was that of
his own destruction through his exploitation of her weakness.

Unique in his fictional representation of these spoiled children is
the intensity of James's anger at the "spoilers," an anger he never
ceased to feel, and one that was to become subsumed in the artist
when, in his maturity, he produced some of the most memorable
children in English and American literature.

An important component of James's theory of education, and
one that in no small measure determined the form it was to take,
was his abiding interest in the French manner of rearing young
girls. As early as 1876, while on holiday in Etrat, the young author
was struck by "the immense difference between the lot of the *jeune
fille* and her American sister."

People went about in compact cohesive groups. . . . The groups
usually formed a solid phalanx around two or three young girls,
compressed into the centre, the preservation of whose innocence
was their chief solicitude.[19]

The notion of the protected young girl appealed to the novelist because it supplied in abundance that which James had missed in his
own childhood—clearly defined expectations on the part of parents as evidence of their concern. He tells us in his autobiography:
"our 'fending'. . . for ourselves didn't so prepare us for invidious
remark . . . as to hush in my breast the appeal to our parents, not
for religious instruction (of which we had plenty, and of the most
charming and familiar) but simply for instruction (a very different
thing) as to where we should say we 'went,' in our world under
cold scrutiny or derisive comment."[20] Henry James, Senior, who
was nothing if not eclectic in his attitude toward the education of
his children, replied that "there was no communion, even that of
the Catholics, even that of the Jews, even that of the Sweden-
borgians, from which we need feel ourselves excluded." But un-
limited freedom of choice is disconcerting to small children and
young Henry's response was predictable: "I not only failed quite to
rise to the parental reasoning, but made out in it rather a certain
sophistry; such prevarication for instance as if we had habitually
said we kept a carriage we obviously didn't keep, kept it because
we sent when we wanted one to University Place, where Mr.
Hathorn had his livery stable."[21] Children infer parental indif-
ference from an excess of freedom, and it was difficult for the sensitive little boy to reconcile his need for established limits with his
appreciation of unfettered opportunities for experience. The liberal
attitude of his parents had many advantages of which he was
aware. "No education," he remarked in adulthood, "avails for the
intelligence that doesn't stir in it some subjective passion." The fact
that his freedom brought him a measure of uncertainty did not di-
minish the pleasure he derived as a child from being free to "dawdle and gape" without the usual parental restrictions. Thus the essential conflict, the ambivalence that found expression in James's
fiction—the American versus the European way—may well have
had its inception in his own childhood experience; it is certainly
reflected in his lifelong preoccupation with the American versus
the European *jeune fille:*

> I used to pity the young ladies at first for this perpetual application
> of the leading-string; but a little reflection showed me that the

French have ordered this as well as they have ordered everything
else . . . if French marriages are almost always arranged, it must be
added that they are in the majority of cases arranged successfully.[22]

The key to the success of the French system was the position of the
mother in the hierarchy of the family. She controlled the destiny of
her daughter but she was obligated to pass the legacy of power
on to her. What James admired most in his own mother was her
strength and devotion. When she died in 1882, he made the following entry in his notebook:

> It was a perfect mother's life. . . . To bring her children into the
> world . . . to expend herself, for years, for their happiness and wel-
> fare—then, when they had reached a full maturity and were ab-
> sorbed in the world and in their own interests—to lay herself down
> in her ebbing strength and yield up her pure soul to the celestial
> power that had given her this divine commission.[23]

Strength and dedication would always be inseparable from the
parental function for James; so, too, would be firmness and control. But of James the sentient observer, the perceptive advocate of
"the felt life," there is another story to be told. The conflict between the novelist's craving for order and limitation and his impulse to experience all is clearly reflected in his fictional representation of the young girl. The discrepancy between the novelist's
nonfictional statements about the *jeune fille* and his finished portraits of adolescent girls stems from his own insatiable need to
"see" and "know" all that life had to offer. Without awareness there
could be no existence for him. Awareness, however, brings with it
recognition of, and exposure to, evil; this threatens contamination.
This problem of the relationship between knowledge of evil and
moral excellence was to occupy James for nearly three decades.
Early in his career it found fictional expression in *Daisy Miller*,
1878, and in Pansy Osmond, of *The Portrait of a Lady*, 1881.

Between 1892 and 1899 James's ambivalent attitude toward the
education of the young girl is exemplified in a series of notebook
entries on the theme of a story he never wrote:

> August 4, 1892
> Last evening at Ouchy, Miss R. said, after the conversation had run
> a little upon the way Americans drag their children about Europe:
> "A girl should be shown Europe—or taken to travel—by her hus-
> band—she has no business to see the world before. *He* takes her—
> he initiates her."

Struck with this as the old-fashioned French view and possible idea for a little tale. The girl whose husband is to show her everything— so she waits at home—and who never gets a husband . . . the daughter of a conservative "frenchified" mother etc. A pretext for the mother's selfishness, neglect, etc.—*she* travelling about. The girl's life—waiting—growing older—death. The husband comes in the form of death, etc.[24]

The passage is richly connotative. Not only does the novelist see marriage as a form of extinction, but the sheltered life suggests the death of the developing sensibility. In an entry dated 21 December 1895, he includes the motif in a list of possible ideas for a tale: "The mother who takes the line that her daughter's husband must show her everything—the husband never comes." Three years later, 7 May 1898, the idea is still with him: "Etta R's case of maturing, withering daughter. 'Her *husband* will show her the world, travel with her—a girl—in our *monde*—waits for that.'" In the fourth and final notebook reference to the theme, it becomes clear why James never made a tale of it:

5 October 1899
the little thing noted a long time ago as on a word dropped by Miss R.—the way for a woman (girl) to see the world, to travel, being for her husband to show her. The foreignized American mother who takes the line—the *un*foreignized ditto—or rather, American girl herself—who represents the idea of the young woman putting in all she can *before*—either to show it herself to her husband, or because she will, *after,* with the shelved and effaced state of so many, precisely, *by* marriage, have no chance. I might give three images: the girl *a la* Miss Reubel (I mean evoked by her words); and the first and second, *both* of these last-mentioned cases. They would make a little presented "scenic" trio.[25]

The story was never written because by the time James had made his last notebook reference to the theme of the sheltered daughter and the problem of what she should or should not be exposed to, he had already produced two major novels based on this motif— *What Maisie Knew,* 1897, and *The Awkward Age,* 1899. Furthermore, the notebook entries of the unwritten tale serve as a gloss to the course he was actually taking in his published fiction; we discern in them the evolution of the girl-heroine he *did* create.

With Maisie Farange, of *What Maisie Knew,* James achieved his most clearly realized representation of a small child's sensibility as well as one of his most scathing indictments of an uncaring, unfeeling adult world. By deciding to use the child's point of view exclusively—"the consciousness, the dim sweet, sacred, wondering, clinging perception of the child"—the author gives Maisie another dimension. She becomes more directly involved with and affected by her experience. Her developing awareness becomes a protective armor against the thoughtless cruelty of the adult world.

"The sensibility of the female young is indubitably, for early youth, the greater," remarks James in his preface to *What Maisie Knew*. However, what differentiates James's little girls of this period from their male counterparts is hardly their degree of sentience. They are differentiated by their ultimate fate. Morgan Moreen of "The Pupil" and little Miles of "The Turn of the Screw" have an abundance of sensibility; what they lack is the physical strength to survive. Comparing his little boys with Maisie and the young telegraphist of "In the Cage," he observes, "The two little spirits of maidens in the group, bear up, oddly enough beyond those of their brothers." [26] It would seem that for James perspicacious little girls are tougher than perspicacious little boys.

Critics have long noted the author's tendency to endow his female characters with physical and intellectual energy denied their male equivalents. Leon Edel's subtle analysis of James's need to hide behind the feminine persona in order to protect himself from female seduction as well as from male competition has given us a new understanding of the novelist's strong, transcendent heroines. What Edel calls James's "spiritual transvestitism" is undoubtedly fundamental to the novelist's projection of his important female characters. There is, however, another influence which could have significantly affected his characterization of young women.

In her perceptive biography of Henry James's young sister, Alice, Jean Strouse gives us a comprehensive view of attitudes toward women in the James household. Henry, Senior, firmly believed that girls were "not cut out for the conscious and continuous cerebration of intellectual endeavor." They were, in his view, spiritually superior but intellectually inferior to men; "selfless and naturally virtuous," woman's role in life was "simply to love and bless man." [27] William's attitude can be inferred from the tone he habitually took with Alice—humorously flirtatious, sometimes overtly sexual, and, in the final analysis, condescending. Wilky and Bob, the two younger brothers, teased her mercilessly with less subtlety and affection than William.

Alice James's short tragic life attests to the effect upon her of

having grown up in an environment which stifled her every creative impulse and engendered ambivalent feelings about herself as a
woman. Initially a bright, energetic child, upon reaching adolescence, she began to suffer "increasing 'nervous' susceptibility."
Her breakdown in 1868 was the first in a recurring pattern throughout her physically and emotionally tortured existence. Of the male
members of the James family, Henry, Junior, alone treated Alice as
an intellectual equal; his letters to and about his sister "assume a
shared world of reference and discrimination." Unlike his brothers
and his father, the novelist believed that women "represented the
dilemma of choice, imagination and knowledge that he saw as the
essence of human experience."[28] Throughout their lives Henry and
Alice shared a deep intellectual and spiritual kinship. He was aware
of the circumscribed nature of Alice's existence. "In our family
group," he wrote, "girls seem scarcely to have had a chance."[29] Not
surprisingly it was Henry, the novelist (not William, the psychologist) who discerned the function of Alice's chronic invalidism and
offered the most penetrating analysis of it. In a letter to William,
after Alice's death in March of 1892, he wrote, "Her disastrous, her
tragic health was in a manner the only solution for her of the practical problem of life."[30] Strouse cogently rephrases James's insight:
"The intelligence and energy Alice might have used in some productive way went into the intricate work of being sick . . . she recognized indirectly that her miserable health *was* her career."[31]

Cognizant of the psychological base for Alice's illness, James
must have reflected upon conditions that drove her to fashion for
herself so destructive a mechanism to ensure survival; he must have
asked himself what alternatives she had had, and he could very well
have concluded that, like so many women in her time and place, they
were stringently limited. The only "chance" then, for a girl would
lie in the broadest possible education, in having insight, awareness—that which, by virtue of her position in nineteenth-century
society generally and in the James household specifically, Alice was
denied. She had never, like her more privileged brothers, been free
to "dawdle" and "gape," free to develop her potential in a world of
men. Unlike the novelist's fictional heroines, Alice did *not* survive
because she was ill equipped to deal with an environment in which
it was considered unthinkable for a woman to compete intellectually with any man, much less with two brilliant and successful
brothers.

It is not unreasonable to suggest that James's empathy for Alice, his painful awareness of his sister's wasted life, affected his fictional representation of women. While Alice lay dying in March of 1892, Henry was in constant and solicitous attendance at her bedside; he wrote William, "They were infinitely pathetic and, to me, most unspeakable hours."[32] His preoccupation with the theme of the young girl who must be exposed to Europe by her husband began with a notebook entry dated 4 August 1892, five months after Alice's death. His interest in the girl who "waits at home—and who never gets a husband," whose life consists of "waiting—growing older" and to whom "the husband comes in the form of death" could very well have had its genesis in the novelist's response to the tragic fate of his sister. In the years between 1892 and 1899, James increasingly endowed his young heroines with that insight, that awareness denied his sister; thus armed, they, unlike Alice, can transcend, at least in the world of the novelist's creative imagination, the repressive forces of the milieu in which they are obliged to live. If Alice could not survive in the real world, she could triumph through her brother's art.

The education Alice James never received becomes the key to Maisie Farange's development and ultimate survival. The little girl's exposure becomes her education. Like Geordie and Ferdy, Morgan and Miles, she is sacrificed on the altar of adult egotism; unlike them (and unlike Alice) she emerges unscathed. The sacrifice brings regeneration to those around her, not by her physical death, but by the "death of her childhood"—by the achievement of maturity. Maisie takes part in shaping her own destiny as well as the destiny of the adults with whom she comes in contact.

What differentiates the novelist's treatment of Maisie from that of his adult heroines is his authoritative documentation of her perceptions which is rooted in his understanding of, and empathy for, the child's sensibility. The author knew—or perhaps he remembered—precisely how the world could look to a child, how experience impinged upon the consciousness of the young, and he communicated this faithfully in his rendering of Maisie:

> Maisie found in her mind a collection of images and echoes to which meanings were attachable—images and echoes kept for her in the childish dusk, the dim closet, the high drawer, like games she wasn't yet big enough to play. The great strain meanwhile was that of carrying by the right end the things her father said about her mother—things mostly indeed that [her governess] on a glimpse of them, as if they had been complicated toys or difficult books, took

out of her hands and put away in the closet. A wonderful assortment
of objects of this kind she was to discover there later, all tumbled up
too with the things shuffled into some receptacle, that her mother
had said about her father.[33]

This re-creation of the repressive mechanism at work presented
in terms of images that are salient for a child is characteristic of
James's sensitive grasp of the child's response to external stimuli.
The moment of Maisie's initiation into total awareness of her function for her divorced parents is recorded with chilling lucidity:

> The theory of her stupidity, eventually embraced by her parents, cor-
> responded with a great date in her small still life: the complete vision,
> private but fierce, of the strange office she filled. It was literally a
> moral revolution accomplished in the depths of her nature . . . old
> forms and phrases began to have a sense that frightened her. She
> had a new feeling, the feeling of danger: on which a new remedy
> rose to meet it, the idea of an inner self or, in other words, of
> concealment.[34]

The little girl's recoil from hostility and rejection is authentically
documented. James goes on to identify the weapon the young child
would forge in order to protect herself:

> She would forget everything, she would repeat nothing, and when,
> as a tribute to the successful application of her system, she began to
> be called a little idiot, she tasted a pleasure new and keen. . . . She
> spoiled their fun, but she practically added to her own. She saw
> more and more; she saw too much.[35]

James's handling of Maisie's early development has a psychological
verisimilitude almost painful in its accuracy. Yet, despite his carefully delineated record of Maisie's reactions to her experience,
there is an essential element missing in his projection of her; this
omission furthers the development of the author's theme but it ultimately robs Maisie of psychological authenticity. Despite the brutality to which the child is exposed, she is completely devoid of
anger or resentment. Because Maisie bears no grudges, her moral
sense is free to develop to its fullest capacity. But her lack of anger,
in view of the emotional lacerations her life experience must have
given her, is difficult to accept. There is a limit to the hate a child
can absorb without having some of it rub off on her little person.
What can a small child be expected to feel when she is told by her
father, "You know your mother loathes you, loathes you simply"?
How can a child ever erase from her memory the words, "Your fa-

ther wishes you were dead—that, my dear, is what your father wishes"? While James dealt magnificently with the causes in his presentation of the child's character and plight, he has not adequately dramatized effects. What Maisie comes to know does not—if we are to think of her in terms of psychological realism—affect her in ways the reader can accept.

There are essentially three ways a child can deal with the inevitable anger provoked by rejection: it might turn the feeling inward and the result would be some form of self-destruction (as was probably the case with James's sister, Alice). These hostile feelings could be projected outward and the result might be a destructive impulse toward society. A third alternative lies in the sublimation of hostile energy into socially sanctioned activity. For Maisie, none of these alternatives exist. The achievement of a state of moral superiority is a result of successful sublimation, not a substitute for it. While James exhibits discernment in his rendering of Maisie's perception of her world, he fails to face the implications of those perceptions for the child. In Maisie the novelist has created what was perhaps for him the ideal child, one that is victimized and aware, yet free from aggression and hostility, one who "live[s] with all intensity and perplexity in its terribly mixed little world," but who could, one suspects, only exist in the world of James's rich and creative imagination. But to leave it at that is to ignore the work of art. The rare quality of the novel lies in the delicacy of response on the part of the novelist to the movement of the child's mind, in the figurative language that so sensitively captures the pain of childhood and growing up, in the author's sustained metaphoric use of the child as a force for spiritual health and moral transcendence. In *What Maisie Knew* the author focused on the most terrible cruelty that can be perpetrated on children—the cruelty of subjecting them to chaos, confusion, and emotional deprivation. Love and order are closely related in the child's world. Maisie alone knows this and she teaches it to Sir Claude. Affection cannot exist without a coherent value system; both are indispensable for the well-being of the young.

Problems of adolescence and the maturing process engaged James's imagination for more than thirty years. His earliest novel, *Watch and Ward,* 1870, touches upon this motif. While Nora, the young heroine, prefigures the observant and intuitively perceptive adolescents of the novelist's mature work, there is little evidence in this early tale of a specific or unique educational philosophy. By the time he created his finished tales of adolescents, he had arrived at a clear concept of what constituted maturity. If the earlier children had their experience of life determined for them by external circumstances beyond their control, the adolescents who followed actively reach out to life in an effort to understand and shape their destinies.

There is a progression in James's treatment of the emerging adult. The movement is from unawareness to self-consciousness, from partial insight to complete vision and from defective perception to full cognition; this ability to perceive the truth about oneself and the actuality of one's condition becomes the gauge of the character's moral worth. The young, inexperienced and avidly curious governess in "The Turn of the Screw," 1898, is an adolescent. Her extremes of sensibility, her passionate dedication to her "cause"—that of "rescuing" Flora and Miles from evil—her unpredictable changes of mood and her insatiable curiosity are all characteristics of the adolescent seeking to come to terms with herself and the reality of life. The governess is, to be sure, more than a typical adolescent; she is the vehicle for James's inquiry into the nature of "seeing" and "knowing," of illusion and reality, of ambiguity and certainty. She raises the question of whether it is enough to desperately want knowledge in order to gain it. What are the necessary conditions for "awareness"? Does the governess have a lucid perception of reality? For James, a prior condition for the acquisition of knowledge about others is self-knowledge, which, in turn, implies a recognition of human fallibility. The young governess is clearly deficient in this area. She never sufficiently questions the reality of the "danger" she senses. Overwhelmed by her emotions, she has lost perspective and cannot understand her inner turmoil. That James meant her to be viewed in this context is clear from the changes he made in the text in 1907. Every alteration he made emphasizes the emotional aspect of the governess's response to the experience she is recounting. If the character of the adolescent governess seems overdrawn, it is because the novelist's major interest was in the theme of transition from innocence to knowledge, from adolescence to maturity. The ambiguity with which the author surrounds his narrator is indispensable to the projection of his epistemological and metaphysical themes.

The young telegraphist of "In the Cage," 1898, is another curious, sensitive girl on the brink of maturity. Unlike the governess, the young telegraphist perceives reality; her problem is to make peace with it. Here is indeed a fine consciousness (perhaps, at times, too fine for credibility) and the reader is exposed to every nuance of it as the girl stands apart, as it were, and takes note of her need to escape from the reality of a humdrum existence. "In the Cage" is a subtle, gentle tale of growth through perception, of the successful synthesis of emotion and intellect, of the achievement of identity through self-knowledge. The telegraphist and the governess represent the obverse and converse of the proposition that true knowledge derives from maximum consciousness and a vision of reality free from distortion. James brought this theme to complete realization in *The Awkward Age,* 1899. Nanda Brookenham is the logical successor to the deluded young governess and the aware but unheroic little telegraphist.

The Awkward Age contains James's most complex and comprehensive epistemological statement. He defines the "well-brought-up" young girl, circumscribes familial responsibility, and characterizes the society in which maximum growth is possible. He creates, finally, his own species of *jeune fille* and contrasts her directly with her more traditional sister. All James's themes of childhood and adolescence come together, all his fictional young people converge in his portrait of Nanda; she is the novelist's final, vigorous affirmation of the moral superiority of the exposed innocent. Where the governess lacked insight and discrimination, Nanda's vision of reality is penetrating. Where the little telegraphist lacked stature, Nanda emerges as morally and intellectually larger than life. Nanda Brookenham is James's tribute to adolescence as Maisie Farange was his panegyric to childhood. The curious, wondering little girl has evolved into the alert young woman who, because of her fine consciousness, is able to face the hypocrisy of her world with equanimity and make the choice that will ensure her moral superiority.

James's notebook entry of 4 March 1895, reads, "The idea of the little London girl who grows up to 'sit in' with the free-talking modern young mother—reaches 17, 18, etc.—comes out—and not marrying, has to 'be there'. . . and though the conversation is supposed to be expurgated for her, she inevitably hears, overhears, guesses, follows, takes in, becomes acquainted with horror."[36] The "horror" lies in the behavior of Nanda's reprehensible family and their hypocritical social set. Nanda lives in a morally dislocated world in which virtue and vice are so thoroughly confused that only a superior mind is capable of penetrating the duplicity which permeates the very air she breathes.

The central problem in the novel is the implication of Nanda's "exposure"—as a young, innocent, unmarried girl—to the intrigue, malicious gossip, and hostile witticisms of her mother's "impossible" drawing room. The problem of Nanda's "sitting downstairs" becomes a metaphor for the larger issue of a society that confuses propriety with morality, that compromises integrity for personal gain and places greater value on meaningless convention than on affection and loyalty. In Nanda's society the conventions of an earlier age have survived, but the integrity which gave substance to them has disappeared, leaving the empty shell of manners and mores and an ethical code observed more in the breach than in the practice. Nanda is of the "new," thinking adolescents who gain perspective through an expanded consciousness and the ability to realistically evaluate the world around them. Old Mr. Longdon, who had been in love with Nanda's grandmother, comes to realize, through his contact with the girl, that integrity can coexist with knowledge of evil in one individual. Vanderbank, the young sophisticate with whom Nanda is in love, appears to know and accept reality, but, in the final analysis, is a captive of his own rigidity; he cannot accept Nanda as his wife because she has "taken in" too much, been too much "exposed." Mr. Longdon, under Nanda's tutelage, exhibits a flexibility of which the younger man is incapable:

> "Girls understand now. It has got to be faced . . . Even Mr. Longdon admits that."
>
> Vanderbank wondered, "You mean you talk over with him—"
>
> "The subject of girls? Why we scarcely discuss anything else . . . "
>
> "But you mean," Vanderbank asked, "that he recognizes the inevitable changes—?"
>
> "He can't shut his eyes to the facts. He sees we're quite a different thing."[37]

Nanda finds her salvation in an unqualified acceptance of herself and in the conviction that true morality lies in the deepest possible perception of life. James is saying through his young heroine that while the educative process requires the broadest exposure, awareness without discrimination, knowledge without responsibility, insight without the will and strength to act is of scant value. Therefore, those accountable to the young must be selflessly involved in their lives, must feel genuine affection for them and set an example worthy of emulation. A highly developed consciousness alone does not secure the child against suffering and defeat; only love and familial responsibility can mitigate the inevitable pain of living. These, then, are the laws which, in James's world, govern emotional and intellectual growth.

The search for the manifest life-myth inherent in James's treatment of children and adolescents in his fiction leads inevitably to the perception that the novelist's artistic temperament found fuller and freer expression through the persona of the strong, triumphant young woman. Seen this way, the author's girl-child becomes emblematic of intellectual, emotional, and spiritual development; all little girls blend to become one little girl who, like her creator, becomes more mature from tale to tale, conscientiously fashioning for herself (and possibly for James) a unique defense against the pain of a basically disillusioned view of life. This defensive mechanism—a fully and completely developed sensibility—assures survival and, because of its moral coloration, transcendence for child and author; in its artistic manifestation, this transcendence becomes immortality through the creative act. Nanda Brookenham is the most convincing product of James's educational theory because she expresses most fully the compromise with the life of the senses James must have reached at the end of the nineteenth century; she dramatizes, as well, the resolution of a problem central to James's thought and feeling—the European as opposed to the American way of preparing the young for adulthood.

By applying the methodology of the "new biography" to the scattered theorizing of James as well as to his fictional representation of children and adolescents, we can, in the end, formulate what the novelist left unformulated. Education is transcendence, awareness the saving and nourishing principle that is nowhere more critical than in the child who is besieged by bewildering and often hostile forces. Ideally, responsible adults will both exemplify and demand adherence to objective moral standards. But as society faces the disintegration of an identifiable social and moral order, as the chasm between what is stated and what is practiced becomes ever wider, the young person becomes increasingly vulnerable. Therefore, in the final analysis, the quality of the perceiving consciousness determines whether the effect of awareness shall be survival against implacable odds, as in Maisie; self-acceptance and moral strength, as in Nanda; or transformation of awareness into creativity, as in James himself.

NOTES

1. Leon Edel, "The Figure under the Carpet," *Telling Lives* (Washington: New Republic Books, 1979), 24–25.

2. Henry James, *Autobiography,* ed. introd. Frederick W. Dupee (New York: Criterion Books, 1956), xiii.

3. James, *Autobiography,* 7–8.

4. Oscar Cargill, *The Novels of Henry James* (New York: The Macmillan Company, 1961), 351.

5. Cargill, 351.

6. Leon Edel, *Henry James The Master: 1901–1916* (New York: J. B. Lippincott Company, 1972), 111.

7. Edel, *Henry James The Master: 1901–1916,* 111–112.

8. Graham Greene, *The Lost Childhood and Other Essays* (New York: The Viking Press, 1951), 26.

9. James Sully, *Studies of Childhood* (New York: Longmans, Green and Company, 1895), 65.

10. Henry James, *What Maisie Knew* (New York: Doubleday and Company, 1954), 23.

11. G. Stanley Hall, *Adolescence* (New York: D. Appleton and Company, 1922), I, 536, 589. Originally published in 1904.

12. Henry James, "The Pupil," *The Complete Tales of Henry James,* ed. Leon Edel, vol. VII (New York: J. B. Lippincott Company, 1963), 411.

13. James, *Complete Tales,* II.

14. James, *Complete Tales,* IV, 143.

15. Henry James, *Literary Reviews and Essays,* ed. Albert Mordell (New York: Twayne Publishers, 1957), 246.

16. Henry James, *A Small Boy and Others* (New York: Charles Scribner's Sons, 1913), 216.

17. James, *Complete Tales,* VII, 106.

18. James, *Complete Tales,* VIII, 451.

19. Henry James, *Portraits of Places* (Boston: James R. Osgood and Company, 1885), 163–164.

20. James, *A Small Boy and Others,* 233–234.

21. James, *A Small Boy and Others,* 235.

22. James, *Portraits of Places,* 163–164.

23. *The Notebooks of Henry James,* ed. F. O. Matthiessen and Kenneth B. Murdock (New York: Charles Braziller, Inc., 1955), 41.

24. James, *Notebooks,* 125.

25. James, *Notebooks,* 295.

26. Henry James, *The Art of the Novel* (New York: Charles Scribner's Sons, 1962), 156.

27. Jean Strouse, *Alice James: A Biography* (Boston: Houghton Mifflin Company, 1980), 45.

28. Strouse, *Alice James,* 50.

29. Leon Edel, *Henry James The Conquest of London: 1870–1881* (New York: J. B. Lippincott Company, 1962), 49.

30. Leon Edel, *Henry James The Middle Years: 1882–1895* (New York: J. B. Lippincott Company, 1962), 306.

31. Strouse, *Alice James,* 291.

32. Strouse, *Alice James,* 314.

33. Henry James, *What Maisie Knew* (New York: Doubleday and Company, 1954), 25.

34. James, *Maisie,* 27.

35. James, *Maisie,* 28.

36. James, *Notebooks,* 192.

37. Henry James, *The Awkward Age* (New York: Harper and Brothers, 1904), 286–287.

THE BIOGRAPHER AS NOVELIST

Harvena Richter

1

In an essay titled "The Art of Biography," Virginia Woolf sets out to prove that the biographer "is a craftsman, not an artist." It may be a superior craft he practices, but "his work is not a work of art, but something betwixt and between."[1] That Woolf should reduce biography to a level lower than that of fiction is curious, considering that much of her time was spent writing nonfiction, most of it biographical in one way or another, and that her closest friend outside the family was Lytton Strachey. Another nearby biographer was Harold Nicolson, the husband of Vita Sackville-West. Woolf's father, Leslie Stephen, had edited the *Dictionary of National Biography*.

Virginia Woolf's feelings about biography, which seemed to increase in intensity as she grew older, point to a curious conflict within Woolf herself: a conflict stemming not only from what she felt was the unbridgeable gulf between "the truth of real life and the truth of fiction,"[2] but from obscure forces involving her own concepts of poetry and fiction, her insistence on the primacy of the imagination, her subterranean jealousies and rivalries of which she was perhaps unaware. To examine, however cursorily, these elements of conflict is to understand more clearly the direction that biography is taking in the latter part of the twentieth century, a direction which, together with Strachey, Woolf pioneered.

What appeared to bother Woolf most about biography was the curtailment of freedom involved; nothing which inhibited the writer could possibly be first class. Although biography had "its new liberties," it was "the most restricted of all the arts." One was restricted by the very subject, as Queen Victoria, for example, "was limited";[3] by family members peering over one's shoulder, as Woolf learned while writing *Roger Fry;* by the fact itself which is not necessarily the truth about the person, if by "truth" one means the essence of that subject's personality which the biographer tries to capture—an achievement reached by a manipulation rather than a simple presentation of the facts. Pressed down by life-facts, which paradoxically she searched for in her novels as well as in her diaries, she wished to escape into an area that posed no controls. The truth of imagination and the truth of life, although they actually met in her novels, seemed poles apart. Her problem in understanding that they exist side by side can be seen in her rejected plan for an essay-novel called *The Pargiters,* in which chapters of fiction and social history would alternate. After writing six essays and five chapters, she abandoned the idea. The essays, it must be noted, have none of the energy and imagination she infuses into her other works of nonfiction. They are the sad, flat result of a preconceived theory which she did not subscribe to in her own literary life. Almost as if those rejected essays had been a penal project to expiate for the guilt of the exuberant biography-fantasy *Flush,* which followed *The Waves,* she had served her time and could now return to fiction. But after *The Years,* which *The Pargiters* became, there was still more discipline ahead: *Three Guineas,* biographical as well as polemical, and after that, *Roger Fry.*

Another factor which may have exacerbated Woolf's conflict is the mental connection which she made between her madness and her imagination. Factual writing may have fulfilled a need to "control" her mind. Seeing it as a personal corrective, part of a fight against her natural inclination to soar too high, she would then relegate factual writing to a lower level. Compounding whatever feeling of guilt she had was her knowledge that the periods of madness became the chrysalis stage of the novels she would write.[4] Her illness caused herself, and others, pain; yet it also helped to produce her finest work. As Lily Briscoe punishes herself for being an artist in *To the Lighthouse* by constantly demeaning herself, so factual writing may have become a corrective in yet another sense.

A further element may have entered Virginia Woolf's feeling that biography was a suspect art. As many critics have commented, her own novels are heavily biographical. Not only her first novel, *The Voyage Out,* had characters whom her sister Vanessa instantly recognized, but subsequent ones portrayed various friends and family members: her brother Thoby, Vanessa, her parents, Lytton Strachey (caricatured in three novels). Woolf's imagination fed on what she knew first hand, which made her intuitively perceive the difference between fact and imagination and perhaps feel oversensitive about the thin line which sometimes separates them. She also knew the transformation which occurs when imagination processes life into art, when a few facts, as both *Orlando* and *Flush* demonstrate, form the base for the most fanciful of structures. Indeed, in most of Woolf's work the borderline between genres is vague. *A Room of One's Own* eludes classification (autobiographical meditation?). Some of her short stories, such as "A Mark on the Wall," resemble essays. *Orlando,* a raffish portrait of her friend Vita Sackville-West, is less biography than a casebook on how to write one; *Flush* is more fiction than biography. Had Woolf read the charge leveled at her by Jean Guiguet that the failure of *Roger Fry* was due to "its hesitation between novel, biography and autobiography,"[5] she would have defended her method as one underlying all her work, suggesting the direction of literature in general and biography in particular.

Before a discussion of *Roger Fry* and the difficulties Woolf encountered writing it, mention must be made of the background of her two essays on biography which appeared some twelve years apart. The earlier essay, "The New Biography," a review of Harold Nicolson's *Some People,* stresses the topics of truth and personality and the "change" which "came over biography, as it came over fiction and poetry." Her mood is mellow; she is at work on *Orlando* and so comments on Nicolson's method "of writing about people . . . as though they were at once real and imaginary," which was just what she was doing in her own novel. She admits that "the biographer's imagination is always being stimulated to use the novelist's art of arrangement, suggestion, dramatic effect to expound the private life." If, in Nicolson's case, "a little fiction mixed with fact can be made to transmit personality very effectively," that is quite all right, as long as he does not "mix the truth of real life and the truth of fiction." Woolf hedges diplomatically, careful not to offend Vita's husband at the time when their relationship (Vita's and Virginia's) was at its most intense. But she cannot help remarking that the method of "the biographer whose art is subtle and bold enough to present that queer amalgamation of dream and reality, that perpetual marriage of granite and rainbow" does not yet exist, though Nicolson "waves his hand airily in a possible direction."[6]

In sharp contrast is her later essay, "The Art of Biography," in which she takes Lytton Strachey to task for inventing too much of *Elizabeth and Essex,* treating biography as an "art" by flouting its limitations.[7] She pronounces it a failure—something she probably would not have done had Strachey been alive. A memory of old resentments seems to surface in this essay, a hint of the competitive rivalry she may have felt when Strachey's *Eminent Victorians* was published to great applause and she was struggling with a minor second novel. That Woolf far surpassed her friend (who had once proposed to her, then shrank with horror from the commitment) might not be guessed at from the tone of her essay. She owed him debts, as Leon Edel observes.[8] She certainly does not pay them here.

Yet if she cuts down Lytton Strachey she is also diminishing herself as biographer, for she was working at that time on *Roger Fry,* trying to suppress the fictional element which Strachey had freely used. A year earlier she had written to Vita, "My God, how does one write a Biography? Tell me. . . . How can one deal with facts—so many and so many and so many? Or ought one, as I incline, to be purely fictitious? And what is a life? And what was Roger?"[9]

It would be 1940 before the book was published and she could leave "the compromise of biography"—a compromise with Roger Fry's family rather than with biography itself—to "rush headlong into a novel; as a relief."[10] Yet her diary confesses to a certain triumph: "I can't help thinking," she wrote on 9 February, "I've caught a good deal of that iridescent man in my oh so laborious butterfly net." And she was furious at Leonard's reaction to the manuscript, feeling as if she were "being pecked by a very hard strong beak" as he judged it to be "'merely analysis, not history. Austere repression. In fact dull to the outsider.'"[11]

Leonard Woolf's unusual criticism—a passage included in *A Writer's Diary* which he himself edited—seemed unfair to Virginia because it appeared to represent a certain "lack of interest in personality" on Leonard's part. Her use of the words "iridescent" and "butterfly net" in the excerpt quoted above reveals that she felt her imagination had been at work—the artist's, not the biographer's. For in *To the Lighthouse,* did she not use the image of the butterfly twice ("the light of the butterfly's wing lying upon the arches of a cathedral") to represent Lily Briscoe's vision of a work of art?[12] And in her essay "On Reading," the netting of moths in the dark forest represents the searching imagination in the forest of the unconscious.[13] The biography *Roger Fry* was no mere show of craftsmanship. With its emphasis on moments of being, its pursuit of personality, its complex synthesis of feeling, it was for her more like a novel, perhaps "too like a novel."[14]

For the outstanding quality of her fiction was just this search for the "iridescence" of the human personality: Clarissa walking down Bond Street; Mrs. Ramsay reading to her son James; Rachel on a Santa Marina hilltop. *Jacob's Room,* an attempt by Virginia to capture the iridescence of her brother Thoby, is crowded with images of butterflies and moths. Early in that novel, the narrator is pictured as a "hawk moth," humming, vibrating "at the mouth of the cavern of mystery" that was Jacob Flanders. Twenty years later that same image of the hawk moth would resurface in *Roger Fry.*[15]

The emphasis on the mystery of the human personality, how it came to be that way, what constituted its elusive essence, marked one of the directions biography would take. It was part of the lesson that *Orlando* offered, for the mystery of Vita Sackville-West was hidden in her family which traced back to the Elizabethans, in the country estate of Knole, in the complexities of her androgynous personality. This quest for the sources of personality which is unfolded page by page—"And what is a life? And what was Roger?"—governs both Woolf's novels and her biographies, quasi-biographies, and essays, and supplies the suspense element as does any mystery, any quest.

Writing was also, for Virginia Woolf, a personal quest for the human being who had lived, then died. *Jacob's Room* was a means of bringing back her dead brother Thoby by giving him a nearly tangible body within the pages of a book. *Orlando* gave permanent shape to what Woolf probably recognized would be a temporary friendship, given Vita's infidelities. *To the Lighthouse* restored her parents in a form that the author/child could deal with. In a sense, what had been lost, or what would be lost to Woolf, was partially returned; the private hurt was redeemed in the public gesture.

Roger Fry, too, had been closely intertwined in her life: her sister Vanessa's lover whom she herself must share in a different but equally intimate relationship as biographer. When in 1934, scarcely two months after Roger's death, she thinks about writing his life, she notes, "I must now do biography and autobiography."[16] In 1940, not long after sending off the page proofs, she writes, "What a curious relation is mine with Roger at this moment—I who have given him a kind of shape after his death. Was he like that? I feel very much in his presence at the moment; as if I were intimately connected with him: as if we together had given birth to this vision of him: a child born of us."[17]

This is a startling quotation, and it is one of a piece with the comments Leon Edel makes regarding Woolf's obsessive rivalry with her sister: the long flirtation with Clive, the almost incestuous desire to possess Thoby, who was closer in age to Vanessa.[18] By writing a book about Roger, she was producing a "child" which Vanessa did not have by him. Even more startling is the image of giving him a "shape," almost as if Roger himself is being reborn through her. The many guises Thoby takes in her novels also fit the subject of "possession" as the magic of a sorceress who can not only summon the disembodied from the void but steal psychic ownership.[19] This topic may be an invitation to discuss the many subterranean motives and drives of the biographer, but that is not part of this essay. The only pertinent point is that the creation of a character by a novelist, from whatever sources, single or multiple, real or imaginary, his model may derive, functions in the same manner, is driven by the same forces that demand punishment, serve aggression, act as wish fulfillment, satisfy complex emotional needs. There is some element of magic here in the more archaic sense of the word. Perry Meisel, in *The Absent Father: Virginia Woolf and Walter Pater,* speaks of the alchemical concept of artistic creation and the figure of Hephaestus, god of fire, who is "the patron of smiths."[20] One remembers Stephen in James Joyce's *A Portrait of the Artist* who goes forth "to forge in the smithy of my soul the uncreated conscience of my race"; Septimus Smith in *Mrs. Dalloway* who partakes of extraterrestrial powers and knowledge; the "bolts of iron" which clamp together the work of art under its butterfly surface in *To the Lighthouse.*

If *Roger Fry* lacks the magic of Woolf's finest fiction, it is nonetheless a portrait of a very alive person, a man himself composed of butterfly and iron, and it seeks the springs of action, the sources of the mystery of personality, as does her other work. Vanessa Bell, who found in Mrs. Ramsay of *To the Lighthouse* her mother "raised from the dead," said to Virginia, after reading *Roger Fry,* "Now you have given him back to me."[21] It is curious that the biography has been so downgraded by the critics (Phyllis Rose terms it "dreary," an attempt "to substitute sheer work for genius"),[22] oblivious of the advanced biographical techniques it demonstrates, techniques certainly learned from Strachey as well as from her own novelistic methods. The biography has the pace of a novel, from the opening image of the Oriental poppy bud with its show of "crumpled scarlet silk" through the conflicts, revolts, and contradictions of his life and personality, to a peaceful end ("On 13th September, a day as it happened of extraordinary beauty, his body was cremated.") which resembles the conclusion of *The Years*. There is story, there is symbolism, there is an adroit handling of relationships, except for the gaps of his liaison with Vanessa and the madness of his wife—material too close to Virginia to be handled by her. And there is a vivid background of Bloomsbury and of the Omega Workshop, a feel of time and place, but above all that "iridescence" of personality which Woolf intuitively felt she had caught. If the book at times seems overweighted with quotations from Fry's own writing, they form part of the granite in the "granite and rainbow" marriage a biography must achieve, and they give, as no paraphrase can, the particular flavor of that person.

2

Roger Fry was to be the first of many biographies of individual members of Bloomsbury by one of the inner circle. Much earlier (1914) Leonard Woolf had written a roman à clef, *The Wise Virgins,* in which he himself, Virginia, Vanessa, and an aura of the Leslie Stephen household appear lightly disguised. In the 1950s the first tentative biography by an outsider, Aileen Pippett's *The Moth and the Star: a Biography of Virginia Woolf,* was published, to be followed by a string of Bloomsbury reminiscences that would furnish later, more meticulous biographers with a solid block of material. Not until the late sixties would the massive two-volume life of Lytton Strachey by Michael Holroyd appear, and in the early seventies an equally long but quite different life of Virginia Woolf by her nephew Quentin Bell.

Between Pippett's loose, rambling account and the Holroyd and Bell biographies a quiet revolution had taken place. The revolutionary was Strachey himself, and his influence came to be felt in the sixties and seventies in a rather circuitous manner. The direction was toward psychology and fiction. The particular route, whether metaphorical or actual, was via Leon Edel's biography of Henry James, three volumes of which had been published by the time Holroyd began his biography of Strachey, giving Holroyd a blueprint of how to write a biography whose tenets derived from Holroyd's subject himself. That Leon Edel would in turn do a cycle of Bloomsbury portraits, which includes Strachey, more than a decade later closes the loop.

To those acquainted with Leon Edel's slim volume *Literary Biography,* the influence of Strachey on his own work should come as no surprise. Strachey's name begins the first sentence of the book, and if Strachey's style now seems dated in comparison to Edel's artfully modern prose, his inventive concepts are not. Edel comments on how the kind of biography Strachey wrote "borrows from the methods of the novelist without, however, being fiction." Those methods, the disengagement of scenes or utilization of "trivial incidents . . . to illuminate character," the very act of being "wholly selective and psychological,"[23] are at the very heart of the James biography. If we are to look at the influence of Edel on Holroyd, it is in the emphasis on psychological drama, the use of a fictionlike series of obstructions and resolutions, a concentration on the density of personal relationships. Holroyd, like Edel, is careful to dramatize the influence of strong women on his subject, to point out how Strachey chose powerful female figures for his own subject matter (as did Henry James).[24] If the James biography has a certain majesty lacking in the Holroyd volumes, part is due to the majestic figure of James himself and the matters of his life and his fiction which so beautifully counterpoint each other. With Strachey as subject, a certain flippancy must be observed. The background itself is not so ordered; shift and sequence do not operate as noiselessly as in Edel's work.

Although Edel's incursion into Strachey territory in *Bloomsbury: A House of Lions* bears little resemblance to his biography of James, there is the same attention to psychology, a sharpened use of fictional modes. In his preface Edel admits to using a form which many novels take, that of "an *Entwicklung,* an unfolding," a following of the character's struggle to maturity. With nine characters to deal with, all of whose lives are closely intertwined, Edel must resort to more than "episodic structure" and "psychological interpretation" to create a work which is both highly compressed and thematically designed. The title itself hints at his methods. *A House of Lions* is no mere amusing phrase borrowed from Virginia Woolf; it becomes a device whose theme, that of power—for what quality more aptly symbolizes the lion—governs the approach to each character in the book. Leonard Woolf, for example, demonstrates the power of the human will over fear and anger; Clive Bell has the power of the hunter's eye over game, women, and art; Lytton Strachey exercises his manipulative power over people, Maynard Keynes over difficult, abstract ideas. Vanessa, in a suggested oxymoron, is the volcano beneath the monolith. Virginia's struggle with, and literary victory over, her madness is another power story, as is Roger Fry's crusade for post-Impressionist art. Only the two lesser lions, Duncan Grant and Desmond MacCarthy, are allowed a gentleness of treatment; perhaps they are powers unto themselves.

This mythologizing, usually found only in the province of the novel, is carried into a recounting of certain myths which the characters created about themselves: Lytton Strachey as both Voltaire and Caliban, Virginia and Leonard Woolf as Pericles and Aspasia. And it serves to compress the vast amount of material with which Edel has to deal. He has not, as Strachey declared of himself in his famous introduction to *Eminent Victorians,* lowered a bucket here and there in the ocean to bring up an exotic specimen. Rather he has selected, filtered, and condensed with the novelist's eye.

If each character appears engaged upon a quest, Edel follows the crisscrossing of those patterns, a configuration more complicated than that of the summer weekend guests in Henry James's *The Sacred Fount.* There is a crossing of career lines (Leonard Woolf and Roger Fry), of marriage lines or taboos to fulfill a compulsive psychological need. Obsessions in the nursery, such as Vanessa's and Virginia's competitive drive for Thoby's attention, grow and change into adult obsessions, such as Virginia's earlier-mentioned urge to share her sister's life and lovers. Strachey's quest for sex embroils a large group of artists and poets on the edge of Bloomsbury; he becomes the center of a whirlpool into which Carrington is fatally drawn. These relationships, whose threads are constantly kept taut, suggest a larger theme in the biography: the nine characters form a composite of man in search of himself. And the representative questing hero, drawn larger than any other portrait in *A House of Lions,* is Leonard Woolf, whose history opens the volume. He forms a counter-rhythm to the rest of Bloomsbury; the most brilliant intellectually of the group, he is an outsider who conquers and endures. Edel lends him the overtones of an existential hero who surmounts a variety of handicaps, operates on a number of levels. He is novelist, socialist, political writer, editor, publisher, husband/nursemaid/companion of a woman whom he must nurture in both a physical and a literary way.[25]

There is a subtle polarization between Leonard, the active hero, and Vanessa, the monolithic heroine, who is the immovable center of the often volatile group. Given to inward rages, in contrast to Leonard's quick outer angers, she maintains a reign of calm. Her quest is for peace and work, which she achieves as Leonard achieves his self-control. There is a suggestion in *The Wise Virgins* that Leonard was much attracted to Vanessa. In his own autobiography Leonard remembers that upon his first meeting the sisters, "It was almost impossible for a man not to fall in love with them, and I think that I did at once."[26] The plural pronoun suggests an interchangeable aspect of the two. If one cannot marry Vanessa (who by the time Leonard returned from Ceylon was married to Clive Bell, whom Leonard disliked), then one marries Virginia. Edel does not mention that Leonard's love for Vanessa may have been sublimated into his love for Virginia. Unspoken plots underlie the suggestive matter of the book.

There is one more aspect of the novel which Edel employs, and that is a tone which may be compared to that of a Victorian novelist, a way of referring to the matter of the book as "our story," to the characters as "our personages." Words like "goodly" and "comely" serve to distance the members of Bloomsbury, many of whom lived on into our own time, and throw over them the fictional aura of "character" rather than of person. This enables Edel to present minianalyses of the members without changing gear; it is the distance of the psychologist who records rather than enters the life of his patients. One may recall the remark that Henry James wrote like a psychologist whereas his brother William James wrote like a novelist. Biographer Edel manages to write like both.

It is perhaps in the compression of material, the sharp focus on personality and its psychological history, that *Bloomsbury: A House of Lions* falls under the latter-day rubric of "portrait." By its very nature the portrait seeks to condense, reduce to essence. The result is not photographic but rather impressionistic, synecdochal. Its ancestry lies in the biographical literary essay; its best practitioner, who loosened and perfected that form, was Virginia Woolf. Curiously, its closest relative in fiction is the plotless novel of that same writer ("Don't bother about the plot: the plot's nothing," thinks Miss La Trobe in *Between the Acts*). But if Woolf sidestepped plot, she adopted design, much as the post-Impressionist painters forsook dimension to concentrate on a carefully created surface pattern. *A House of Lions* insists on such a pattern to the lives and takes great care in delineating it. The figure in the carpet, to echo a phrase of Henry James, is as important as those who walk that carpet.

Because of its freedom—anything is permitted—the portrait appears to be the biographical form that most books about Bloomsbury assume. There are Ur-portraits in the academic profiles of J. K. Johnstone's *The Bloomsbury Group*. Quentin Bell's brief *Bloomsbury* presents the picture of an attitude and an ambience. The form turns to group portraiture in David Gadd's *The Loving Friends*, becomes melodrama in Nigel Nicolson's *Portrait of a Marriage,* reaches a definitive shape in Richard Shone's *Bloomsbury Portraits: Vanessa Bell, Duncan Grant and Their Circle.* The last three have strong aspects of the novel, as does *A House of Lions.* And it is impossible not to speculate that in part this is because Bloomsbury itself is the very stuff of fiction. The characters are appealing, brilliant, original. Their actions and ideals—a combination of vague indecency with high-minded motive—form an exotic paradox. In the background, a constant parade of English notables or titled families move to and fro. A tangle of unholy alliances—transsexual, complicated, often multiple—result in a net of relationships which any novelist might aspire to invent. There is not only wry comedy but tragedy: madness, suicide, sudden death. Just to sort out the complexity and characterize the members and their actions takes a certain talent. It is the new biographer's paradise: a blend of extravagance and reality, a reservoir of ready-made stories.

Indeed, Bloomsbury seems destined to become one of those great matters of history and legend that engage the imagination in other than purely sociohistorical ways. Bloomsbury already has its saints; new feminist critics, for example, have compared Virginia Woolf to Joan of Arc. Although this may appear to take things a little too far (I think the idea would have amused if not horrified Virginia), it is emblematic of the curious attraction Bloomsbury has in our time, a laying hold of a legend whose personages linger in the memory of their living descendants. To plunge into that legend as recorder is to take part in a time and place that the biographer passionately wants to make his own. The reflected light is dazzling, the movement into myth spontaneous. To use modes of imagination, as the novelist does, to record Bloomsbury is only to act in the spirit of its time. The new biography is far removed from the mechanical nonfiction novel that American journalism has produced. It manages to accomplish what Virginia Woolf herself deemed impossible, a marriage of the truth of fact with the truth of fiction. This is, after all, close to what she envisioned the biographer as doing: "He can give us the creative fact; the fertile fact; the fact that suggests and engenders." [27]

This appears the direction in which biography as a whole is headed: a movement toward fictional modes, a quest for the mystery of the personality with which it deals. If the biographers of Bloomsbury appear absorbed with who *and* why—not only what a person is but why he is that way—others are equally adventurous. David McCullough, in his preface to *Mornings on Horseback,* concerning the early life of Theodore Roosevelt, claims that his "intention was not to write a biography of him. What intrigued me was how he came to be." This *how* includes familial, social, political, and psychological history. As Virginia Woolf's *Orlando* only too clearly teaches, a man *is* his time, both past and present. Good fiction demonstrates this, as does good biography. In recognizing the inherent closeness of the two disciplines, the biographer can feel free to enter into his proper domain of art.

NOTES

1. *Collected Essays,* vol. 4, ed. Leonard Woolf (London: Hogarth Press, 1967), 227.
2. Virginia Woolf, "The New Biography," *Collected Essays,* vol. 4, 233–234 (written for the *New York Herald Tribune,* 30 October 1927).
3. Virginia Woolf, "The Art of Biography," *Collected Essays,* vol. 4, 221, 224.
4. See my essay "Hunting the Moth: Virginia Woolf and the Creative Imagination," in *Virginia Woolf: Revaluation and Continuity,* ed. Ralph Freedman (Berkeley: University of California Press, 1980), 18 and 19, which cites diary entries of 10 September 1929 and 16 February 1930. Also *The Letters of Virginia Woolf,* vol. IV, ed. Nigel Nicolson and Joanne Trautmann (New York: Harcourt Brace Jovanovich, 1978), 180 (22 June 1930): "As an experience, madness is terrific I can assure you . . . and in its lava I still find most of the things I write about. It shoots out of one everything shaped, final, not in mere driblets, as sanity does."
5. *Virginia Woolf and Her Works,* trans. Jean Stewart (London: Hogarth Press, 1965), 351.
6. Woolf, "The New Biography," 231–235. In this essay she calls the new biographer "an artist," a viewpoint she would later change as the opening paragraph shows.
7. Woolf, "The Art of Biography," 223.
8. Leon Edel, *Literary Biography* (Toronto: University of Toronto Press, 1957), 93.
9. Woolf, *Letters,* vol. VI, 226 (3 May 1938).
10. Woolf, *Letters,* vol. VI, 294 (24 October 1938).
11. Virginia Woolf, *A Writer's Diary* (New York: Harcourt, Brace, 1954), 313–314 (9 February 1940) and 316 (20 March 1940).
12. Virginia Woolf, *To the Lighthouse* (London: Hogarth Press, 1963), 78 and 264 ("Beautiful and bright it should be on the surface, feathery and evanescent, one colour melting into another like the colours on a butterfly's wing; but beneath the fabric must be clamped together with bolts of iron").
13. Richter, "Hunting the Moth," 14–15.
14. Woolf, *A Writer's Diary,* 302 (15 April 1939).

15. Virginia Woolf, *Roger Fry* (New York: Harcourt Brace Jovanovich, 1976), 152. The context of the image is different, but the quest for the meaning of the mystery is the same.

16. Woolf, *A Writer's Diary,* 223 (1 November 1934).

17. Woolf, *A Writer's Diary,* 326–327 (25 July 1940).

18. Leon Edel, *Bloomsbury: A House of Lions* (New York: J. B. Lippincott, 1979), 79, 136–138.

19. In *To the Lighthouse* Lilly Briscoe literally summons Mrs. Ramsay from the Elysian Fields (she appears at the window), demonstrating the magic power of the artist.

20. Perry Meisel, *The Absent Father: Virginia Woolf and Walter Pater* (New Haven: Yale University Press, 1980), 57 and 61.

21. Quentin Bell, *Virginia Woolf: A Biography,* vol. II (New York: Harcourt Brace Jovanovich, 1972), 128 and 214.

22. Phyllis Rose, *Woman of Letters: A Life of Virginia Woolf* (New York: Oxford University Press, 1979), 222.

23. Edel, *Literary Biography,* 87, 88.

24. Note also the similarity of the titles of the first volumes: *Henry James: the Untried Years; Lytton Strachey: the Unknown Years.* Headings of chapter sections have a certain witty gaiety: "The Besotted Mandarins"; "The Peacock and the Butterfly" (Leon Edel). "Palpitations, French and English"; "A Rose-water Revolution" (Michael Holroyd).

25. Several ideas in this discussion are included in a passage on *A House of Lions* in my "Virginia Woolf and the Creative Critic," *Review,* no. 2(1981).

26. Leonard Woolf, *Sowing: An Autobiography of the Years 1880 to 1904* (London: Hogarth Press, 1960), 186.

27. Woolf, "The Art of Biography," 228.

III
AMERICANA

ON WRITING
WALDO EMERSON

GAY WILSON ALLEN

1

CRITICS OF Edgar Allan Poe are often skeptical of his explanation of how he wrote "The Raven," and it is doubtful that many authors of literary stature either plan their works as schematically as Poe claimed he did or can follow a blueprint in the actual writing. Unexpected thoughts, insights, discoveries suddenly appear in the act of creation; this is why writing can be so exciting and pleasurable. Of course, in writing *Waldo Emerson, a Biography* I began with a general outline; and preceding that I had built an Emerson library, consisting not only of editions of his journals, letters, lectures, poems, and prose works, but also of important secondary sources. I like to write in my own study, with everything (so far as possible) in easy reach. The unpublished manuscripts (letters, sermons, unfinished or discarded poems, diaries, etc.) had to be used in the Houghton Library at Harvard, though I was permitted photocopies, making it possible for me to quote directly, not from a four by six card.

After surveying the logistic problems, I estimated recklessly that I could finish the research and write the book in three years; I had retired from teaching and could give full time to the project. Actually, it took me ten years! What went wrong with my calculations? Mainly, I had not realized how long it would take me to assimilate Emerson's writings; how many times I would reread and mull over certain poems and essays. It seemed to me that neither I nor anyone else had fully appreciated his complexity, though his contradictions and paradoxes were notorious, and more than one person had suggested that his mind worked dialectically.

In brief, my first task was to understand Emerson, and I found that I could only do that progressively, step by step, reading everything in the order of his writing and experience. A chronological narrative may not be essential for every biographical subject, but Emerson's development was as sequential as the transformation of a tadpole into a frog, or any other of nature's metamorphoses—a phenomenon, by the way, which fascinated him: "nothing stands still in Nature but death, . . . the creation is on wheels, in transit, always passing into something else."

I not only found it necessary to trace Emerson's intellectual and emotional growth from childhood to maturity, and inevitable decline; I vicariously lived with him through his unpromising youth, his difficult young manhood, the crises following the death of his child-wife and his resignation from his pastorate, his finding a new vocation on the lecture platform, the traumatic years of the Civil War, when he became so impatient with President Lincoln for delay in issuing a proclamation freeing the slaves, and the relaxation of his mind and will when the proclamation finally came. As his anger cooled, so did his artistic creativity; but by this time I sympathized so deeply with the weary man that I rejoiced in his ease and comfort, so hard-earned and so well deserved. Living in imagination through every stage of this man's life and writings was one of the richest experiences of my life, the most rewarding decade in my education.

Any author whose writings are quoted as scripture, by friend or foe, is sure to be misunderstood, whether he be Jesus or Nietzsche the AntiChrist. Misunderstanding of Emerson comes most frequently when he is quoted out of context, and by context I mean not only a given literary work but also the context of his experiences. A good example is Robert Penn Warren's interpretation of Emerson's remark on carrying an armful of wood into the kitchen: "I suppose we must do this as if it were real." Warren says this remark reveals Emerson perching "above the issues of the untidy—and unreal—world," indifferent to human events and their urgencies.

Of course Emerson wrote several poems and an essay on the Hindu concept of life as illusion, and was strongly attracted by the philosophical "Idealism" of Plato and the Neoplatonists, Plotinus especially; but he also had so strong a sense of *reality,* I found, that he could make fun of the Ideal theory, as in the wood-carrying joke—and it was a joke. He also satirized the absurdities of the young Transcendentalists "who eat clouds, and drink wind"; who feel that they are too good for the world, refuse to vote, and disdain work unworthy of their "genius." Emerson did not include himself among these overrefined idealists, though his critics continue to do so. Horace Mann, the activist reformer, once complained that Emerson's idea of living was to sit alone and keep a journal. This is a half-truth.

Emerson's sense of humor has been too rarely recognized. I admit it was not hilarious, or even always immediately obvious, as in the poet's debate with the sphinx (in "The Sphinx"), but he was a master of ridicule, sarcasm, irony, comic exaggeration, and wry humor, as when he recorded in his journal: "The man I saw believed that his suspenders would hold up his pantaloons & that his straps would hold them down. His creed went little farther." Or this "transcendental" thought in "Nature" (the essay): "the maples and ferns are still uncorrupt; yet when they come to consciousness, they too will curse and swear." In the same essay he makes fun of the scientific utopians: "They say that by electro-magnetism your salad shall be grown from seed, whilst your fowl is roasting for dinner." The whole poem "Alphonso of Castille" is a satire on human pretensions and expectations (I quote from my biography):

> the king is vexed that nature lets things degenerate, and he asks the gods, whom he addresses sarcastically as "Seigniors," whether *they* or "Mildew" are in charge of the world. He will give them some good advice. No more famine: "Ply us with a full diet." Too many people in the world? Simple: "kill nine in ten" and "Stuff their nine brains in one hat. . . . " Also make man more durable, as long-lived as the marble statues he erects: "So shall ye have a man of the sphere/Fit to grace the solar year.

Emerson's language is so pungent and arresting that nearly everyone is tempted to quote him without regard to source or circumstance. His remark on carrying in wood is a good example. Or, "Traveling is a fool's paradise," in "Self-Reliance." In fact Emerson made three trips to Europe, the last extended to Egypt, and traveled widely in his own country. What he meant was that no one can escape his own character, his *self,* by going to distant places; therefore, "the wise man stays at home with his soul"; though when necessity carries him abroad, "he is at home still."

And in that often-quoted saying about consistency, Emerson says a "foolish consistency," that is, fear of being criticized for changing one's mind in the light of new experience. Perhaps only a foolish reader would misinterpret so obvious an assertion, but then Emerson has had many foolish readers. The point I wish to make is that Emerson's life illustrates his ideas, and a responsible biography can clarify his words, regardless of what the "New Critics" were saying a few years ago. In fact, I believe the best reasons for writing a literary biography are: (1) to show a creative mind at work and (2) to relate the author's experience and his art in such a way that the biography provides the best critical guide to his writings.

If one did not know Emerson's moral rectitude and tender conscience, one might misunderstand his assertion in "Spiritual Laws" that "our moral nature is vitiated by any interference of our will." This sounds like a license for irresponsibility, following whims and fleeting impulses. And he does say puckishly in another passage that he would like to write "whim" on the lintel of his door. Yvor Winters was right in declaring that a life actually lived on such a principle (or lack of principle) would end in madness; therefore he called Emerson insane, and Walt Whitman and Hart Crane also for accepting his ideas. Emerson further taunts such people as Winters by declaring in "Self-Reliance" that he does not care whether his impulses come from God or the Devil. But the biographical evidence is overwhelming that he did not think they came from the Devil.

The clue to Emerson's misleading witticisms about the malicious will is his profound belief in the wisdom of his intuitions. He did not, like Jones Very, believe that God literally put thoughts into his mind and activated muscles (though his comments on his unconscious mind, discussed below, might lead to this impression). He had found by experience that he more often made mistakes by following the advice of friends and relatives, or by simply conforming to what society expected of him, instead of acting on his own judgment. He went into the Unitarian ministry because his family expected him to follow in the footsteps of his father, grandfather, and five generations of clergymen. Yet by temperament and character he was wholly unfitted to be pastor of a church, and resigned ostensibly over his unwillingness to administer the rites of the Lord's Supper, but his journals show that he had been dissatisfied almost from his ordination.

After his resignation, Emerson became severely ill. For weeks he suffered from diarrhea, which appears to have had some connection with his inability "to eat or drink religiously." (Of course it is also true that nerves affect the digestive processes.) Emerson thought of joining his two younger brothers in Puerto Rico, where they were seeking a cure for tuberculosis of the lungs, but on a sudden impulse he decided to engage passage on a small merchant brigantine preparing to sail to Malta.

On a Christmas morning, with gale winds rising, the little ship sailed out of the Boston harbor and was soon overtaken by a storm which lasted a week, for Emerson a week of unremitting nausea and tossing in his bunk. But when the seas subsided and food could be prepared, he found that he had a sailor's appetite, and no sign of diarrhea. The fasting had also purged his mind of his worries. For nearly a year he would be able to travel in Europe, often under exhausting and uncomfortable conditions, without once being ill. In fact, he would never be seriously ill again until his old age.

Emerson's faith in conscience as God-inspired began in his devoutly religious home; his parents believed God to be near enough to them to make His presence felt. Prayer was the instrument by which they communicated with Him, and He answered them by altering their state of mind or touching their emotions. A skeptic might call this self-hypnosis, but believing Christians had no doubt that God answered prayers, though what He wanted for their good might not turn out to be what they thought they wanted.

For Emerson this faith became less naive and more psychological after he met the Hicksite Quakers in New Bedford, to whom he preached before becoming pastor of the Second Church in Boston. He was especially impressed by the testimony of a remarkable woman named Mary Rotch, who said that in times of difficulty she found herself "Driven inward, driven home, to find an answer, until she learned to have *no choice,* to acquiesce without understanding the reason when she found an obstruction to any particular course of action." She refused to call it divine spiritual direction, or even "an intimation." It was more like *"a healthy state of mind."* But she did agree with Emerson that it came from a "higher direction." Later Emerson would think of this vague "direction" in terms of his unconscious mind, and always from *above,* never from *below,* like Freud's suppressed unconscious, a den of terrors.

Previous biographers of Emerson, and most of his critics down to the present day, have called him a "mystic," and tried to explain his ideas and his delight in solitude and meditation in terms of "mysticism." Of course, he was a mystic in the sense that he believed an unseen power (whether God or Spirit) energized the universe. His "Ideal" philosophy came from Plato, the Neoplatonists (Plotinus, Proclus, Porphyry, and Iamblicus, in Thomas Taylor's translations), from Christian theology, and the Natural Supernaturalism of Coleridge and Carlyle, which they had adapted from German Transcendentalism. (However, when Emerson read Carlyle's *Sartor Resartus,* he found the ideas already familiar to him.) But to interpret Emerson's writings largely in terms of these Platonic and Transcendental theories misses the empirical immediacy of his psychological observations; whatever philosophical ideas he borrowed were tested and modified by his own experiences. He used introspection to discover how a supposed infinite mind operates in or through a finite mind. He was not satisfied with abstractions.

Emerson's interest in this subject, and his own thinking on it, underwent vast and rapid changes after the death of his first wife, Ellen Tucker, the most traumatic experience of his life. She had tuberculosis of the lungs when he married her, and both knew that she might die in a few months. Their adoration of each other was so strong that they could not bear the thought of separation. Thus, both clung desperately to the conventional Christian beliefs in immortality, and she promised that she would not forget him in heaven. Shortly before her death, which she knew was imminent, she begged him not to grieve for her, that she was merely going before him to "prepare the way."

Two hours after Ellen's death, Emerson wrote his Aunt Mary, "My angel is gone to heaven this morning," and he felt "rich in her memory." Two nights later he dreamed of her, and on waking prayed, "Dear Ellen (for that is your name in heaven) shall we not be united even now more & more?" He said she knew his mind and would "suggest good thoughts as you promised, & show me the truth." But days and nights passed and he did not receive any telepathic messages. She did not even visit him in his dreams, and he began to wonder, almost in panic, if she had forgotten him. This inability to communicate with his "sainted wife" in heaven brought about nothing short of an intellectual revolution in Emerson's life. He did not become an atheist or an agnostic, but God became to him an impersonal spirit or power. He found increasing satisfaction in reading the Neoplatonists and the "Hindu Scriptures." His pastoral duties were boring and burdensome, and he began to wish he could get rid not only of his Second Church but all churches.

After Emerson's return from Europe, he found a new vocation in lecturing—significantly, first on natural science. He now looked for evidence of God's existence and benevolence in His Creation. He still preached occasionally, and in a sermon on "The Person-ality of God" he said, "the soul knows no persons." His little book on *Nature* set forth his new natural theology. In an address to Har-vard divinity students he rejected the miracles of the New Testa-ment and the divinity of Jesus; the orthodox were profoundly shocked. Like Socrates, one of Emerson's greatest heroes since his college days, he identified the "soul" with the moral power of in-telligence and character. Like Plato, he argued that "Truth" lies al-ready in the human mind, waiting to be discovered, or recognized: "We know better than we do." In a lecture on "The Head" he de-clared that "God comes in by a private door," never consciously left open. In the same lecture:

> Always our thinking is an observing. Into us flows the stream ever-more of thought from we know not whence. We do not determine what we will think; we only open our senses, clear away as we can all obstruction from the facts, and let God think through us. Then we carry away in the ineffaceable memory the result, and all men and all the ages confirm it. It is called Truth.

Perhaps the reference to God in this statement has prevented Emerson's biographers and critics from seeing that he is describing a psychological phenomenon, what William James would later call the "stream of consciousness"; it is significant that both use the same metaphor. James found by introspection that his waking mind, or consciousness, was never empty; he was constantly aware of images, sensations, and "thoughts" following each other in an endless succession, like detritus in a stream of water flowing down hill. By exercise of the will he could shift his attention to other objects in the stream, but he could not stop the onward movement. Apparently it went on even in sleep, though the objects then jostled and merged into each other in an irrational manner. When he tried to recover previous stages of the flow, he could only glimpse, as it were, a few, and they mingled with present sensations and emerg-ing "thoughts." The stream flowed only one way.

James in the role of scientist professed ignorance of the origin of consciousness, which he called a miracle in nature; he presumed that it had developed in biological evolution because it had survival value. But in the "overbeliefs" which he confessed to holding in the conclusion of his *Varieties of Religious Experience,* James speculated that the "unconscious" mind (though he preferred "subconscious" or "subliminal") is a doorway between "the finite self" and the "absolute self . . . one with God and the soul of the world."

Perhaps when Emerson described letting "God think through us," he was not describing all states of consciousness, but those rare occasions when "Truth" is discovered—an epiphany. But at least this observation explains why he thought spontaneous action and intuitive cerebration so valuable. He was deeply interested in the psychology of the unconscious, regarding it as a reservoir of psychic or creative energy. "We are always on the brink of an ocean of thought into which we do not yet swim." How to plunge in was the problem, but he did not wait for a miraculous revelation; he stalked it with dogged persistence:

> Set out to study a particular truth. Read upon it. Walk to think upon it. Talk of it. Write about it. The thing will not much manifest itself, at least not much in accommodation to your studying arrangements. The gleams you do get, out they will flash, as likely at dinner, or in the roar of Faneuil Hall, as in your painfullest abstraction.

Believing as he did that the unconscious is "the doorway to God," Emerson expected the gift of health and happiness from it, if only the conscious mind, warped by society and deference to the physical life, did not thwart it. Carlyle had written in an anonymous essay called "Characteristics" (*Edinburgh Review,* December, 1831) that "The healthy know not of their health, but only the sick . . . the first condition of complete health, is, that each organ perform its function unconsciously, unheeded" by the conscious mind. The importance of this statement to Emerson was that some kind of seemingly intelligent unconscious coordinated the functioning of his biological self.

What interested Emerson especially, however, was how he might use his unconscious to protect him from the errors of his conscious will. "Could it be made apparent," he wrote in his journal, "what is really true, that the whole future is in the bottom of the heart, that, in proportion as your life is spent within,—in that measure you are invulnerable." Invulnerable to mistakes of judgment, and actions harmful to health or peace of mind. Emerson also believed that the artist can make conscious the unconscious life. In this sense he is a psychologist of the soul.

Emerson seems to anticipate both Freud and Jung in his description of the unconscious or hidden memory: "The dark walls of your mind are scrawled all over with facts, with thoughts. Bring a lanthorn and read the inscriptions." But his desire to read these inscriptions in the dungeon of memory was not exactly that of a protopsychoanalyst:

> It is long ere we discover how rich we are. Our history we are sure is quite tame. We have nothing to write, nothing to infer. But our wiser years still turn back to the before despised recollections of childhood and always we are fishing up some wonderful article out of that pond, until by and by we begin to suspect that the biography of the one foolish person we know, is in reality nothing less than a miniature paraphrase of the hundred volumes of the Universal History.

This is much more like Jung's "collective unconscious" than Freud's suppressed and festering desires. But Emerson's method of recalling and using the memories engraved on the dark walls of his mind at least suggests the use of the psychoanalytic couch. He encourages the flow of memory, a "silent stream ever flowing from above" [note again, *above*]: in solitude sit alone and listen to your own thoughts; "keep a journal" and record "the visits of Truth to your mind."

A few years earlier Emerson had heard of a certain Frenchman (unnamed) who had advanced the theory that the human body had "two souls . . . which never suspended action, & had the care of what we call the involuntary motions." One of these souls "knew a good deal of Natural magic, antipathies, instincts, divination & the like." In psychoanalytic terminology: neuroses, hysteria, amnesia, delusions, and so forth. The only time Emerson discussed this "soul" so dangerous to sanity was in a lecture on "Demonology"; and he had no sympathy for, or much interest in, psychic phenomena which seemed to violate the laws of nature. He did think, however, that dreams might be useful in giving clues to character.

2

Granted that Emerson sought harmony between his unconscious and conscious mind, were there instances of experiences inscribed on the dark walls of his memory which influenced his later life? I begin my biography with an experience which could have profoundly influenced his whole adult life; however, one he had not forgotten—quite the contrary—though he may not have been aware that it still influenced his judgment. In 1850 when Emerson was forty-seven, his brother William conveyed to him an urgent request from the historian of the First Church in Boston for a biographical essay on their father.

Emerson was not pleased by this request, and replied with obvious irritation that his father had died when he was eight, and "I have no recollections of him that can serve me." Actually, he remembered his father quite well, but not kindly. When he was six he had had a skin eruption, for which a physician had recommended saltwater bathing. To carry out this therapy, the boy's father taught him to swim in the ocean by pushing him into the water "off some wharf or bathing house" and letting him swim for his life. Now in middle age, he could still hear his father's voice, like "Adam that of the Lord God in the garden," calling him for the swimming lesson, and like Adam trying to hide.

Perhaps Emerson characterized his father correctly as a "social gentleman" who never wrote anything worth remembering: "his printed or written papers as far as I know, only show candour & taste, or I should almost say docility." By "docility" he probably meant conformity to current social and religious thought. Such facts as I was able to find supported Emerson's opinion of his father, but this lifelong grudge doubtless had a personal basis.

Emerson remembered quite well marching in his father's funeral procession, which he recalled as an impressive spectacle, not as a time of personal grief. He may even at the time have felt relieved to be rid of that unwelcomed voice of authority. A week before his fourth birthday, his father had apologized to a friend, "Ralph does not read very well yet." This was not a joke, as the minister's treatment of his other children shows. As soon as they could read, all the Emerson children were required to recite passages from Shakespeare, Addison, or the Bible before breakfast; normal play was denied them. A psychoanalytic biographer might trace Emerson's nonconformity in religion, education, and literature back to his resentment in childhood of the paternal authority which seemed to him unreasonable and harsh.

To some extent this was probably true, but I suspect also that a disposition for independence was in Emerson's genes, inherited from the grandfather who led the Concord revolt against British tyranny, or some other freedom-loving ancestor. For whatever reason, he was endowed with a mind which saw through shams and pretenses, and resented unreasonable restrictions. His three brothers (not counting the youngest, an imbecile) dutifully obeyed their parents and teachers, excelled in Latin School and Harvard College, and competed frantically for academic honors. Ralph (or Waldo, as he chose to be called while in college) did not have their competitive spirit; he preferred to compose verses, read books not assigned by his teachers, or simply daydream. His younger brothers Edward and Charles drove themselves to an early grave, and even William, the oldest, died fourteen years before Waldo.

Emerson was not robust in his youth and early manhood, and needed to set his own pace. Soon after he entered the Divinity School at Harvard, he had to drop out because of some kind of eye affliction. At the time he had doubts about his qualifications for the ministry, and the eye-trouble could have been psychosomatic; but I rejected that guess because a few months later operations on his eyes enabled him to recover full use of them.

After he was "approbated" to preach in the Unitarian ministry, Emerson also began to suffer chest pains which threatened his ministerial career, if not his life. Boston physicians thought he had bronchial tuberculosis, the disease which later killed his two younger brothers, and they recommended a mild climate. After spending the winter in Charleston, South Carolina, and St. Augustine, Florida, Emerson returned to Massachusetts in better health, and eventually was completely cured. He either conquered his fear of the ministry, or he had actually been physically ill. I found it impossible to say which, but there seemed no doubt that he aided his recovery by deliberately cultivating a healthy attitude of mind and will.

Emerson's childhood afflictions and disappointments encouraged him to find "compensations" for them. The easiest way was to escape into a world of fantasy, but as he grew up he adjusted himself to the world he had to live in. On his first trip to Europe, after losing wife, church, and profession, he hoped to find a "teacher" (say "surrogate father," if you wish, though he was thirty years old); but after meeting the leading writers in England, he realized that no one could help him but himself. This was the origin of his great essay on "Self-Reliance."

On returning to America, he found a profession, as mentioned above, in giving public lectures, first on natural science. His subject was not as strange as it may sound, for he had long been interested in the discoveries and theories of modern science. He had preached several sermons on astronomy, and in the 1830–decade

Charles Lyell was teaching him the basic facts and theories of modern geology. The realization that the world was not six thousand years old, as the Christian Church had taught for centuries, but millions of years old revolutionized Emerson's conception of nature, God, and the universe. During his travels in Europe he had found visiting scientists, museums of scientific objects, and botanical gardens more exciting than art galleries and historic places. He saw no conflict between religion and science; in fact, he hoped science would suggest analogies for "moral philosophy." Before his death, some British scientists would turn to materialism and agnosticism, but he would always be too convinced of a purposeful universe to be tempted by such views. Science, he believed, was a liberating force for mankind, and in this he was a nineteenth-century optimist.

Science was also an influence on Emerson's poetry—along with Neoplatonism and Persian poetry; again what would seem to be the most unlikely combination of sources. As early as 1907 George Woodberry in a short biography pointed out that "Emerson always thinks of the process of Nature as a dance of atoms," and "the energy of Nature as a Dionysiac force, with overflow and intoxication in it." This observation went unnoticed by Emerson's critics, but it gave me a hint for a new interpretation of his poetry. The key words are *ecstasy* and *intoxication*. Most readers have found neither in Emerson's poems, perhaps because they were looking for ideas—especially "transcendental" ideas. On 6 July 1841, Emerson confessed in his journal: "In every week there is some hour when I read my commission in every cipher of nature, and know that I was made for another office, a professor of the Joyous Science, a detector & delineator of occult harmonies & unpublished beauties." A few months later in a lecture on "Prospects" he repeated this ambition, and in "Poetry and Imagination" he called poetry "the *gai science*." He got these phrases, apparently, from reading an article on Zoroaster (Nietzsche's Zarathustra, using the Greek spelling). However, his favorite Neoplatonists also gave him the idea that a poet's senses should be intoxicated: "I read Proclus for my opium," he confessed in his journal in 1843. "I am filled with hilarity & spring, my heart dances, my sight is quickened, I behold shining relations between all things, and am impelled to write and almost to sing."

In his "Bacchus" poem Emerson borrowed the Persian conceit of inspiration as vinous intoxication. "Bring me wine, but wine which never grew/ In the belly of the grape." He admired the sensual abandon of Hafiz in his dancing rhythms. In 1943 Professor John D. Yohannan pointed out that "Emerson's interest in Persian poetry" coincided with his first significant poetic productions. His knowledge of Persian poetry came from the translations into German by Joseph von Hammer (later von Hammer-Purgstall), from which he made his own translations into English. Yohannan examined these roundabout translations and decided that they had strongly influenced Emerson's own poems. Many critics have commented upon the cryptic and asymmetrical phrasing in Emerson's diction, often regarding these effects as prosodic ineptitude or the result of a poor ear for music. Yohannan found the same effects in von Hammer's translations (or sometimes in Emerson's awkward versions of them). This observation suggested to me a new approach to Emerson's poems, one combining the Dionysiac ecstasy of the atom with the Neoplatonic intoxication of the senses and the imagery and rhythms of Persian poetry. An example is "Merlin," Emerson's archetype poet, who would not "his brain encumber/ With the coil of rhythm and number." "Merlin" has been called a "Bardic" poem (influenced by tribal Welsh poets), but the imagery is strongly Persian:

> He shall aye climb
> For his rhyme,
> 'Pass in, pass out' the angels say,
> 'In to the upper doors;
> Nor count compartments of the floors,
> But mount to paradise
> By the stairway of surprise.'

Though Emerson admired Hafiz, his favorite was Saadi (his spelling), whose name he borrowed for himself. He especially approved Saadi's dwelling alone in order to bring the wisdom of the gods to the race of men, which was the motif of Emerson's early poem "The Apology," probably written before he had heard of Saadi. The vicarious kinship went even further: just as Emerson scorned the Calvinists, so did Saadi the sad-eyed Fakirs who preached the decay of the world and said Allah wanted men to drink wormwood. Saadi-Emerson replies:

> And yet it seemeth not to me
> That the high gods love tragedy;
> For Saadi sat in the sun,
> And thanks was his contrition.

3

Nearly everyone who has studied Emerson's life and writings has been impressed by his contradictions and paradoxes: fond of Plotinus, Montaigne, and the Persian poets; student of natural science and a strong believer in intuition; symbolist in poetry and master of the American idiom in his prose; tender lover of his first girl-wife but unable to give his second wife the affection she craved— the list could be extended indefinitely.

It was not my intention to write psychography; however, many of my interpretations started from assumptions about the influence of Emerson's unconscious on his conduct and thinking. For example, Emerson remained all his life so in love with the memory of Ellen that he could never fully love another woman. Unlike Poe, however, in love with his dead mother, this memory did not make Emerson sexually impotent; he fathered four children and led a comfortable domestic life with Lidian Jackson, though more satisfying for him than for her. He could never write her the "one letter" for which she begged. Even his letter of proposal (withheld from Rusk by the family) clearly reveals a psychic dilemma. In apology for his lack of emotional ardor, he says he loves her "after a new and higher way."

Emerson's essay on "Love" also clearly shows his inhibitions. At the age of thirty-five he associates erotic love with youth and springtime, when "a simple tone of one voice makes the heart beat" faster, and "the most trivial circumstance associated with one form is put in the amber of memory." His first and only love was embalmed, and it created problems, which he attempted to solve by philosophical evasion. "There are moments," he says in "Love," when "the affections rule and absorb the man, and make his happiness dependent on a person or persons. But in health the mind is presently seen again," meaning that these finite things are seen as only finite, and their loss no tragedy. He believed that he had progressed from love of beauty in one person to love of universal beauty.

Emerson also "compensated" for his other failures and limitations. He was sensitive and easily hurt. His mediocre record at Harvard made him feel inferior and depressed. His illness after he was licensed to preach undermined his self-confidence, and it was only the strong desire to marry and protect Ellen that enabled him to forget himself and gain strength. To buffer the pain of disappointments, he cultivated stoic attitudes, such as: keep expectations low; bear pain with fortitude, reminding himself that it is only physical and therefore endurable; the soul is unaffected by pain, by failure of the body, or the opinions of society; it is immortal and unconquerable, and is the only "real" reality. To dampen grief, Emerson convinced himself that his emotions were sluggish and his power of sympathy low. After the death of his first son, he berated himself for not feeling the loss more keenly; actually, his mind was numb with the emotional pain.

Emerson never lost his philosophical Idealism, out of which he wrote some of his finest essays, such as "The Over-Soul," "Spiritual Laws," and "Intellect." But his Idealism was balanced by an increasing desire, beginning as early as 1839, "to go straight into life . . . to the hodiernal facts." Concern with the actualities of American life led him to condemn the removal of the Cherokee Indians from their ancestral lands, and to befriend John Brown, both before and after his raid on Harper's Ferry. While Brown was being tried for murder, Emerson said that if he were hanged Brown would make the gallows glorious like the Cross. These examples, two among many, contradict those critics who say Emerson had no sense of evil and was indifferent to the wrongs of his contemporary world. No one more strongly condemned the war with Mexico, slavery, and political corruption in the Jackson and Polk administrations.

For a decade and a half before the Civil War Emerson advocated buying black slaves from their southern owners in order to free them, as Great Britain had done in the British West Indies. Visionary as this proposal seemed to the politicians, it could have prevented a tragic Civil War. Then during the war Emerson became so impatient with President Lincoln for delay in issuing a proclamation freeing the slaves that he even talked anarchism. However, the day the proclamation was published, his faith in Lincoln, the Republic, and the future of the American people returned. Yet, ironically, almost from that day his creative mind began to slow down and his art to degenerate. Possibly this might have happened anyway, for in a short time his memory began to fail, and in the last decade of his life he would be able to produce little of consequence.

Ralph Rusk in his *Life* of Emerson covered the years of decline in such detail that he emphasized the pathos. I wanted to avoid that kind of ending because I felt it to be a literary mistake, giving an otherwise upbeat narrative a negative reversal; furthermore, it was a distortion of Emerson's life as he experienced it. Of course, every human life is a tragedy in the sense that death, the ultimate failure of the body, is inevitable, predestined by the order of nature; but the failure can be made less painful if met with courage and fortitude, virtues which Emerson possessed undiminished until the end of his life. He accepted his limitations without flinching, made a joke of his loss of memory, and never felt sorry for himself.

To de-emphasize the pathos, I hastened the narrative pace and covered the last ten years of Emerson's life in as few pages as possible, with concise sentences. But I did not skimp his few old-age triumphs and his happiness in his friendships. His "compensation" principle never failed him. When he bogged down in his lectures at Harvard on the "Natural History of the Intellect," his daughter's father-in-law, John M. Forbes, the railroad magnate, took him on a rejuvenating trip by train to California, during which he visited Brigham Young, lectured in San Francisco, and toured the Yosemite Valley on horseback. When his house burned, friends sent him on a trip to Egypt while they completely restored his house. On his return to Concord, Emerson's neighbors welcomed him with the exuberance they had shown when Concord soldiers returned from the war, and he asked in bewilderment what they were celebrating.

It is probable that Emerson's stoicism shortened his life by a few months or years, but it was part of his character. On a Sunday in April 1882 he attended church (unheated, as was the custom) and caught a cold, which he tried to cure by walks to Walden Pond without an overcoat to protect him against the wind blowing off the frozen water. His cold quickly turned into acute pneumonia, which no medicine of the time could cure. Near the end he suffered great pain, and his friend and doctor James Putnam gave him ether to ease his final hours. He was buried in Sleepy Hollow Cemetery, which he had dedicated nearly three decades earlier, saying, "In this quiet valley, as in the palm of Nature's hand, we shall sleep well when we have finished the day." Thus I had only to state the simple facts of Emerson's death and burial to give my biography a pastoral ending, appropriate for the man who had preferred, of all places he could have chosen for his home, Concord, Massachusetts, a town as peaceful and restful as its name.

STYLE AND SINCERITY
IN THE LETTERS
OF HENRY ADAMS

VIOLA HOPKINS WINNER

THE LETTERS OF Henry Adams present a special but not unique biographical problem. Like other narrators, letter writers can be un-
reliable—their comments conditioned by passing moods, their
relation to a recipient, and other such contingencies. With letters in
general, as with autobiography, the interpreter must learn to read
between the lines. When an author regards letter writing as a form
of literary expression and consciously aims at stylistic perfection,
then the problem of distinguishing between the "real" person and
the persona of the letter is compounded.

So it is with Henry Adams. Letter writing was for him a literary
activity, less demanding than formal kinds but not essentially different. In the 1890s and other fallow periods in his career, it was his
main literary occupation. Of his total output, about forty-five
hundred letters have survived, spanning the years from 1858 when
he first left home to study in Germany to shortly before his death
in 1918. These letters are in a class of their own in nineteenth-
century American literature, comprising a major literary work
equal to, if not surpassing, *The Education of Henry Adams* and
Mont-Saint-Michel and Chartres. The intellectual vigor and documentary importance of his correspondence have long been recognized; its literary significance has not been equally appreciated.
With the publication in 1982 of three of the projected six volumes
of the first comprehensive edition of the letters, Henry Adams's
epistolary art is coming into its own.

"Nobody else—except your Historian—writes letters; it is a
lost art," John Hay remarked to Henry Adams's wife, Marian, ap-
ropos a mutual friend's letter.[1] What Hay meant was not that people

no longer wrote letters to keep in touch or for more utilitarian purposes, but rather that the kind of letter that had flourished in the eighteenth century as a social art, private entertainment, and literary genre had gone to seed. Viewing Adams within this epistolary tradition—and as an exception to its decline—we may come to an understanding of the relationship of artifice to sincerity in his letters that may have wider application.

Until 1868, Henry Adams's closest and most frequent correspondent was his older brother Charles Francis Adams, Jr. Up to a certain point, the two young men agreed on the conventions and the aesthetic of the "familiar," as against the public, letter, of which the first rule was that its language was the spoken word. From the assumption that letters are a form of conversation between intimates, it follows that the dialogue should be informal and candid. Even a letter intended for circulation among friends and family—travel letters especially are expected to be read aloud or passed around—is supposed to seem improvised, unpondered. Display of learning, ornate rhetoric, anything suggesting premeditation or studied effect is to be avoided. In *Pride and Prejudice,* when Elizabeth Bennet finds "something very pompous" in the style of Mr. Collins's letter, she is prompted to ask her father "Can he be a sensible man, sir?" Covert gestures toward a posterity presumed to be reading over one's shoulder may be less easy to detect. As the Adamses were a family of diarists, letter writers, memorialists, and publishers for the public record Henry Adams was aware that his letters would become part of the family archives and did not shrink from the prospect of posthumous publication. To what degree this expectation influenced his epistolary style is a moot question.

Clearly from the beginning Henry aimed at writing good letters and also realized that, as with good conversation, artifice is involved. When from Dresden (15–17 May 1859) he wrote expressing admiration for "the first-rate letter" Charles had made from the "commonplace materials" of Boston life, he was in effect congratulating him on his literary skill in treating a barren subject.[2] There was the further implication that a letter should be concerned with more than private matters, that it should also, as the old formula goes, amuse and instruct. His half-apology that his letter of 8 August 1859 had to be "short and personal" was not just prompted by New England moral earnestness and reserve. It was taken for granted that the letter was a medium for reflection on current events, books, letters, politics, art, or whatever else engaged one at the time and would also interest one's reader. Typically, as in an 1868 letter to his English friend Charles Milnes Gaskell, he moved from comments on his sister's social activities to generalizations about American and English manners. From Polynesia in 1891, he sent a twenty-three page letter on the results of his exploration of coral reefs to the geologist Clarence King, one of the "five of hearts" as King, the Hays, and the Adamses had dubbed themselves in 1883.

The art of the letter is difficult to define, for it is a hybrid of actual experience, mixed personal motives, and literary intentions. It is especially dependent in its contents and in the very preservation of its text on the vicissitudes of life. It verges on the informal and expository essay, as in the instances just mentioned, and on fiction when a writer is given to psychological analysis or to depiction of people in a social setting. The epistolary novel *Pamela,* it will be recalled, evolved from a manual on letter writing that Richardson was working on at the time. When the letter writer's impulse is to record the events of the day, his letters come close to being history or a journal.

The letter partakes of the novel, history, and the essay, but the more a writer is inclined toward deliberately working to make his letters informative, well written, entertaining, or documentary, the greater the danger of falling away from the primary ideal of spontaneity and of candor. In the opinion of his brother Charles, Henry had in 1867 succumbed to style at the expense of sincerity. Charles's view was occasioned by a letter from Henry that appeared to him to have been "copied in cold blood." He showed it to a friend who thereupon pronounced Henry a "humbug," an epithet that Charles thought was deserved.

The significance of Henry's reply to the charge is not his denial that he had ever, except for a letter to Secretary of State Seward, reworked his letters, but rather his expression of regret that he did not do so. "If I only could manage to endure the drudgery of copying and recopying every word I write, there would be a good chance for me yet to leave half a dozen agreeable volumes in the family library." His polished style was not the result of revision, for "when a man has been worried by a subject and thought it over till he does what few people will ever do—that is, knows something about it, his words and sentences flow easily enough, even into 'antitheses and rhetorical finish'." He went on to answer the further criticism of having "written a familiar letter like an essay, or rather an essay like a familiar letter," by advising his brother to attack him for "employing art badly" but not to be "so intolerably barbarous as to fancy that art itself is bad" (22 October 1867).

Henry Adams took letters seriously, finding in them a writer's essential qualities of mind and art. He admired, somewhat perversely, Henry James's writing after having read only his letters and considered Flaubert's as representative of his style as *Madame Bovary*. He placed the letters of his great-grandmother Abigail Adams on a short list of works representative of the best of American literature.

Henry's earliest letters certainly gave no reason for complaint on the score of being too Ciceronian, as these two passages from letters from Germany to Charles in Boston indicate:

My dear fellow

Your letter dated Thanksgiving Day arrived yesterday, and I give you my word that though I have been having a delightful time here and have enjoyed life to the hubs, still I have never felt quite so glad at being out of Boston as I felt after reading that epistle. There was in it a sort of contented despair, an unfathomable depth of quiet misery that gave me a placid feeling of thankfulness at being where I am. (17–18 December 1858)

By jingo, your balls, your canvass-backs [ducks] (they never saw a decent supper here) your girls, your dancing is tantalization. . . . You blasé dog! Just come to Europe and if you don't get into good trim to appreciate [Boston] society, then this 'ere child must be rather out of the way. Well, well, well! We can't have all that we want. I'd give fifty thalers for a real piece of roast mutton and caper sauce, and a talk and a walz with a pretty girl. Oh! the wasteful vilyan that I was in old times to go to a ball and be cross. Verily now could I dance like the agile roe-buck and talk words softer than the down of the eider-duck. Which is a rhyme though not meant. Haven't I been staring all the afternoon at a pretty girl across the concert room! And didn't she give the shyest glances back! And *wasn't* her ma a watchin of me! Well you had better believe. No use though. I never shall know her unless I can grind her. (6 April 1859)

The humorous ease of the first passage is notable. The Thanksgiving date of his brother's last starts a train of thought worked out to a rounded conclusion of thankfulness with a pun on Boston as the hub and witty antithesis and hyperbole along the way. The second seems to have been dashed off from the very scene, but the style is also far from naive. High and low diction are playfully employed: "by jingo" juxtaposed to "Oh! the wasteful vilyan." The voice of present feelings cuts across both with the allusion to "roast mutton and caper sauce" and the flirtation with the pretty girl at the concert. Henry almost certainly did not write the letter at the concert, but gave the effect of immediacy by shifting to the progressive tense—"Haven't I been staring. . . . " Casual as this writing is, it shows Henry Adams already had at his command a fluent, variable style, both colloquial and rhetorically effective. The facetiousness of the second passage thinly masks, and the tinny tone gives away, the depth of his despondency and homesickness at the time. He was to become more skillful in making humorous capital of misery.

Another aspect of Adams's epistolary style developed from his attempt to record political events on the model of Horace Walpole. In late 1860, Adams was in Washington on the scene of history in the making, the eve of the Civil War. From his front seat in the political arena, as private secretary to his father just re-elected to Congress, Henry proposed sending Charles a series of private letters "to show how things look. I fairly confess that I want to have a record of this winter on file, and though I have no ambition nor hope to become a Horace Walpole, I still would like to think that a century or two hence when everything else about us is forgotten, my letters might still be read and quoted as a memorial of manners and habits at the time of the great secession of 1860" (9 December 1860). Walpole left in his letters a vivid record of the life of his times, remarkable for its inner view of public figures. He was particularly adept at dramatizing and elaborating anecdotes and at portraying people in a social setting. Adams experimented with Walpole's method somewhat awkwardly in these 1860 letters, focussing chiefly on Secretary of State Seward as seen at dinner parties and other occasions. In urbanity and visual fullness, Adams fell short of Walpole, as his initial description of Seward suggests: "I sat and watched the old fellow with his big nose and his wire hair and grizzly eyebrows and miserable dress, and listened to him rolling out his grand, broad ideas that would inspire a cow with statesmanship if she understood our language." Walpole no doubt would have made us see what in the cut or fashion of the dress made it "miserable" and would have re-created the scene with novelistic texture. In Henry's account, the detail is vivid enough, however, for what seems to be his purpose—to convey the impression

of the incongruity between Seward's homely, folksy appearance and
his sublime oratory. The culminating image of the hypothetical
cow humorously clinches the idea.

In his mature manner when recounting similar occasions, Adams
likewise assimilated reportorial, descriptive detail to a larger imaginative, intellectual, or satiric purpose. Describing a reception at
Theodore Roosevelt's White House which he reluctantly attended,
he wrote:

> You cannot conceive how night-mared I was. An Indian from the
> plains would not have felt quite so ghostly. . . . Received with war-
> hoops by the President and bidden to supper, we found ourselves
> penned into the next room with a hundred people who were perfect
> strangers to me and bowed and smiled and said: "You don't remem-
> ber me"; and ended by making me think my social vogue was
> boundless. The Chinese minister in marvelous dragons and jewels
> embraced me tenderly; Mrs Whitelaw Reid in a harness of diamonds
> and rubies graciously allowed me to do homage; Mrs Patterson,
> collared with solitaires, received me as a friend of the family.

He then goes on to describe himself seated across from the President and defenseless against his monologue: "we were straws in
Niagara. . . . We were overwhelmed in a torrent of oratory . . ."
There is social documentation—where the guests assembled, how
they dressed, the seating at the table—but observation is subordi-
nate to perception and judgment. The "harness" of diamonds and
rubies worn by Mrs. Reid, the diamonds in which Mrs. Patterson
is "collared" suggest bondage to display. The imagery of the wild
west and untamed nature—"an Indian from the plains," "the war-
hoops by the President," "straws in Niagara," "overwhelmed in
a torrent of oratory"—is ironically incompatible with the osten-
tatious trappings of an "imperial court" (10 January 1904). The advance in drama and metaphoric interplay of this vignette over that
of the secession winter is apparent; it stands in relation to the latter
as a Sargent portrait to a Nast caricature. On the other hand, the
sophisticated and arch use of western hyperbole lacks the Mark
Twain freshness of Adams's earlier and cruder style. The personality of the young Adams who modestly "sat and watched" Seward,
whom he hero-worshipped, is also often more appealing than the
old Adams, the sage of 1603 H Street, who thought Roosevelt a
dangerously insane egotist.

In between his two careers, the first culminating in his *History of
the United States* and the second in *Mont-Saint-Michel and Chartres*

and the *Education of Henry Adams,* Adams devoted his talents chiefly to the writing of travel letters. Usually day-by-day accounts, they have a distinct character even to the size paper used. They hold a special place in his correspondence. His travels in the 1890s took him through the South Seas, Mexico, Cuba, Sicily, the Near East, Scandinavia, and Russia, not to mention familiar European grounds. He wrote voluminous journal letters from wherever he happened to be and if he had put together the travel book he toyed with writing, he no doubt would have drawn largely on the letters.[3] They show in their solidity of information and breadth of speculation that he applied himself with Bostonian high seriousness and a Faustian appetite for all knowledge as vigorously to the study of alien cultures as he did to his own.

The travel letters are more discursive and pictorial than his others written from places familiar to his readers. His description of natural scenery is precise and atmospheric. "The sense of space, light and color, in front, is superb," he writes of a Hawaiian landscape, "and the greater from the contrast behind, where the eye rests on a Scotch mountain-valley, ending in clouds and mist, and green mountain-sides absolutely velvety with the liquid softness of its lights and shadows" (31 August 1890). His sense perceptions are keen and discriminating. The story of his arrival and first night at Nikko, in Japan, is a panorama of smells, sights, sounds, tastes, and sensations; he evokes "open privies," "an open bath-house where naked men and women were splashing," the "clack-clack— like castanets" of the "watchman on pattens," the midnight "pain internal, passing into desperate nausea; then into drenching perspiration, and lastly into a violent diarhoea" (24 July 1886).

As a descriptive writer, Adams is more closely related to the introspective symbolic style, without the transcendental underpinnings, of Emerson and Thoreau, than to European or American realism. His response to weather and landscape recalls Emerson's definition of the lover of nature as "he whose inward and outward senses are still truly adjusted to each other." His account, for instance, of his nieces' introduction to the Scottish moors, is striking for its fluid blend of the "inward and outward senses":

> To the children everything was new, exciting and delightful: the yellow broom, the purple heather, the strange stillness of the air, the outlines of the mountains, and the sense of novelty with the feeling of freedom that always comes with the moors. They were delighted with everything, and on Sunday afternoon when the sun shone

bright for a few lovely hours, I took them up to the top of the hills, and turned them loose to wander where they liked over the heather. They started off in two different directions, and except as dots on distant hillsides I did not see them again till I got back to the house, two hours after. (20 July 1892)

He presents initially what the eye sees without feeling—the immediate sensory impact—"the yellow broom, the purple heather"; the psychological effect of the moors is introduced with the modifier "strange" of "stillness of the air"; "outlines of the mountains" is another visual detail but more abstract and distanced than the opening color images. The concluding generalization follows logically and euphoniously; the alliteration of *l*'s, *s*'s, and *f*'s is noteworthy. The next sentence returns to the specifics: "on a Sunday afternoon. . . . " The phrasing "I took them" and "turned them loose," a faintly humorous allusion to the children as caged animals, and the concluding vision of them straying off "in two different directions" dramatizes the "feeling of freedom" while the "dots on the distant hillsides" keeps the experience within the narrator's perception. Similarly, this notation on a London fog fuses the sensuous response with the psychological: "A lovely dark day, black as night, and full of refined feeling" (21 January 1892).

Adams put some of his best creative energy into his letters, though he corresponded nonetheless for practical and social reasons. Writing to keep in touch with family and friends, he dealt in the staples of friendly exchange—gossip, weather, plans, work, visitors, the trivia of daily life. To intimates, he wrote about himself with surprising candor. Henry James, a friend but not of Adams's inner circle, was struck by the self-disclosure of the South Sea letters that Hay had let him read: "What a *baring* of one's self— hitherto unsuspected in H. A."[4] Though the baring is relative to contemporary standards of decorum and Adams's personal reserve, the letters chart his shifting moods as well as prolonged emotional states. Applying his analytical imagination and historian's sense of fact, he wrote about himself with subtlety and detachment. In the later years, especially after 1893, formulaic ennui, combined with obsessive screeds against the degeneracy of the age, blotches his letters. How he successfully sublimated emotions in style may be seen in the following extract from a letter of 18 January 1892 to Elizabeth Cameron, the wife of Senator James Donald Cameron. She and their daughter, Martha, had become after his wife's death the center of Adams's emotional life.

Adams had not been in England for over a decade and this was the first time there since the suicide of Marian Adams seven years before, in 1885. She is the most living ghostly presence at the teatable. About Mrs. Cameron, Adams was in baffled turmoil. With her encouragement, he had hurried half way around the world from the South Pacific to meet her in Paris the previous October. The reunion was not a success. Accompanied by her stepdaughter Rachel and Martha, she seems to have arranged her schedule so that he saw more of them than of her. She returned to the United States a few weeks later; he stayed on in England, not sure whether to return himself, and if he did, on what footing.

Monday, Jan. 18. [1892] Gaskell came up on Saturday, and we have been knocking about town renewing our old acquaintances who are packed away into odd corners out of sight like broken bric-à-brac.[5] None are fashionable; a few are respectable and well-to-do; some are struggling under the heels of the horses. We dined with May Lacaita, the daughter of our old uncle Sir Francis Doyle, a favorite cousin of ours, and still full of Irish charm. She declares she once sat next John Hay at a dinner at the Farrars, and he gave her a book. We sat an hour yesterday with Augusta Hervey who now gives music lessons; but is, I think, rather better off than her cousins the Bristols who are obliged to let Ickworth as well as the house in St James's Square, and live on husks in the dark. I have just come from an effort of piety—a call on old Thomson Hankey, my contemporary, now eightysix years old, with a memory gone to the bowwows, who succeeded at last in remembering my father, but still is hazy as to my identity, and persists in repeating that I am a professor at Harvard College. He was delighted at telling how he had buried all his contemporaries. I have also sat an hour with the Woolners, to bid them good-bye. Queer sensation, this coming to life again in a dead world. People are rather glad to see one; ask no questions; slide silently over all that has come between, as though all the ghosts were taking tea with us, and needed no introductions; and so we rattle on about today and tomorrow, with just a word thrown in from time to time to explain some chasm too broad to be jumped. I feel even deader than I did in the South Seas, but here I feel that all the others are as dead as I. Even Harry James, with whom I lunch Sundays, is only a figure in the same old wall-paper, and really pretends to belong to a world which is extinct as Queen Elizabeth. I enjoy it. Seriously, I have been amused, and have felt a sense of rest such as I have not known for seven years. These preposterous British social conventions; church and state; Prince of Wales, Mr Gladstone, the Royal Academy and Mr Ruskin, the London fog and St James's

Street, are all abstractions which I like to accept as I do the sun and the moon, not because they are reasonable but because they are not. They ask me no questions and need no answers. Just the opposite of Paris and the French, they do not fret me with howling for applause because they are original. My only sorrow is to see no footmen in powder, no small-clothes and silk-stockings; no yellow chariots, and no fat coachmen in three-cornered hats. Much has gone, but thank the British Constitution, nothing new has come, and I sleep in peace with all the Georges and Queen Anne.

The passage opens as if it were to be an account of social activities of the weekend, but the unusual metaphor relating "old acquaintances" to "broken bric-à-brac" indicates that this delving into the past was a more complex experience than that suggested by the casual "knocking about town." Like the subsequent allusion to Henry James as "a figure in the same old wall-paper," the bric-à-brac image relegates the acquaintances and their society to a decorative function; the "odd corners out of sight" implies that they have even lost their value as curios; what is left is the pretense of an order that is actually shattered. The formal generalization "none are fashionable; a few are respectable and well-to-do; some are struggling under the heels of the horses" is exemplified first with May Lacaita as one of the "well-to-do" and then with the Herveys and Bristols representing those down in the world, climaxed with the apocalyptic image of "living on husks in the dark." The examples proceed logically but the progression does not stiffen into cold rational exposition. May Lacaita's remarks and social exaggeration are mimicked with the choice of the word "declares." The scene of the visit to Thomson Hankey, "my contemporary," is evoked. Henry Adams, at the time fifty-four years old, now mocks himself and dramatizes his dislocation. His identity as a "professor at Harvard College" was in another age; he is now in his dotage. Then, the unadorned allusion to the Woolners, unrhetorical perhaps because he realized that Woolner was not well. "Queer sensation, this coming to life again in a dead world," referring to his feeling that his life ended with his wife's death, shifts the focus back on himself; the allusion to the way in which his personal tragedy is glided over in social intercourse but remains in the air explains the "queer sensation" of the return after long absence in his peculiar circumstances. The polite evasion of "all that has come between" in his life is an instance of the restful hypocrisy and conservatism of British society as a whole: British social conventions and political forms are so preposterously fixed and divorced from any reality that one can no more question their rationality than one could the sun and the moon. Echoing the prayer for the souls of the dead in his concluding sentence, he pronounces his benediction on the society and on his past.

The deftly handled layering and mingling of past and present, personal feelings and social judgments; the thumbnail sketches airy yet sharply delineated; the mockery and self-mockery; the polished but supple and colloquial phrasings; the startling metaphors and poetic evocation of a vanished world in the conclusion make this a virtuoso rhetorical performance. At the same time, while the presence of the recipient is not as strongly felt as it is in the early letters of Henry to Charles, there is the sense of address to a sympathetic reader. The bravura aspects of the account need not be taken as a disguise of feeling; elegance of form and richness of allusion both in sentence structure and in the larger units of paragraphs and the essay-letter had become for Adams second nature.

Adams also wrote about himself directly, without such elaboration. In response to a troubled letter from a young friend who lived in Florida, he wrote: "Life is running pretty dry to me, and, except for a half a dozen friends, it had better be over. . . . You are still in the midst of it, with all it can give that is worth having. You, in your Florida swamp, make it go perfectly well. I, with every possible advantage, have failed to make it go at all" (16 March 1893). Paradoxically, direct statements of world-weariness, nihilism, and alienation seem more often to be tainted with pose than those in which he dramatized these emotions. Turning to inflated imagery and humor to raise his spirits, he followed the advice of the heroine's father in *Esther,* "Laugh, Esther when you're in trouble. Say something droll! Then you're safe!" So he would write, "As for me, I crawl in corners and lie in dark holes like a mangy and worn-out rabbit, and play pretend to be alive when noticed; but it is rather ghastly, and I wish you were here to protect me" (25 June 1893). Or he would express his fears about social chaos and personal collapse in conceits such as the following: "I am in a panic of terror about finance, politics, society and the solar system, with ultimate fears for the Milky Way, and the Nebula of Orion. The sun-spots scare me. Ruin hangs over the Pole Star. Of course this means the approach of old age and senility . . . " (9 September 1893). Underlying the humor and hyperbole is a pervasive ironic self-depreciation. As early as 1862, he was troubled by dejection and puzzled by a feeling of duality. As he put it to his brother Charles,

> You find fault with my desponding tone of mind. So do I. But the evil is one that probably lies where I can't get at it. I've disappointed myself, and experience the curious sensation of discovering myself to be a humbug. How is this possible? Do you understand how, without a double personality, *I* can feel that *I* am a failure? One would think that the *I* which could feel that, must be a different *ego* from the *I* of which it is felt. (14 February 1862)

Typically, especially after his wife's death broke in him the spring of resilience against despondency and the completion of his *History* took away his occupation, he exaggerated and dramatized his anxieties, loneliness, and boredom, simultaneously expressing his feelings and mocking them.

After more than forty years of letter writing, Adams found in the recently published letters of Robert Louis Stevenson reason for pause. "They exaggerate all one's bigness, brutality and coarseness; they perpetuate all one's mistakes, blunders and carelessnesses. No one can talk or write letters all the time without the effect of egotism and error" (5 March 1900). The essaylike, narrative cast of his letters, his humorous detachment from himself, and his empathy with the people to whom he wrote, saved Adams from the worst effects of egotism.

The person Adams unwittingly revealed in his letters was not free of self-deception and pose. The insistent energy with which he asserted fin-de-siècle nihilism and his credo of silence betrayed a hardening into attitudes of which he seemed unaware. Assuming an Olympian freedom from illusion, he condescended to those like Henry James who had not relinquished theirs. His stated detachment was at odds with the force of his rhetoric, as when, referring to Washington social and political figures, he wrote: "All this is little to me, to be sure,—almost as little as English affairs; yet I am amused too at the hog-like scramble of our English friends back into the public trough, and the silent scrunch with which they thrust their snouts into public patronage" (18 August 1892).

If Henry Adams, especially late in life, seems to have been confined in a carapace of style, it would be a mistake to equate style totally with the man. His style was a flexible instrument for the expression of his highly intellectual, ironic, and paradoxical vision as well as of tenderness and affection in a quiet domestic way, as for instance in his letters to Marian Adams in 1885 when she was away nursing her dying father. It was their first separation of any length since their marriage in 1872. The first letter, dated 14 March begins: "Madam/As it is now thirteen years since my last letter to you, possibly you may have forgotten my name. If so, please try to recall it. For a time we were somewhat intimate." Another, dated 12 April, 9 A.M., begins "Dear Mistress/The dogs and I have just come in from picking some violets for you, which we have put in your little Hizan tea-pot on our desk. The violets are only now in flower." The rest of the letter is mostly chit-chat about people he had been seeing, up to the final paragraph:

> I am not prepared to deny or assert any proposition which concerns myself; but certainly this solitary struggle with platitudinous atoms, called men and women by courtesy, leads me to wish for my wife again. How did I ever hit on the only woman in the world who fits my cravings and never sounds hollow anywhere? Social chemistry—the mutual attraction of equivalent human molecules—is a science yet to be created, for the fact is my daily study and only satisfaction in life.
>
> Ever Your H.

As an expression of feeling, the passage read in the cold light of criticism appears stiff, contrived, clumsy. We have, however, every reason to believe that Adams's love and affection for his wife was genuine. The failure to convey emotion is a stylistic one, though of course deeper psychological forces may be involved. The conclusion to be drawn is that style may become second nature, but it is also artifice. Letters, partaking of both life and fiction, hover between the randomness, untidiness, and mystery of life and such order, clarity, and conclusiveness as art imposes on life. The biographer of a subject whose letters are consciously literary has the task of discriminating between sincerity subverted by style and sincerity expressed through style.

NOTES

1. *The Correspondence of Henry Adams and John Hay, 1881–1892,* ed. Philip Blair Eppard (Ann Arbor, Michigan: University Microfilms International, 1979), 165.
2. All quotations from Henry Adams's letters through 18 January 1892 are from volumes 1–3 of *The Letters of Henry Adams,* ed. J. C. Levenson, Ernest Samuels, Charles Vandersee, and Viola Hopkins Winner (Cambridge, Massachusetts: Harvard University Press, 1982). Letters dated subsequently are from manuscripts to be published in volumes 4–6. Quotations are reproduced here with the permission of Harvard University Press. Adams's punctuation and spelling have been retained throughout.

3. Letters from the South Seas have been published in French, *Lettres des Mers du Sud, Hawaii, Samoa, Tahiti, Fidji 1890–1891,* ed. Evelyne de Chazeaux (Paris: Publications de la Société des Océanistes, no. 34, 1974).

4. George Monteiro, *Henry James and John Hay, The Record of a Friendship* (Providence, Rhode Island: Brown University Press, 1965), 109.

5. Adams's friendship with Charles Milnes Gaskell went back to the mid-1860s when as young men about town they flirted with Augusta Hervey at balls and country houses. Adams was half in love with her sister Mina, and Gaskell was jilted by her cousin, Lady Mary Hervey, the sister of the Marquis of Bristol. May Lacaita was Gaskell's cousin. Thomson Hankey was a family friend when Charles Francis Adams was minister to England. Thomas Woolner was the pre-Raphaelite sculptor and personal friend of the Adamses.

THE BEAT
BROTHERHOOD

JOHN TYTELL

> In fact, a biography cannot imitate life; it has to
> get rid of the chaos and the clutter; it rejects the
> habitual and the extraneous detail of our days; it
> rearranges its material; it tells a flowing story—
> something our lives never were.
>
> Leon Edel, *The Age Of The Archive*

THE HISTORY of any literary movement is at best a precarious adventure. Writers detest categories and groupings; like Faulkner
claiming not to have read *Ulysses,* they ingeniously deny influences
even as literary critics determine them. And since writers devote
their waking moments to developing difference and dream about
uniqueness, it is no wonder that they resist the linkings and contexts that can occasionally clarify their efforts.

The term *movement,* applied to a chain of literary circumstance,
implies a tension between past tradition and a particular turn in the
present. There was a time, when events moved more slowly, when
a single set of attitudes could dominate the literary community for
long periods. So we can see the continuity of sensibility connecting a Matthew Arnold to Wordsworth, for example, just as we can
retrospectively recognize that when Arnold tells us in his preface
to *Empedocles On Etna* that his own poetic voice has lost its authority, he is tacitly acknowledging the end of the romantic mood.

Our century has been considerably less unified in literature as
well as everything else, and literary movements, like celebratory
fireworks in the night, are often transient spectacles. In our time,
writers have paraded under the banners of Naturalism, Imagism,
Modernism, Vorticism, and Surrealism, and they have affiliated
themselves with groups like Bloomsbury or the Lost Generation.

Often, an especially dynamic figure like Ezra Pound may be associated with several of these movements, and the interchangeability is an index of the tremendous diversity of artistic enterprise in the twentieth century. In any such movement there exist the seminal thinkers, the genuine innovators, the impresarios, and the crowd of parrots. Imagism transformed modern poetry but who, except for Pound or William Carlos Williams, was able to write a poem fulfilling Imagist principles that had any lasting value as a poem? The charisma of art is usually a seductive blandishment as the followers of any literary style can attest, but imitation itself has its significance, and does exist as one sort of barometer of the informing power of any new view.

I offer these remarks on the momentum of literary movement out of my interest in a recent American manifestation—the Beat Generation. This movement, controversially greeted, radical in its view of America and in its esthetic, has had great cultural impact during the past twenty years. Jack Kerouac, who named the movement and who has been called the spokesman of his generation, died in 1969 at the end of a turbulent decade that he, in part, may have helped to bring about even as he despised its excesses. Many of his friends, writers like William Burroughs, Allen Ginsberg, Gary Snyder, and Lawrence Ferlinghetti, are still alive, agitating for their own causes and advocating what may be called Beat consciousness. While the movement involved a broad spectrum of writers in New York and San Francisco, in places like Kansas City, in small corners of the country like Reed College, and in centers of intellectual opinion like the University of Chicago, I have chosen to focus exclusively on the lives of the three major figures: Burroughs, Kerouac, and Ginsberg.

Like the ambulance drivers of the Lost Generation, Burroughs, Kerouac, and Ginsberg met during a period of national crisis. They began as a sort of brotherhood of ebullience and despair: three young men living in New York City during the Second World War with intimacy, intensity, and an unusual reciprocity of interest. The oldest was William Seward Burroughs, a Harvard graduate from a proper establishment family who had come to New York out of a perverse inclination to consort with criminals. Jack Kerouac had come to Columbia University on a football scholarship from the provincial factory town of Lowell, Massachusetts. The youngest member of this group was Allen Ginsberg, an eagerly serious aspiring poet studying with Mark Van Doren and Lionel Trilling at Columbia. These three men were almost as hetero-geneous as the American nation: Burroughs, a crusty, genteel WASP; Kerouac, a redneck confused by the clash between his Catholic conditioning and the emerging hipster values he detected in New York City; and Ginsberg, a Jewish intellectual from New Jersey whose father wrote poetry and whose mother was to be confined in a madhouse. Burroughs, who had read more, who had been psychoanalyzed, and who had traveled to Europe, became a kind of informal mentor for Kerouac and Ginsberg, introducing them to books like Spengler's *The Decline Of The West* and Wilhelm Reich's *The Cancer Biopathy,* and to writers like Céline, Cocteau, and Kafka. These men were surprisingly open with each other, and their discussions moved from books and ideas to more personal realities. Soon, Burroughs was psychoanalyzing Allen Ginsberg and initiating his younger friends with drugs like morphine and marijuana which he had just discovered through his underworld contacts. Before long, they were all sharing a large apartment near Columbia, communally experiencing the generational giddiness of Americans who first combined elements of surrealism and existentialism.

The rebellious camaraderie was partly a comfort in the presence of terrific pain. Burroughs was especially isolated and intent on repudiating his caste and its respectability. He was a marvelous raconteur, but a blocked writer who would not begin his first novel until his mid-thirties. All of them struggled with writing, and the problems they felt were connected to what they saw as a paralysis in the culture and the need to make new selves. Kerouac's French-Canadian mother had a peasant's outlook and little sympathy for his ambitions; his father, dying of stomach cancer after the Second World War, saw his son as a failure while Kerouac spent years trying to justify himself with a sprawling apprenticeship in fiction, *The Town and the City,* a first novel influenced by Wolfe, Fitzgerald, and Hemingway. And Ginsberg, troubled by his mad mother, pressured by a cautiously conservative father, was anxious about his own homosexuality, and dissatisfied with his ornate imitations of sixteenth-century English verse, efforts that made him feel like a "ventriloquist of other voices."

Much of the pain and motive for rebellion was a mutual refusal to accept the shell-shocked values of postwar American culture. The war years had been a time of great national sacrifice; it seemed, afterwards, that an enormous affluence was possible, but at certain costs. Part of a special new anxiety that dominated the postwar era has been noticed by E. L. Doctorow, who has offered one of the best accounts of the frozen fifties in *The Book of Daniel,* a novel which imagines the trial and execution of the Rosenbergs for allegedly passing atomic secrets to the Russians. Early in his novel, Doctorow comments on the political hysteria of the moment:

> Many historians have noted an interesting phenomenon in American life in the years immediately after a war. In the councils of government fierce partisanship replaces the necessary political coalitions of wartime. In the greater arena of social relations—business, labor, the community—violence rises, fear and recrimination dominate public discussion, passion prevails over reason. Many historians have noted this phenomenon. It is attributed to the continuance beyond the end of the war of the war hysteria. Unfortunately, the necessary emotional fever for fighting a war cannot be turned off like a water faucet. Enemies must continue to be found. The mind and heart cannot be demobilized as quickly as the platoon. On the contrary, like a fiery furnace at white heat, it takes a considerable time to cool.

The grey flannel suit culture that William H. Whyte described in *The Organization Man* had little appeal for the Beats. Instead of repression, respectability, and careerism, their priorities were pleasure and freedom of expression. Kerouac spent his undergraduate nights at Minton's, a jazz joint in Harlem, listening to Charlie Parker and Lester Young, trying to adapt the inspired spontaneous beat of black American music to his own prose rhythms. Ginsberg complained to Mark Van Doren that Whitman and Henry Miller were ignored or disparaged by the Columbia academicians. Burroughs scorned American institutions and values, and in seeking out criminals and drugs was making of himself an untouchable. These men formed the vanguard of an underground generation in absolute revolt from unprecedented pressures for conformity, from the phlegmatically bovine dullness of the Eisenhower era. Instead of security, the Beats began a search for ecstasy, mystical experience, sexual release, and emotional honesty.

These were clearly unpopular ambitions during the Cold War years, a time of extraordinary insecurity and profound individual powerlessness, a perilous time when old-fashioned notions of personal responsibility were being rationalized in the interests of corporate growth, when the catchwords were coordination and adjustment, and when the idea of individuality no longer seemed to matter. Ironically, after the war, the emphasis for the victors was on fear—of nuclear annihilation, of Russian spies and expansionism—and the social cost seemed to be perpetual rearmament. Internally, the mania of rabid anticommunism fostered more fear and distrust as the accusations of Joseph McCarthy and the red-witch hunts in Hollywood and the universities created an atmosphere of coercion and conspiracy.

The Beats responded to what they perceived as the stifling qualities of the fifties with a passionate roar. Each of their major works during this period, Ginsberg's *Howl*, Kerouac's *On the Road*, and Burroughs's *Naked Lunch* caused publication difficulties or actual censorship proceedings: two thousand copies of *Howl* were burned by customs police in San Francisco in 1955 (the volume had been printed in England) and, like *Naked Lunch*, it could only be released after court tests. When *On the Road* appeared in 1957, it was villified by many critics who called it hedonistic, nihilistic, and onanistic. They especially deplored the delirious manners and reckless mores of headstrong characters who seemed able to sacrifice conventional bonds for the sake of change. Even so, Gilbert Millstein in *The New York Times* recognized the novel as an "historic occasion" and compared it to *The Sun Also Rises* as a sign of generational identity.

Apparently, some taboo had been threatened, some nerve in the cultural nexus had been exposed, some tacit agreement between artist and audience had been spurned, and the critics saw the young Beats as barbarians storming the literary citadel. Indeed, the Beats had returned to a romantic perspective (just about one hundred years after Arnold gave us his touchstone for the end of Romanticism) in a time when expansive attitudes and lyrical expression were suspect, when literature was dominated by the narrow theoretical limits of the "new criticism": irony, strict formal adherence to literary convention, proper taste in subject matter. Postwar poetry was mandarin, decorative, diffident, difficult sometimes, it seemed, only for the sake of difficulty, ponderously symbolic with the weight of Eliot's influence. A model is Robert Lowell's admired early volume, *Lord Weary's Castle*—even its title connotes a fatigued elitism lost in a remote intellectual idyll that took shelter in abstraction. The change in American poetry would begin with the confessional ardor of Ginsberg's *Howl*, and it is clearly reflected in Lowell's next and best book, *Life Studies*.

The Renegade Path

Instead of the mannered tradition of Henry James and Virginia Woolf, the perspective that carefully applied fineness of sensibility and discrimination of feelings as a source of illumination about character and culture, the Beats followed the more rambunctiously renegade path of Whitman, Rimbaud, and Henry Miller. Regarding themselves as exiles within the culture, they rejected middle-class values for a bohemian libertarianism that romantically idealized freedom and spontaneity and saw, sometimes with a paranoiac terror, social controls at every corner.

The emancipation that so dissident a stance implies came as no sudden discovery, but as the result of a long history of travail and grief in the world. I want to chart some of the steps in this history—not for its sensational aspects, though Beat style was to use sensation, never to flee from it in shame, as a hieroglyph of life in a time of apathy—but to show how by transcending the values they opposed, they helped alter what they feared and affected their age. Of course, it is practically a given that modern artists find themselves in a situation antagonistic to culture. But the Beats were singular in that they were given to more extreme gestures and actions than their contemporaries. The biographical focus with rebellious artists is always on the struggle with conditioning, the ways that the mores and thought patterns of a culture and one's parents subtly influence action and insinuate guilt with each departure from the circumscribed order. To put it simply, each of the Beats was willing to take enormous risks and to gamble with potentially dangerous experiences in order to transcend that conditioning. The routes, perhaps inevitably, were traditional and as old as the prophets: travel, drugs, spiritual quest, and a profound argument with what it meant to be "sane" in a time when all definitions were shifting.

No contemporary writer has endangered his mind and body as has William Burroughs who remained addicted to morphine, heroin, and other drugs from 1943 to 1958. Writers often choose their metier because of the power of personality and a desire to affect the world through the word; Burroughs, however, spent fifteen years in pursuit of obliteration. In one sense, he became a writer in spite of himself, and the drug experience which consumed him for so long, with its deprivations and special transports, became his story.

Burroughs's childhood in St. Louis represented another extreme, the claustrophobic terrors of upper-class gentility. His grandfather had perfected the adding machine and founded the giant Burroughs corporation, and that instilled a clear legacy for the entire family. Burroughs's father, as is often the case with the children of fortune and power, was retiring and ineffectual; he spent his time collecting and selling antiques. Burroughs's mother was a direct descendant of Robert E. Lee. She wrote a little book on floral arrangement and smothered her son with an overdeveloped sense of Victorian propriety—a trait, incidentally, which was not especially characteristic of the Lee family as her brother, Ivy Lee, became John D. Rockefeller's chief publicist. Later on, Burroughs's own fiction would become a savagely inspired departure from his mother's mannered conventionality.

As an adolescent, Burroughs was fragile and sickly. Sent to a boarding school to practice sports, he instead read de Maupassant, Baudelaire, Wilde, and Gide, gradually developing an interest in crime. The title of his first literary essay, "The Autobiography of a Wolf," offers a clue to his loneliness and isolation. Remote, laconic, easily embarrassed by sentiment but attracted to other men, Burroughs attended Harvard during the Depression where he studied literature, linguistics, and anthropology. T. S. Eliot was in residence at Harvard during one of Burroughs's years as an undergraduate, and Burroughs must have been influenced when he heard Eliot read—his own fiction later reflects this.

After graduating from Harvard, Burroughs, supported by a modest trust fund, went to Europe where he began medical studies in Vienna. He met a young Jewish woman who feared for her safety because of the Nazis; Burroughs married her so that he could bring her to the United States where their arrangement of convenience was immediately dissolved.

War seemed imminent and Burroughs tried to join the newly formed Office of Secret Services. He had the right credentials and appropriate family connections—his uncle, Ivy Lee, was a good friend of William Donovan who had organized the agency. While Burroughs passed all the intelligence tests, his application was denied when on his physical he admitted to having sliced off the tip of a finger with a chicken shears to see what the sensation would be like. Burroughs was then drafted, but received a psychological discharge after six months, and began psychoanalysis with a psychiatrist who had been analyzed by Freud. After his analysis, he drifted to Chicago to find the criminal elements which by now had begun to obsess him; he worked as a bartender, an exterminator, and a private detective, but encountered no gangsters in the town of Al Capone.

He did find some in New York City just at the time that he met Kerouac and Ginsberg. His introduction to the world of petty criminality came through a Times Square hustler and hipster named Herbert Huncke (who, a few years later, became one of Alfred Kinsey's first subjects in his study of the sexual habits of the American male; Huncke then recruited subjects for Kinsey's interviews). Burroughs rented a flat on the lower East Side of Manhattan for Huncke where he hoped to meet more underworld figures. In the meantime, Huncke introduced him to morphine injections. This was the time when Burroughs, Kerouac, and Ginsberg formed what I have already called a brotherhood, sharing a large apartment near Columbia with several women. One of them was Joan Adams, a graduate student of journalism at Columbia who fell in love with Burroughs, left her husband, and lived with Burroughs for the next seven years.

After the war, Burroughs and Joan Adams began to fear police apprehension because of their drug use, and they moved to a little farming community north of Houston, Texas. Burroughs's intentions were not particularly pastoral: he believed he could cultivate opium on his land so as to have the raw material for morphine and heroin. While he could not grow opium, he did succeed in raising a quantity of marijuana secreted between rows of alfalfa which he harvested and sold in New York.

At every step along the way, Burroughs was challenging authority and testing legal limits. Slicing his finger was a rejection of parental protection; marketing marijuana (even though it may have predicted a billion dollar business) placed him outside the law. While in Texas he became especially sensitive to the farm bureaucracy organized during the New Deal, and he chafed under its agricultural controls. He also noticed the way in which such controls could be relaxed for the big farmer when they seasonally imported Mexican wetbacks, and decided that since the law was so relative and so selectively applied, it had little inherent validity.

It is clear that Burroughs was following a path that would set him apart from the social compact binding men under government. In 1951, living now in Mexico City and studying Mayan history and archeology on the G.I. Bill, he committed the act that effectively ruptured all remaining ties to family and state when he shot Joan Adams. Whether the act was or was not premeditated seems almost unimportant from a psychological perspective. The couple had a love/hate relationship, and Joan depended on Burroughs more than he needed her. They had a son, but Burroughs's inclinations were homosexual; in his fiction and later interviews he has expressed his misogyny. The unhappy couple had been mixing champagne and drugs at an all night party when Joan put a glass on her head and dared Burroughs to shoot it off at close range. He missed the glass.

The trial lasted almost a year. During this period, Burroughs finally broke through the barriers that had for so long blocked his dark vision, and he began writing *Junkie*. The book had none of the experimental features of his subsequent work, but naturalistically recorded the seedy world of addiction. Burroughs sent chapters to Allen Ginsberg who interested a publisher and the book appeared under the pseudonym of William Lee. Kerouac had been encouraging Burroughs to write for years, but except for a sketch written at Harvard, he had done very little. Suddenly, as if the last totem of respectability had been demolished, as if the death of Joan Adams had somehow finally released him from the obligations of his own conditioning, he was able to write.

Burroughs now intensified his drug use. Leaving Mexico before the court's verdict, he voyaged into the backwaters of Colombia and Peru in search of *ayahuasca*, a South American psychedelic prepared and administered by tribal medicine men. He described some of his terrifying experiences in letters to Ginsberg, and his trip into the Conradian inferno seemed like some sort of purgation or expiation, as if the body itself was a treacherous vessel that had to succumb to natural law so that the vision could be released.

This is hardly offered as romantic rationalization. The fruit of Burroughs's new perspective is evident in *Naked Lunch*, a major esthetic advance in the form and content of the novel. Burroughs's addiction became even more serious after his South American travels. He moved to North Africa where drugs and young boys were cheap and available and began taking notes on his own disintegration. These notes, some of them written during the delirium of drug addiction, became *Naked Lunch*, which itself is perhaps the most powerful artistic warning of the dangers of drugs in our time. *Naked Lunch*, partly because of its censorship case, attracted great notice and affected the literary world. In a tremendous act of self-assertion, Burroughs broke his addiction to devote himself to writing. He had become the outsider incarnate, and his antagonism to the world would be expressed in a series of alarming apocalyptic auguries of Western breakdown. His telegraphic style and kaleidoscopic structure was one early demonstration that fiction could move beyond Joyce, that a new postmodernist mode had begun.

One of the intriguing aspects of Burroughs's novels is the absence of any authorial presence, a character who might be seen as speaking his views. By inventing a panoply of changing characters and setting them in a mosaic architecture, by refusing to develop character in the way a more traditional writer might, Burroughs manages a harrowing invisibility. But the act of writing, especially fiction, is so intimately a reflection of how a writer wants to see himself, a projection that may be idealized or exaggerated, but is usually dependent on some significantly revealing distortion. In this respect, Burroughs follows the modernist line of T. S. Eliot, the position that requires effacement of personality. But a literature of consistent invective and rage is itself a sufficient barometer of Burroughs's sensibility.

We all, of course, fashion personae for different occasions; some of us act to heighten our fantasies, even if only in some small token way. It is the business of fiction, however, to fabricate the fantasy, to weave an artifice, to embellish and give power to what might otherwise seem ordinary. Part of the purpose of criticism is to clarify the distance between person and persona, a distance the artist often confuses. For any biographer, the mask, the projection, may reveal how an artist sees himself: is he rejected, self-loathing, aggressively proud, maniacally inspired? The possibilities are as vast as the range of personality, and they naturally determine the biographer's perspective.

In Kerouac's case, persona is more drastically present than in Burroughs's, more romantically pronounced and engaging, more enthusiastically the first-person "I" than the camera eye of the modernist esthetic. His fiction suggests an almost insatiable quest for experience, at times beyond normative moral parameters, and always moving toward the release of feeling. The myth behind the books is that of the adventurer who knows no horizon, the American pioneer who heads for the territories, the man who when he reaches the top of the mountain tries to keep on climbing. Late in his life, when Kerouac was living in almost reclusive retirement in

St. Petersburg, Florida, he was haunted by youths who would knock on his door expecting to be regaled by the characters he had conceived. It was the kind of anomaly familiar to writers who have been too convincing with their fantasies.

That fantasy life began rather early for Kerouac. He started writing prior to his teenage years: family newsletters, journals, stories. His father was a small-time printer who set type himself and taught his son to do it in the factory town of Lowell, Massachusetts. Kerouac's parents were French-Canadians and they lived in the "Canuck" ghetto of Lowell until the Merrimack River flooded during the Depression and swamped Leo Kerouac's print shop. Kerouac's first language was French-Canadian, and he only started using English in grade school.

As a young man in high school, Kerouac showed early signs of willfullness. He trained so hard for the running team that he subsequently developed thrombophlebitis, an illness which he knew could terminate his life at any moment. When he wanted to play football for Lowell High, the coach told him he was not big enough for the team. Kerouac trained on his own and became a star running back, so good that he was offered an athletic scholarship by Notre Dame and Columbia.

The Kerouacs were Catholic and Gabrielle, the mother, had a peasant sensibility: cautious, conservative, and very religious, she wanted her son to attend Notre Dame. Leo, more impulsive and carefree, a man with many friends in Lowell who loved the track and the barroom, wanted his son to be a football hero in New York. Kerouac wanted to write and realized that New York City offered more opportunity; his mother saw writing only as a disreputable possibility.

Kerouac's life was as inconsistent and as contradictory as his literary career. After leaving Columbia University in the wake of scandal—his friend Lucien Carr had murdered a man and Kerouac was arrested as a material witness—and joining the merchant marines during the war, Kerouac spent five years toiling on his first novel, *The Town and the City,* which appeared in 1951 to favorable reviews but limited sales. The book was written in a conventional style; Kerouac was still learning how to write fiction, but he knew how important it was to discover a new form and a new way of storytelling. His catalyst was a young friend named Neal Cassady, a reform school delinquent who read Proust and wanted to become a writer. Cassady, who became a model of activity for the

Beat Brotherhood, sent Kerouac a forty page, single-spaced, un-punctuated letter describing his sexual exploits, and Kerouac saw in its colloquial naturalness of expression an energy that could transform his own prose. Cassady was a nonstop talker of inexhaustible velocity, and he encouraged Kerouac to travel to the American west to discover the virtues of the open road. Actually, Kerouac came to hate the vulnerability of the hitchhiking that he later popularized and much preferred the security of the Greyhound bus, but he allowed himself to be lured from his worktable on many occasions because he realized that Cassady had become his subject. However, the writer who made a myth out of the gregarious adventures of his friends spent most of his time living with his mother in Queens, then the lower-middle-class section of New York City, writing in her kitchen. And after each trip to Cassady's home town of Denver, to Mexico to visit Burroughs, to California, Kerouac would return to the sanctuary of his mother's kitchen to assimilate his experiences and record them. He had vowed to his dying father, as a Catholic, that he would protect his mother always, and he remained faithful to this vow, abortively ending his first two marriages because of it, and marrying again near the end of his life the sister of a childhood friend whom he knew would continue to care for his mother after his death. Since Kerouac was largely responsible for creating an interest in Buddhism during the sixties (because of his novel *The Dharma Bums*), a view which accepts the inevitability of suffering and the importance of detachment, the tie to his mother represents yet another aspect of contradiction.

Kerouac's life presents problems for any biographer because he claimed to write directly from experience, without revision (which he saw as a subtle form of censorship) or otherwise altering the actual. To an amazing extent, he succeeded, but the game of fiction with the distorting roles of memory and ego projection inevitably affects any historical record. As a man, Kerouac was afflicted with deep feelings of loss and estrangement; as a writer, he created a spectacle of Whitmanic union, merging, identification in love. So the fiction was the exact reverse of the man. The power of the book for which he became famous, *On the Road,* depends much more on Kerouac's myth-making ability than on his confessional imperative. What his audience really cared about was a version of Huck Finn who actually did light out for the territories to find a dream of lost freedom and innocence. What made that audience feel his story was the manner in which Kerouac set it down, with a rhythmic, rhapsodically lyrical sweep and an excited American vernacular.

On the Road was written in a three-week burst of inspiration in 1951, but published only in 1957 after Malcolm Cowley succeeded in convincing the editors at Viking Press that Kerouac had written an important book. During the six years that Kerouac had to wait for the acceptance and publication of *On the Road,* he wrote another dozen books convinced of his own genius but feeling it would not be recognized in his time. One act that seems suggestive of Kerouac's situation at this time was his decision to work as a fire lookout for the forestry service, spending months on the tops of desolate mountain peaks in Oregon and Washington, writing, meditating, observing nature, and generally living like a monk in communion with the starry universe. Kerouac had accepted his anonymity and weathered it with a kind of homespun Buddhist nature worship. When *On the Road* appeared, it aroused a storm of controversy and publicity for which Kerouac was entirely unprepared. Some self-destructive inclination, which perhaps is the edge to living for the sake of experience anyway, caused him to drink more and more heavily, and the alcoholism began to warp him, to sour his writing, to close him to the very friends who had once so filled him with a sense of possibility. Like Melville, who sought (according to Hawthorne) to annihilate his sensibility, Kerouac retreated from the world. At the age of forty-seven, consumed by his drinking, bitter, angry and still confused, his body collapsed and he died of abdominal hemorrhaging.

Allen Ginsberg has led a life as full of vicissitude as Kerouac's. When he met Kerouac and Burroughs, he was full of nervous intensity and shyness and an eagerness to be accepted. His own childhood, as his poem "Kaddish" attests, had been scarred by a mother whose paranoia was so developed she believed that Roosevelt was eavesdropping on her secret thoughts. Naomi Ginsberg became an inmate of mental institutions and eventually received a frontal lobotomy. Ginsberg's father, Louis, a high school English teacher and poet, encouraged his son to follow convention in his life as well as in his poetry. It would seem that Ginsberg has devoted his life to a refutation of that paternal position.

At Columbia University, Ginsberg won literary prizes but was dissatisfied by what he considered to be the manneristic inferiority

of his poetry. He was also anxious and unsure about his own homosexuality. He felt that his poetic ambitions would never be realized unless he received psychoanalytic assistance. After graduating
from Columbia in 1948, he was galvanized by an auditory halluci-
nation of William Blake's voice, an experience that terrified him
but also excited him to the possibility of participating in the prophetic tradition of poetry. Through a Chaplinesque involvement
with Herbert Huncke and a band of petty thieves, Ginsberg spent
almost a year at Columbia Psychiatric Institute, sent there instead
of to prison when Lionel Trilling interceded on his behalf. Later,
he would receive treatment at the Langley-Porter Clinic in San
Francisco. The lesson he took from all his analysis was what Burroughs had told him when he performed an amateur analysis in the
first year of their friendship: accept himself as he was, without
shame. This realization led, in San Francisco in 1955, to the spontaneous transcription in the style Kerouac had taught him which
we know as "Howl"—a brilliant and overwhelming release of
sheer feeling and rhythm that changed the direction of American
poetry. At that time, Ginsberg met Peter Orlovsky, a younger man
with whom he lived and loved for over two decades.

During the sixties, Ginsberg continued to write poems, appearing frequently before large gatherings, and soon gaining the reputation of being the most powerful reader of poetry since Dylan
Thomas. Much more overt politically than either Burroughs or
Kerouac, he devoted himself to the effort against the war in Vietnam and, in *The Fall of America* (1974), documented the internal
consequences of that era. He traveled to India, mixing morphine
with guru searches and learning to chant mantras. After visiting
Cuba and Czechoslovakia, he was expelled because the libertarian
consciousness that he advocated is anathema for any totalitarian re-
gime. Returning to the United States, he participated in the psychedelic movement. Ginsberg seemed to be simultaneously reaching in a number of directions, all of which affected what he was
writing: living on a farm in upstate New York, learning to make
music with Bob Dylan, intensifying his Buddhist study and meditation. He consistently expanded the frontiers for poetry, in the
seventies, by experimenting with blues improvisations and Blakean
homosexual songs full of tender harmony and unprecedented
revelation.

Ginsberg's imperative has always been to transform normative
consciousness so as to shock free a visionary possibility, and the

kind of confrontational, personal politics he has pursued—most recently he was arrested for blocking a train carrying Plutonium—has been a crucial factor in discovering such vision. Indeed, what some might call Ginsberg's outrageousness can be seen as the paradigm of Beat consciousness, devoted to the expression of direct feeling of love or fear, no matter what the cost to public image or convention.

The Biographical Journey

I offer these three vignettes as an instance of passionate literary moment in our time. Part of the difficulty in presenting them is that excess is often mistrusted and usually feared. During the fifties, a time of many silent omissions, the Beat polemic was release. Their politics were not leftist as much as libertarian and the purpose was to rouse, to challenge, to question the changes caused by the new technologies, to help Americans remember that this too was once a place where men could dream of a better future. Such visions as they managed occurred as the consequence of a struggle with their own conditioning at great psychic cost. In Kerouac's case, the struggle burned him out before he was fifty. The value of such suffering for the community, however, is whatever spiritual insight may ensue, particularly if the sufferer seeks to record the changes along the way. In this sense Burroughs, Kerouac, and Ginsberg share a communion of perception.

When I began my work on the writers of the Beat Generation, as a young scholar who had written about Henry James and Ford Madox Ford, about Baron Corvo and Richard Crashaw, there was virtually nothing useful on the subject. My interest began when I was asked, during the time of troubles in American universities at the end of the sixties, to deliver a lecture as if it were my last opportunity to address a university audience. I felt my own literary interests might not be immediate enough for the concerns of students and faculty anguished over our involvement in Southeast Asia. The Beats were political and engaged; their work had power though it was then unappreciated and misunderstood.

I began with some of the novels and poems, only intending to speak my piece and move on to other areas of literary endeavor. But when I realized how maligned and patronized the Beats had been throughout the various controversies concerning them, I decided to write an essay on their origins and importance. This appeared in *The American Scholar* and provoked interest. Before I knew it, I was reading all the available literature and embarked on *Naked Angels,* the first comprehensive account of the Beats.

I was fortunate in living in New York City since Allen Ginsberg had deposited there his letters and papers as well as whatever he had saved of Kerouac's and Burroughs's—but the collection was a chaotic quagmire without collation or chronology, a disorder of undated notes and fading letters stuffed in shoeboxes. The awful state of the Ginsberg papers seemed to be an index of how the Beats were then regarded. After a year of reading this material, making several trips to other university collections like the one at the Humanities Research Center in Austin, and using private collections like the one owned by Kerouac's friend John Clellon Holmes, I knew enough to begin interviewing various Beat writers. What I had to learn was how to ask the questions (often despite the feeling that I was just blundering into the trivial) that could serve to break through the surface of events as they inevitably become fogged in time and memory, and the mistrust of the man asking the questions.

I sent *The American Scholar* essay to Ginsberg and to Burroughs, and they each liked it enough to make themselves available. Ginsberg was full of articulated memory and valuable assistance; Burroughs was much more distant, having the fear of biographical treachery that may be instinctive with certain writers. I used my tape recorder and I remember the way Burroughs would stiffly rise and walk twelve feet away from my machine so that it could not possibly pick up his murmured reply to a question that might have been too personal, too close to the bone of past suffering. But I regarded whatever I got as an advantage, for no one had previously been permitted even to sketch the details of his life. I suppose my greatest luck, however, was in locating and interviewing the lesser figures in the Beat group: men like Huncke (whom I reached only through a fluke of friendship and after enough negotiation to end a small war); Lucien Carr (who tried to get me drunk when I met him in a bar near the *Daily News* building, and who only began to trust me after a former student, a New York City fireman in uniform, came over to greet me); John Clellon Holmes, Kerouac's novelist friend who offered me grace and hospitality; and Carl Solomon, whom Ginsberg had met at Columbia Psychiatric Institute and who then spent eight years in other institutions, still afflicted and still on tranquilizers, and still asking the same unanswerable questions one would expect to read only in a novel by Dostoevski.

There was a surfeit of material, but my real lesson was the understanding that not all of it could be used without losing my readers in an avalanche of detail. I suppose this is the perennial lesson of biography. It was only after I completed my first draft that I was able to eliminate entire sections of my book, chapters on the poets Gary Snyder, Lawrence Ferlinghetti, and Gregory Corso, for example, which blurred my perspective. What Burroughs, Kerouac, and Ginsberg had begun in New York City during the Second World War eventually affected writers all over America, and the decision to focus on them was not reached without circumspection—for one thing, the Puritan in me shuddered at rejecting months of my own work—but it did respond to a clear chronological and geographical validity.

What was much more difficult was the fact of my own conditioning, the years reading more classical forms of expression which had helped to form my taste as well as that of the Western world, and an academic process which reveres the past while almost always condescending to the present. It is easier to idealize the dead; the living can be querulous. As a graduate student, I had been warned by Oscar Cargill, a well-known Americanist, that positions teaching modern or especially contemporary literature were practically unobtainable, and it would be more pragmatic for me to devote my studious ambitions to the nineteenth century. Professor Cargill was right since contemporary literature as a subject for university study was another postwar phenomenon that was only beginning to catch on. Later, when I went to Columbia to ask Lionel Trilling about his former students, Kerouac and Ginsberg, he told me that in their time no one got past the Victorians in literature classes, that Matthew Arnold was considered modern.

Another barrier was a general disdain among the academic critics for the Beats. The Beats had so violated the idea of literary decorum that seemed so important in the fifties by their personal appearances (Ginsberg undressing after reading "Howl" in answer to a questioning professor who wanted to know what he meant by nakedness; Kerouac, who wore open-necked checkered shirts and presented himself more as woodsman than wordsman) and what they set down in print that few critics (even the more rebellious ones like Leslie Fiedler) had the courage to take them seriously. There was little sympathy for the sheer absurdity causing the improvised playfulness evident in Robert Frank's film, "Pull My

Daisy," which allowed the inspired antics of Ginsberg and Corso to the music of Kerouac's narration. At that time, there was little precedent on these shores for writers who psychoanalyzed each other or who so openly used their experiences with drugs or homosexuality as subject matter—that Verlaine had once shot and seriously wounded Rimbaud in Belgium was the sort of scandal that seemed unmentionable in American art, as if the critics believed that the passions of life were somehow separated from what writers wrote about. The late fifties, when *Howl, On the Road,* and *Naked Lunch* appeared, have been characterized by Ginsberg as a time vexed by the "syndrome of shutdown," but it was apparent that the genteel strictures which had for so long governed public taste and publishing were ready to be challenged. In 1960, when I was still an eager undergraduate, two events signaled that change: the ransacking of the offices of the House Un-American Activities Committee in San Francisco by an unruly mob, and the publication of *Tropic of Cancer* (to the accompaniment of sixty local legal contentions).

What was interesting to me was that the established critics seemed threatened by the quality and character of Beat writing, appalled as Allen Tate was by Burroughs's scatological sexuality, his scenes of sadistic terror presented in a scary moral vacuum with what must have seemed gratuitous shocks like the following line from *Naked Lunch:* "We see God through our assholes in the flashbulb of orgasm." Others, like Norman Podhoretz in his piece "The Know Nothing Bohemians," impugned Kerouac's ebullience, his romantic declaration that the writer should accept his original notation, that revision was a subtle form of censorship, an accommodation to satisfy an editor or public taste. Since revision is a writer's shibboleth, a sacred cow of literary enterprise, we can retrospectively understand why Kerouac caused such an uproar, why he was so suspected and outcast by both the critics and some of his fellow craftsmen, writers like Truman Capote who quipped that Kerouac's writing was only typewriting, or Randall Jarrell, who, when accepting The National Book Award in 1960, castigated Kerouac, arguing that the quality of personal revelation in *On the Road* was more suitable to successful psychoanalysis than fiction.

As a graduate student, reading Northrup Frye or R. P. Blackmur on James, schooled in the fastidious euphonics of the New Criticism, I was taught to believe that literary credibility was in large part a function of critical authority. But the Beat writers were almost universally deplored and, by some, clearly despised. The early reviews of *Howl,* the first major publication by a Beat writer, and a book that changed the direction of American poetry in the mid-fifties, document this. John Hollander, writing about his own Columbia classmate in a spirit of evident distrust for what he saw as modish avant-garde posturing, complained in *Partisan Review* of the "utter lack of decorum of any kind in this dreadful little volume." James Dickey, in *Sewanee Review,* established Ginsberg as the tower of contemporary Babel, finding the poem full of meaningless utterance. Ginsberg's own self-assumed role of media clown in the sixties did little to redeem or improve this reputation. For some time, the critics could not fathom the poetic precedents for his long lines, just as they were put off by his blatant message of apocalypse, and the hysterically strident condemnation of the very institutions that fostered their efforts.

I suppose it was partly a response to the nearly unanimous rejection of Beat writing by the critics, the view that they were philistines without a viable literary past, some species of distasteful and aberrant contemporary anomaly, that caused me to discover their lineage. Also, given the tempest of the late sixties, my own radical sympathies may have consumed the more genteel aspects of my calling. In Ginsberg's case that lineage included Blake, Whitman, eastern Buddhism, and the French Surrealism that also affected Burroughs and Kerouac. Burroughs, perhaps because of his postmodernist experimentalism, had received some intelligent criticism from the British critic Tony Tanner. With Kerouac, who had tried so hard to create an authentically American voice (but who in *On the Road* also wrote a book with deep layers of picaresque convention), it was the romantic legacy of spontaneity, the rhythms of jazz, an evocation of natural speech as opposed to literary inflection that finds antecedents in Twain and William Carlos Williams, and in a novel only published posthumously, *Visions of Cody,* what I saw as a neglected masterpiece in the Joycean mode.

Kerouac's reputation is changing in the literary community, and some of those who formerly disparaged him are now out of print while most of his work has been brought back (with *On the Road* selling over fifty thousand copies a year). There has been considerable critical interest in his work lately; several books have been written about him and others are projected. Burroughs and Ginsberg are still writing, as are Snyder, Ferlinghetti, and Corso, so the Beat phenomenon is now in its fourth decade and much of the enormous change in small press and alternative publishing is a testament to its continuing presence.

IV
EXEMPLA

KATHARINE JAMES PRINCE: A PARTIAL PORTRAIT

Jean Strouse

THE STORY of Katharine James Prince bears some striking resemblances to the tales of her novelist cousin, Henry James. It features an attractive, sensitive young woman struggling with ill-health and love. Its drama lies not in action but in perception and the nuances of internal conflict. The narrative emerges through the voices of its characters, each with a limited, specific point of view. Unlike a James tale, however, this story has no central narrator, no moral design, no artistic direction; nor does it have the satisfying resolution of fiction, for information about Katharine James Prince (known as "Kitty") is sparse and incomplete. The voices telling the story come from letters I found in researching the life of her cousin (and Henry's sister), Alice James. I collected them thinking that the life of another woman in the James family with "nervous" disorders might help illuminate aspects of Alice's life; in the end, however, the letters seemed to make up a special little tale of their own. Here, then, is a partial portrait of Kitty Prince.

Born in Albany, New York, on 6 December 1834, Katharine Barber James was the fourth and youngest child of the Reverend William James and Marcia Lucretia Ames. Her paternal grandfather, William James of Albany (1771–1832), had come to upstate New York from Ireland in 1789 and made $3 million in merchandising, banking, real estate, and public utilities. His first wife, Elizabeth Tillman, died in 1797, eight days after giving birth to Kitty's father and his twin brother, Robert. The senior William married twice more, and had a total of thirteen children; among his offspring by his third wife, Catharine Barber (for whom Kitty was named), was Henry (1811–1882), the father of the Henry and

William who made the family famous in American intellectual history.

The education of William, Kitty's father, was strictly Presbyterian. At sixteen, he graduated from Princeton and entered the Princeton Theological Seminary; he was ordained in 1820 by the Presbytery at Albany, went to Scotland for two years' further study, preached all over New York State, and gradually withdrew from active ministerial life to concern himself with philanthropy after his father's death in 1832. He had, apparently, a great gift for public speaking and was, like his brother Henry, a brilliant, fervent, highly eccentric character. One day he interrupted himself in the middle of a sermon and marched up the church aisle to greet a parishioner he hadn't seen for some time.[1] Like many men who are preoccupied with God, he tended toward the absent-minded in daily life: another day, on a trip up New York's Fifth Avenue, he passed the door of a friend's house where a servant was sweeping the steps, and suddenly decided it would be more convenient to leave his suitcase there than to carry it around all day. He called out to the servant and tossed the bag over the top of the bus. Later, when he arrived at the house, no one had seen his bag. In the ensuing search, the missing item was found lodged in a large tree in front of the house: James hadn't bothered to watch where it fell, nor to make sure the servant had heard him.

In 1824 he married Marcia Ames. According to yet another Henry James—the eldest son of William the psychologist—Marcia A. James "became insane" some time after her marriage, and her husband, on being told it was "a case of inheritance," lamented: "Everybody in New York knew it but I, and there was nobody who would tell me."[2]

William and Marcia James had four children between 1826 and 1834: Anna McBride, a son who died at birth, Elizabeth Tillman, and Kitty. I found no letters telling the story of Kitty's early years. We see her first at age sixteen, away at boarding school and in "delicate" health. On 8 October 1850, her mother wrote her a letter that sheds some light on the family concern about "inherited" insanity; it also, in its admonitory tone, echoes the advice a great many middle- and upper-class mothers were giving to their daughters at mid-century—about woman's proper sphere (which did not include book-learning), the dangers of excitement, and the virtues of moderation.

[In all these letters I have retained the original spelling and punctuation, and have not used the indicative *sic* since it would have to appear so often. All the peculiarities that follow, then, appear in the originals.]

Albany   Tuesday Oct. 8, 1850

My dear Kitty,

My youngest and my loveliest my darling precious one. I am happy to retire a few moments from my many cares to write you a few lines. There are so many persons interested in your education that I do not feel myself at liberty to suggest anything new upon that subject. My only concern is your health and happiness. If possible, retire early at night, and do not burden your mind with study. Your ambition will naturally prompt you to be at least equal with your companions. There is much to learn to make us useful in life besides *mere* book knowledge. Avoid everything like affectation, be simple and pure in your manners and neat in your person. . . . Avoid if possible those naughty head aches a disordered stomach or undue excitement will probably bring them on. My poor Mother has several times been deprived of her reason in consequence of severe nervous headaches—avoid all extremes be temperate in all things, and consistent in every thing.[3]

A month later, Mrs. James sent Kitty a glimpse of her own life and some religious reflections, as well as more motherly exhortations to virtue—in run-on sentences. The Rev. James and Anna were traveling in the West, Elizabeth was away at school,

and I spend my time in domestic business. . . . In early life I had so many trials perplexities and disappointments that I learnt to expect nothing else from the world and it was only by looking to God alone that I could live. He often told me in His blessed word that all things work together for good to them that love him yes they all have a tendency to arrest the evils of our hearts and teach us that we are sinners we need much discipline to make us realize this solemn truth. I fear you do not have retirement enough to get acquainted with the motives and principles that govern your life. Self knowledge is a very difficult and humbling study it is rarely learnt except in the school of affliction hence the necessity of our trials.

Be good dear Kitty be good, return good for evil, few can be great all can be good if any unpleasant thing takes place among the young ladies say nothing about it have but one Confidant that your Heavenly Father tell him everything he will listen to all your supplications and give you his blessing.[4]

Ten years go by before the thread of Kitty's story picks up again, and this time the narrator is Kitty herself. On 5 March 1860, age twenty-six, she wrote to her sister Elizabeth (she addressed her as "lambie"), who was married to Julius Hawley Seelye, then Professor of Mental and Moral Philosophy at Amherst College and later (from 1876 to 1890) President of the College. Kitty reported from her family's home in Albany that she had just been leeched—the practice of applying leeches for medicinal bleeding was fairly common as a treatment for a variety of physical and "nervous" ailments in the nineteenth century—and that she had received a letter from her doctor, William Henry Prince,* a psychiatrist who practiced at the Northampton Hospital for the Insane in Massachusetts. Kitty told her sister:

> I pray every day that I may not be selfish about anything, and though I get ashamed of myself very often, I start fresh every day— Dear Lambie, I pray also that I may have discretion about using this terribly intense nature just as Christ would have me use it.[5]

Nine days later, Kitty was a patient at the Northampton Hospital for the Insane. In his official capacity as her physician, Dr. Prince wrote to Mrs. Seelye:

> Dear Madam—
> At the request of Dr. James I write to inform you of your sister's condition, and am happy to be able to say, she continues quite as comfortable as she has been.
> She slept this morning from 4-1/2 to 9-1/2, eats well, and is in good spirits and strength.
> I shall in a few days, if nothing happens, take her out to ride in the hope of giving a natural outlet to the excessive nervous energy.
> Tomorrow, if possible, I will write you more fully.[6]

Four days later, Prince reported to Mrs. Seelye that Kitty was improving daily "in general strength," and indicated that one of her symptoms had been physical violence: "She has now a good appetite, and sleeps part of every night—walks with more strength, and has lost those sudden impulses to strike and throw things from her, she had when she first came here." He had already discussed with Mrs. Seelye the "mental peculiarities" of "your mercurial little sister," and now inquired about Kitty's "physical condition during her childhood and maturing." Clearly he was searching for some organic explanation of her troubles:

---

*Prince, born in Salem, Mass., in 1817, was the son of John Prince, Jr. and Louise Lander of Salem. His grandfather was the Rev. John Prince, a brilliant clergyman and imaginative individual who invented an air pump. William Henry Prince attended Harvard and graduated with an M.D. in 1841.

Can you tell me at what age the curvature of her spine first showed itself? And at what age the deformity in her ribs, or rather the costal cartilagea near the breast bone? And will you have the kindness to add what you may have known of the unnatural tenderness or pressure over the spine, and of the oppression at the chest with wheezing respiration and inability to fully inflate the lungs? Was she ever thought to have a tendency to tubercle of the lungs, or were they ever suspected to exist? Was she subject to cough or difficulty of breathing, in any state of the atmosphere? Had she ever swelled tonsils to affect her breathing? Was any attention ever paid to physical training as a balance to her mental activity? Did she keep late hours? Was she an early riser? Did she bear exposure to weather? Was she an incessant and brilliant talker? I find I cannot rely on her answers and must therefore trouble you.[7]

There is no mention in the rest of the correspondence of a physical illness causing Kitty's troubles. Kitty's next letter to her sister, written from Northampton four months later, in July, shows the slow process of her recovery and her increasingly strong attachment to Dr. Prince. She had "perfect health, but no strength," felt content to stay at the hospital as long as necessary, and described Dr. Prince, a widower,* as her "dear kind father whom I love very much." She was quite concerned with his deceased wife:

He told me today that he had a dear wife in Heaven, who was just as dear to him as if she was on the earth, only he did not see her. Then I was perfectly happy, for I knew he felt about her as I do about [various friends and relatives who had died].

Dr. Prince's wife knows that I have delivered him & Johnnie & Louise [his children] & myself from a terrible spell of some kind—I don't know what, & she loves me very much.

Kitty had no idea how she would occupy herself after leaving the hospital: "the order of my life henceforth must be any little thing that my hand finds to do." All decisions about her future seemed to depend on her personal relations with Prince, which she characterized as entirely innocent and pure: she is his savior, his daughter, the virtuous deserver of his first wife's love. She went on to Mrs. Seelye:

As to whether I shall go or stay, I will leave it with my dear father. If I stay, I must stay *always,* & be his oldest daughter. He has a stronger

---

*Prince had married Elizabeth Lucretia Bullard Parker in Boston in 1843. They had two children, Louise Lander in 1848 and John in 1850. Elizabeth Parker Prince died in 1859, at Northampton.

claim on me than my dear father in Albany, for he never gets angry
with me, & never scolds, or misunderstands me. We are as sure that
we were father & daughter *somewhere, once,* as I am sure that you are
my sister Libby now. If I go away, he has nobody to talk to about
any thing that interests him personally . . .

    We will think this matter over, deliberating, & pray for Divine
Right & settle it *permanently.* I must stay, or I must go *now.*

When she had filled the pages of her letter, Kitty turned the paper
sideways and added some afterthoughts in the margin: she asked
her sister to send her a likeness of Napoleon which was "haunting
me all the time," and then wrote:

> One of the most ludicrous things connected with this delirium of
> mine has been the kind of interest I have taken in young men. I
> thought I must ship them all off for Heaven before I could get there
> myself! How much real service I have done for God in this strange
> state of mind is not for us to know here. My thoughts have run all
> the time in their ordinary channel—How I could get every body off
> to Heaven. Especially, how I could ship off Dr. Prince & his chil-
> dren—they are on the way now, I am very sure, so I think my last
> mission is accomplished.[8]

What Kitty probably meant about her "interest in young men"
was that she had an obsessive desire to proselytize—to lead everyone toward virtue and God. However, she refers to this interest as
"ludicrous" and "strange," and it focuses primarily on young men
and Prince. Whereas in her life at this time she had to be quite pas-
sive and patient, waiting to get out of the hospital, waiting to find
out about her future with or without Dr. Prince, in the "delirium"
she describes, she takes positive action—shipping "every body"
(not the same as everybody) off to heaven. If there was a sexual
subtext in Kitty's "ludicrous" interest in young men, it is neatly
sanctified as missionary zeal; and if she could ship Prince, his children, and those interesting men off to heaven, she would be triply
good—saving their souls, serving God, and removing all danger
of succumbing to something evil in herself. (People generally die
before they get to Heaven, and perhaps there is a murderous subtext here, too; but it seems more likely that she means setting
people on the path to God.)

    Although she professed to be content to occupy herself, from
now on, with "any little thing that my hand finds to do," Kitty
had had some larger ambition. During her time at the Northampton Hospital, she had completed two autobiographical novels,

and crowed to her sister in July of 1860, "My life *work* is finished."
She claimed not to care about publication: her whole concern "was
to finish them, according to my own ideas of novels, 'F.C.' order."
("F.C." stood for the fur cape she frequently wore—Prince had
nicknamed her accordingly.) Just what her ideas of novels were
comes through only indirectly in these letters. One of the books
featured "Mabel," and Kitty told her sister that she thought "Mabel's life is better incomplete than complete—I was running at the
end into things unlawful to be uttered." In an undated letter to her
father, she elaborated. She had apparently showed him one manuscript, and now said:

> Dear Father, I was writing another book—far more human, far
> better in many respects than the other; perhaps it will be too human
> to suit you—but so far as it goes it is the essence of real life—I had
> no will about finishing it; what I have written may be useful to some
> young people. It is *only* written for *young* people: it is the kind of
> book for which I was famishing when I was a little young thing; but
> tho' I was trying every way to avoid it, it was getting intensely per-
> sonal—not in form—I tried every way to make 'Mabel' seem out-
> wardly different from me—but the essence of the thing was in me &
> on the whole, even if you are dead it seems dreadful to think of
> having every body know what sort of person you were—unless it
> would do worlds of good. As to the other book, if it would do any
> good, I suppose it had better be published. It will never be popular,
> but I think it might meet some of the necessities of young persons.

Despite her professed reluctance to publish, she had sent the
first manuscript, with the assistance of Prince ("my dear new father") to the Boston publisher James T. Fields. She told her biological father that Fields's "objection to the book was almost solely
to the orthodox doctrines & not to the artistic defect; at least so I
understand it. . . . What ever it may be, it has not one tenth part
the inspiration of the second book. I do not care much if it will be
of any use, I wrote it before I had suffered & what a difference *that*
has made!"[9]

If those manuscripts still exist somewhere, they have not turned
up; whatever their artistic merits, they would present fascinating
evidence of Kitty's lonely struggle to understand and express what
was going on inside her.

A year later, in March 1861, Kitty was at home and euphoric—
"I feel like a lark, & fly around, & sing and dance. I have not a care

or a fear. Everything is beautiful, *beautiful, beautiful.*" She repeatedly referred to her illness as a dark thunder cloud, and when
she felt better she described the sensation of clouds rolling away.
Once the clouds lifted, she called her happiness "a kind of heavenly calm."[10]

She had no control over these violently alternating moods, and
tried to accept her suffering as intended by God for her instruction. In an undated letter to her father, she told him that God

> has led me to Himself; I knew from the beginning I must suffer,
> more perhaps than most persons, from a sensitiveness I never dared
> to express to myself—something inherited from you—but I never
> thought much about it; I laughed it off, worked it off, prayed it
> off. . . . I never had a trial that I did not understand, so of course the
> *sting* of trial was removed. . . . Dear Father, I never had a bit of
> logic in me! I used to make the most desperate efforts to be logi-
> cal because I thought you would like it. I don't think I succeeded at
> all. Everything in me was intuitive—God taught me everything I
> knew—& for the last few years I have not cared much for books,
> except as they would excite & suggest. I read everything most rav-
> enously when I was a little girl & after I was older constructed a
> good deal on that scaffolding—dear Father I must hurry on. This
> sickness has been unutterably blessed; God tested & *tested* & *tested*
> me in ways it would only harrow up your feelings to specify; but He
> was by my side every moment & gave me supernatural support, so
> that I often wondered if it were suffering! And after a while it all
> ceased, every pain. . . . And Christ came to me and said—"Now
> you are mine—mine for ever, life nor death nor things present nor
> things to come shall separate you from my love"—I thought it
> would only last a minute but it has been flowing on, on, ever
> since—so quietly, so intensely! It is the first freedom from excite-
> ment I ever had in all my life—And how I used to *hate* this idea of
> quiet! Nothing excites me in the least, except opposition—That
> does not irratate, but the least vestige of it makes me feel I will
> break; as if I would break right down and die.

Kitty was longing for sympathetic understanding, not opposition,
and she preached a little sermon to her father on the subject: "Oh!
Father, sympathy, *sympathy* not only in spiritual things but in tem-
poral—is what people we call sinners (how that epithet has always
revolted me) need to bring them to Christ."[11]

She felt a special kinship with her father: her sensitiveness was
"something inherited from you." However, her letters to him also
sound strong notes of reproach: her novel, clearly about herself,

might be "too human for you," she wrote, and she tried to fight bravely against her "intuitive" nature and be "logical" because "I thought you would like it." She fell in love with a man much older than she was, and referred to him constantly as her "dear, kind father." Kitty was quite explicit about why Prince had "a stronger claim on me than my dear father in Albany"—"he never gets angry with me, & never scolds, or misunderstands me."

Jesus, too, took care of Kitty in just the way she wanted: God had tested her mightily, but also gave her "supernatural support"—Christ came to say that she was His forever and nothing could separate her from His love. Kitty longed for this kind of engulfing, unconditional love. She closed her letter to her father: "I am made just like you, & when I can find the proper person to talk to I never want to keep anything in." Perhaps her message about the love of Christ, and her exhortatory prescription for sympathy on behalf of sinners, were pleas for more of those rare commodities—love and sympathy—from her real father.

When Kitty went with her father to visit her aunt and uncle, Mary and Henry James, Sr., at Newport, Rhode Island, in August 1861, she had two large problems on her mind: her health and her relations with Dr. Prince. Trying earnestly to prevent a repetition of her breakdown the previous year, she vowed to "take it quietly if sent, but not to bring it on." She was corresponding with Prince, and thinking of him constantly, but she was keeping her feelings under control. "I am so glad that God makes me willing to be happy whenever I have a chance," she told her sister. "Though one thought does not leave me—scarcely for a minute ever [presumably, the thought of marrying Prince]—I can take hold of things with real interest, & enjoy . . . everything sometimes. Resignation never seemed anything very great to me—It is better than rebellion & that is all."[12]

Her father and others urged her to stay on at Newport for the beneficial climate, but Kitty may have known more about her own peculiar illness than her relatives, doctors, or clergymen did, for she rejected the purely physical as an explanation or cause: "My health is much more dependent upon circumstances than upon climate,"[13] she told Seelye, her brother-in-law.

She did not stay at Newport for the climate. Instead, she returned to Albany and wrote to Seelye about her "perplexity" over Prince. At some point in the preceding months, the doctor had de-

cided not to marry her, but the decision had not put his conflict to
rest. For some time Kitty had thought there was nothing she could
do with regard to Prince's solitary soul-searching; now, she told
Seelye, she felt differently:

> I think Dr. Prince is making a mistake. Whether he loves me hu-
> manly or divinely, it is a kind of love which makes life desolation
> without me—& before long I have reason to think it will be worse
> than desolation. This is a strange kind of life, but some things,
> terrible as they seem at first are no doubt wisely ordered. His [here
> she wrote "life" and crossed it out] love for his wife was as strong &
> deep, I suppose, as it is possible for love to be. God saw best to take
> her to Heaven—why we don't know. He saw best to send me over
> there "to help him get well," perhaps, for one reason, as he wrote in
> his last letter. He can never love me as he did his wife. God does not
> intend it. Whether it is less, or more, or just as much, I never con-
> cern myself. It is certainly as much as I deserve [here she careted "or
> want" in above the line as an afterthought]. It is as different from his
> love for little Louise, to which he is all the time comparing it, as it is
> from that for his wife. Whatever sort of love it is, it is the only thing
> which keeps him alive now. . . . When his little girl [i.e., Kitty her-
> self] is with him, he is another being. His young life comes back, he
> can enjoy a great deal with her & work is a delight. . . . If God
> places in his reach a way of making life sweet & desirable again, to a
> certain extent, is it not a morbid sensitiveness that makes him push
> it away—which God does not intend, which his wife if she could
> speak from her bright Home would tell him to overcome and thus
> be better fitted for the duties of life. Moreover he has children. He
> wants them to know about the Savior. At present they know as
> much about Him as two little hottentots. In every way they want
> some one to look after them, in a way he says he cannot. . . . He
> wrote a little while ago that he thought he would be better fitted to
> live, & would ripen sooner, & all that, if I were with him, but I do
> not feel as though he were going to change his mind.

Prince wanted to take her on a trip, Kitty told Seelye, "Oh how
much"—but "you are my guardian you know, & I do nothing of
this kind without your sanction & Lambie's." She did not think her
father would like her taking a journey with Prince, and said "I
think I would rather keep quiet, & give occasion to no kind of remark from father, or any one else, & let the slow death work on,
with all the sweet alleviations that God sends."

She had thought of breaking off relations with Prince altogether
the previous summer, and now told Seelye:

I feel *sure* I did right in not breaking away entirely last summer. This is very much easier for both of us, & better, than that would have been. If in view of all these things he decides 'no' again, I will never, come what will to either of us or both of us, or the children, regard it as anything but an error of judgment perhaps, but perfectly excusable. There shall never be one shadow of blame attached to him, but that a shadow will fall somewhere in our vicinity before long in consequence I feel is very probable.[14]

One of the striking things about the painful little drama Kitty narrates here is her failure to express directly any desire, anger, or will of her own: she is concerned purely for Prince and *his* struggle; she endorses and echoes his view of her as his "little girl"; she would marry him only in order to "save" him and his children; she will accept whatever kind of love he can give her (though it would never compare with his feelings for his first wife and his daughter); she will not blame him, whatever happens; she will do what Seelye advises, and wants not to incur her father's disapproval. She was trying, in short, to be the good little girl her mother had exhorted her to be at age sixteen—to submit to the wills of others and want nothing for herself. Yet between the lines of her letter, in spite of her claim to resignation, is a strong will that argues against Prince's qualms, calls attention to her own suffering ("this slow death"), and tries to enlist her brother-in-law on her behalf against both Prince and her biological father. And perhaps her exaggerated self-lessness amounts to a tacit indictment—perhaps the fury that seems to have found expression in Kitty's illnesses was originally aimed, at least in part, at these loved ones for whom she was trying so hard, and at such private cost, to be "good."

Two weeks after Kitty sent this last letter to Seelye, her father wrote congratulating her on her engagement. The Rev. William James was staying at Amherst with Libby and Dr. Seelye, and had seen Prince. Kitty was with her mother in Albany. "My youngest my loveliest," wrote Rev. James on 10 September 1861: "And is this the last letter which I shall ever address to Kitty *James*? Is Kitty *Prince* to be no longer a pleasant vagary? to be a fact—." He had "not the slightest belief" that things would come to this pass, he somewhat ambiguously told her now. She had sent him a letter of her own with one from Prince three months before, in June, and he confessed that he had received them "but being advised of the nature of their contents & being uncertain how I should be affected by them, I never read either of them untill this morning when I read both with greatest delight." He then explained the nature of his apprehensions:

> My impression through the summer has been a very decided one (though I see now that it was founded in ignorance of facts) that Dr. P.'s sincere desire was to have you weaned from him—I found it very difficult to reconcile this with his constantly writing to you—& I was more than once on the point of writing to him to explain himself—But afraid I might do mischief I did nothing—till last Sunday night I felt myself prompted to ask him distinctly whether he had any serious purpose with respect to you—He then gave me a full account of the matter from the beginning leaving on my mind the strongest impression both of the strength & the purity of his affection for you & also of his having acted throughout with the most scrupulous honor.

In closing this odd congratulatory letter, Rev. James wrote: "My work all day and company this evening has left me but a few moments to write & that with impaired strength and spirit—In that I can do little more darling one, than wish you joy which I do from the bottom of my heart on this *Providential* fulfilment of your dearest earthly hopes. May God bless your prosperity as he has your adversity, & give you grace to act in all conditions worthy of your high vocation." He did not, he said, intend to accompany her and Prince on their nuptial tour of Niagara and Canada—had he been invited?—and concluded, "In great haste, Your father." [15]

Kitty did marry Prince that fall, and the record is silent on their first years together. They lived for the most part at the Northampton Hospital, and retreated as often as possible to Prince's farm in the country nearby. In September 1863, the young William James wrote to Kitty, his favorite cousin, about his agonies over choosing a career. He had finished a "pre-medical" course in comparative anatomy at Harvard's Scientific School, but could not see his way clearly to the next step. He was most drawn to natural science, but knew it wouldn't pay well enough to support a family; medicine had some attractions—and a good deal of "unpleasant drudgery," he wrote: "Of all departments of Medicine, that to which Dr. Prince devotes himself is, I should think, the most interesting. And I should like to see him and his patients at Northampton very much before coming to a decision." He had had—and would continue to have—acute psychological difficulties of his own, and he told Kitty, with that twinge of truth that gives jokes extra force, that he had often meant to visit her but feared she might "chain me up in your asylum." He went on, still in an antic tone, to describe his dilemma and to envy the sheltered position of women—unaware of how problematic that shelter was for Kitty:

> I am obliged before the 15th of January to make finally and irre-vocably the "choice of a profession." I suppose your sex, which has, or should have, its bread brought to it, instead of having to go in search of it, has no idea of the awful responsibility of such a choice. I have four alternatives: Natural History, Medicine, Print-ing, Beggary. Much may be said in favor of each. I have named them in ascending order of their pecuniary invitingness.[16]

Kitty, always moved and amused by William, was struggling with choices of her own. In February 1864, Prince wrote to Mrs. Seelye that "our little girl" was now doing well but she had been in a passionate "religious frenzy" and he did not dare leave her in such a state. She became (he told her sister) "entirely uncontrollable, even by me, without physical restraint. She will be quiet in my arms, but not otherwise." He saw no dangerous "excitement" in her, "excepting the ever-present strong desire to do the Master's will, and she sees Him & the Angels and everything beautiful. . . . Most of the time, however, she will take my advice, and exert con-trol over her thoughts but thinks it wicked to drive Jesus away when He comes to her, even to please me!"[17]

Two weeks later, Kitty was in a mental hospital called the Hart-ford Retreat in Hartford, Conn. Prince had heard from Dr. John S. Butler, former Superintendent of the Retreat, and he passed his news along to Mrs. Seelye: "Our dear child is much better, in every way, than when I left her." She was eating and sleeping, talk-ing "a great deal," wrote her husband—"but (better than all) (a di-rect blessing from the Father)—she 'speaks no unkind word to anyone,'" according to Dr. Butler. Prince then reflected: "How good is God so to guide her drifting spirit that she may avoid the rocks & shoals on which so many, in her condition are thumped & battered. [Butler] says, 'she is cheerful, bright & happy,' What con-solation—what a silver lining to the cloud." Prince was coming to Amherst to talk everything over with Seelye: "Nothing now is clear to me except that dear Kitty is not to be again subjected to the temptations of our former life at the Hospital, for whether she yields or fights, it is too great a risk, & too hard a struggle."[18]

Four days later, Kitty wrote to Prince from Hartford. She sent the letter in care of Dr. Butler, and submitted it for the former su-perintendent's approval, writing "Dr. Butler's copy" across the top. In this sad missive, Kitty was convinced that Prince was Louis Napoleon and she the Empress Eugénie. She wrote (all parenthetical question marks are hers):

Hartford
Feb. 20th (?) 1864

My dear Husband,

I will be very happy to see you as soon as it is convenient for you to come. My pen & ink are not of the finest calibre, but I feel sure that you will make allowances, as my heart is

"True as the needle to the pole."

The expression is sentimental, but I think that Dr. Porter* will say that sentimentality is a pardonable weakness under some circumstances—I will restrict it to one single circumstance—When a true, faithful, & loving wife is through nervous debility, regarded by a husband of judgment competent to decide in such a matter, as unfitted for discharging (for a short time) the duties of wife & mother,—who is the proper judge to decide when she is to return home? The husband himself, or the physician to whose care she (against her own wishes & womanly instincts) was confided? Dr. Porter (the assistant physician at the time I was brought to the Hartford Retreat) & who is now by a unanimous vote of the patients still unable to be returned to their homes appointed superintendent of the Hartford Retreat (being an impartial compère), we leave the question entirely in his hands, until the arrival of my dear husband: William Henry Prince, Emperor of France, son of Napoleon Bonaparte† avec sang froid et savoir faire—to whom I am sure Dr. Butler's good sense & Christian principle (?) will restore the only solace of a long dreary life, with "Merci bien" to have her leave—with tender love & dutiful respects to [Prince's] far Elder Brother Frederick Huntington Prince,

I am sincerely Yours the

P.S. Dr. Butler, that is a very poor representation of a fur cape.— the name by which my husband can always distinguish me from a crowd of sentimental admirers, who think it would be "très jolie" to take the place of poor Eugénie—who shall receive the most tender care from our hands when we ascend our throne—As for

*Porter was the recently appointed superintendent of the Retreat.
†Louis Napoleon was in fact the nephew, not the son, of Bonaparte.

Louis Napoleon, we will shake hands with him, & say, "Comment vous partez-vous nôtre Chrétien frère?" "Très bien?" and he will answer, "Oui; très bien."[19]

Two days later, she wrote another copy of this letter, this time "Dr. Porter's Copy," with some changes. She asked the same question about who could properly decide about her discharge from the hospital—and this time she answered: "The unanimous verdict appears to be, that a truely Christian husband, is the proper protector of a truly amiable wife, whose affections are strongly bound up in her husband." And she signed this letter with a list that reflects her confusion about who she was:

> Eugénie (otherwise called)
> Mrs. William Henry Prince
> Katharine Barber Prince
> Kitty B. Prince
> K.B. Prince
> K.J. Prince
> Kitty Prince
> Little Kitty
> Little baby wife
>   of the right royal
>   William Henry
> Emperor in his own right
>   of both sides of the
> Continent of
>   North America &
>   South America
>   otherwise called
> North and South Columbia.[20]

Several weeks later, Kitty wrote again to her husband—this time a polite, formal, pointedly self-controlled and submissive letter acknowledging a note from him. Dr. Butler had just told her that he did not always inspect patients' letters, but Kitty said she had "nothing private to communicate to you, my dear husband," and "under the circumstances, I would simply wish you a very pleasant good morning, & say I would be very happy to see you as soon as it is convenient for you to call: to leave me again, or to take me home (to Northampton), just as you think will most tend to the glory of our Lord & Savior Jesus Christ."[21]

By the end of April she was writing to her sister (still from the Hartford Retreat) in much her old tone of voice. She missed her "dear lambie" terribly, and now gave Prince's diagnosis of her recent troubles: "It was an hysterical affection of the heart—a kind of thing which very rarely proves fatal—(does not that sound like dear mother) but is connected with a good deal of palpitation and faintness." She had found it hard to breathe and sleep—"It seemed as if I had to live on colder & colder air, until I thought I would freeze the poor people who were taking care of me. I never had that feeling about my dear husband, because he having the real, genuine heart disease, which *does* ultimately prove fatal, enjoyed the nice cold air more than other people could." She was singing, drawing, dancing, and trying to be patient until the day Prince would come for his "little girl." [22]

Kitty's troubles had parallels in the lives of many other women during the late nineteenth century. A great variety of ailments, ranging from headaches and general weakness to paralysis, raging fits, and full-blown psychoses, were termed nervous hyperesthesia, neuralgia, neurasthenia, gout, morbid oversensitivity, and hysteria ("It were as well called 'mysteria,'" wrote Dr. S. Weir Mitchell, a noted authority on the subject[23]). After Freud and Breuer published "Studies on Hysteria" in 1895, the medical world began to understand a good deal more than it did in Kitty's lifetime about the complex connections between physical symptoms and emotional conflicts—particularly about the ways in which these symptoms indirectly expressed emotional conflicts. In the 1860s, however, most doctors were mystified, and hysterical illnesses like Kitty's were treated with varying doses of sympathy, skepticism, condescension, and frustration.

There isn't enough information about Kitty to afford much insight into her conflicts, but the clues repeatedly point in the direction of a muffled rage at those around her. She couldn't breathe except in air so cold that she thought it might freeze the "poor people" who took care of her—and while she insists that "I never had that feeling about my dear husband," he was certainly the chief person responsible for her care, and she draws a neat parallel between her hysterical heart trouble and his "real, genuine heart disease which *does* . . . prove fatal." Cold air might not be the best thing for a weak heart, and besides, as Freud pointed out, there is no negative in the unconscious. [24]

The record in Kitty's own voice here comes to an end. She did eventually leave the Hartford Asylum and move with her husband to Clifton Springs, New York, where he served as Superintendent of the Clifton Asylum. In the summer of 1872 they visited friends in Cambridge, Massachusetts. Kitty's "nerves" still apparently troubled her, for she found the friends' house too noisy for comfort, and took to spending her nights at the home of her father's brother, Henry James, Sr., at 20 Quincy Street. She had long, confidential chats with this genial uncle, and he reported them in detail to his daughter, Alice, who was traveling in Europe with Henry Jr. and their aunt, Catharine Walsh. James Sr. noted to Alice how meek, cheerful, and innocent his troubled niece appeared, and went on to draw a skillful sketch of her character:

> Kitty was talking freely yesterday afternoon of her life at Clifton Springs; and she said it was entirely what they would have it to be save that Dr. Foster and Dr. Prince were both in universal demand, and that things would work better if they had a divided empire. I asked her whether Dr. Prince wasn't a very easy man to get along with. She said yes, remarkably so, having such perfect self-control as he had. She said: "his lips are the thinnest you ever saw, more like a thread than a lip; but I have never seen him excited to resentment now for nine years and a half that I have known him, and I have seen him put to very severe trials. The most severe I ever saw him put to, Unkle Henry, was this: a lady, a patient at Clifton, and a very good person otherwise no doubt, but fond of talking, too fond, in full assembly, began one day to talk to him, not knowing anything of his history, about the superiority of second marriages to first. I said to myself what *are* people made of? But she went on, the doctor looking as placidly as if that volcano underneath were not surging and fermenting to sweep away everything before it. I was on the point at last of screaming, to see the poor man so tortured, but happily the conversation changed." She seems to keep up her ardent sympathy, you see, for the doctor's conjugal bereavement in old days. The doctor himself must be very jolly in his own bosom over this sympathy. She evidently fancies him the greatest hero that ever lived, and is proud to be a ministering housemaid to such stupendous sorrows. I don't think I could conceive of such innocence, if I hadn't seen it. [25]

When Dr. Prince retired from Clifton Springs, he and Kitty moved to Newton, Massachusetts, not far from her James relatives. Mary and Henry James, Sr., both died in 1882, she at the end of

January and he the following December. Kitty traveled frequently
to Cambridge to see William, who now had a wife and two sons
and was teaching at Harvard. William's eldest son, Harry, later remembered her "visiting the house in Garden Street when I was
small, & its being explained to me that she was insane and in an
asylum much of the time, but out during lucid intervals. . . . She
was slight and dark & pretty—a shy, feint, quiet little lady." [26] In
1883 Dr. Prince died. Kitty moved to Amherst to be with her sister, and William wrote her regularly in the combined capacities of
cousin, friend, and physician: he prescribed sedative bromides
early in 1885, and said: "Were it anyone else than you, I should say
that you were suffering from *intellectual* inanation, not enough new
things given to your naturally active mind to think about. . . . But
yours is so very peculiar a temperament, and was so carefully studied by so wise a Doctor [i.e., Prince], that I will not give the least
advice." [27]

He continued whenever she had a crisis to supervise her medica-
tion and consult with her physicians. Her Boston doctor thought
she should "keep steadily under the influence of some sedation,"
and since Prince had found that valerian agreed with her, William
sent on a bottle from Cambridge. Kitty feared she might be heading for another full collapse in 1885, but her attending cousin re-
minded her that present symptoms might not develop the way they
had in the past: "You know the law of these nervous diseases is
lawlessness." [28]

Kitty was also afraid of depending too much on William, but he
responded gallantly: "I wish I could believe myself worthy of
being depended on." [29] In August, 1886, he paid the bill for an inscription on Dr. Prince's tombstone, then went out to visit the
grave in Newton. He told Kitty: "The inscription, 'A new song
before the throne,' looked beautiful, and just fitted rightly into its
place. I hope the blessed Doctor in some way takes cognizance of
its being there." [30]

On November 23, 1890, William James wrote from 95 Irving
Street to his brother, Henry, in London: "Poor Kitty Prince faded
out last Wednesday. For months past some happy delusion had
kept her speechless and motionless with shut eyes in bed, and her
end was practically from starvation. It is a most blest relief to all
concerned. . . . She was buried from this house, Mr. Hornbrook,
her Newton minister, performing a most well chosen service."
President and Mrs. Seelye (he "now no longer President but af-

flicted with shaking palsy"), and Prince's two children were there, and "we all rode out in two carriages through the magnificent afternoon to the beautiful Newton cemetery." And William concluded: "When I saw her lowered into the grave beside her dear Dr. for the first time in my life did the grave seem a *cosy* thing."[31]

NOTES

Individual letter writers are identified by their full names the first time they appear below, and thereafter by their initials. I would like to thank Alexander James, literary executor, for permission to quote from materials in the James family archives at Harvard. I am very grateful to the Houghton Library of Harvard College, the Miller Library of Colby College, and the Amherst College Library for permission to quote from letters in their collections. The libraries are cited in full the first time they appear, and are thereafter referred to as Houghton, Colby, and Amherst.

1. *William James of Albany (1771–1832) and His Descendants,* comp. and contr. by Katharine Bagg Hastings. The New York Genealogical and Biographical Record, 1924.

2. Henry James (1879–1947), "Reverend William James," an unpublished memoir. Alexander James and the Houghton Library of Harvard College Library.

3. Marcia A. James to Katharine James Prince, 8 October 1850. Miller Library, Colby College, Waterville, Maine.

4. MAJ to KJP, 20 November 1850. Colby.

5. KJP to Elizabeth James Seelye, 5 March 1860. Colby.

6. William Henry Prince to EJS, 14 March 1860. The Julius Hawley Seelye Papers, Amherst College Archives.

7. WHP to EJS, 18 March 1860. Amherst.

8. KJP to EJS, 16 July 1860. Amherst.

9. KJP to Reverend William James [undated: probably spring, 1861]. Amherst.

10. KJP to EJS, 12 March 1861. Colby.

11. KJP to Rev. WJ [undated]. Amherst.

12. KJP to EJS, 1 August 1861. Amherst.

13. KJP to Julius Hawley Seelye, 3 August 1861. Amherst.

14. KJP to JHS, 20 August 1861. Amherst.

15. Rev. WJ to KJP, 10 September 1861. Amherst.

16. *The Letters of William James,* ed. by his son Henry James (Boston: Atlantic Monthly Press, 1920), vol. I, 43–44.

17. WHP to EJS, 1 February 1864. Amherst.

18. WHP to EJS, 16 February 1864. Amherst.

19. KJP to WHP, 20 February 1864. Amherst.

20. KJP to WHP, 22 February 1864. Amherst.

21. KJP to WHP, 4 April 1864. Amherst.

22. KJP to EJS, 27 April 1864. Colby.

23. S. Weir Mitchell, "Rest in Nervous Disease: Its Use and Abuse," *A Series of American Clinical Lectures,* I, ed. E. C. Sequin (New York, 1875).

24. Sigmund Freud, "On Negation" (1925), *The Standard Edition of the Complete Psychological Works of Sigmund Freud,* vol. XIX, ed. James Strachey (London: The Hogarth Press).

25. Henry James, Sr., to Alice James, 1 July [1872]. Houghton.

26. Henry James (1879–1947), "Reverend William James."
27. William James to KJP, 10 March 1885. Houghton.
28. WJ to KJP, 12 June 1885. Colby.
29. WJ to KJP, 23 June, 1885. Colby.
30. Gay Wilson Allen, *William James* (New York: Viking, 1967), 96.
31. WJ to Henry James, 23 November 1890. Houghton.

WILLIAM MACMILLAN: THE RELUCTANT HEALER

Gloria G. Fromm

In 1951 the Christmas number of a popular English monthly carried the story of William Macmillan, healer, describing him as "a man with the gift of grace." An American citizen, he had been allowed to practice as a psychotherapist for the past eighteen years because in the judgment of certain medical and theological authorities in England he was one of the most powerful healers of this century. The results he achieved were said to verge on the miraculous: restoring to use a little boy's withered arm, for example, and putting back on his feet a man with tuberculosis so advanced that he had to be carried into the treatment room on a stretcher.

Describing himself to his interviewer as a servant of humanity, with a gift (or perhaps an ability) that was also a heavy burden, Macmillan looked like a prosperous businessman and talked like a man of the world. But he claimed to have reached a turning point in his spectacular career. He was writing a book, he said, in which he would tell the full story of his great conflict during the years when his healing-powers were first discovered. Once the book was finished he did not know whether he would return to healing. He might become a teacher instead, along the lines set down in the inspirational book about healing he had published only a few years before. Or, now that he was nearing fifty, he might resume his interrupted life as a private citizen.

Fond of the pleasures of the world—good food, the music of Mozart, travel as well as silks and cashmeres—his secret wish, he said, was for freedom to indulge the tastes which were all too apparent in both his conversation and the cut of his suit. But since 1933 and his struggle with the strange power working through him, he had bowed to duty and given up even the vestige of a personal life, besieged as he constantly was by desperately ill people who saw him as their last hope.

If Macmillan was seeking respite from hordes of patients, this did not seem the way to get it—by advertising all the dramatic reversals he had brought about during the past eighteen years. Indeed, the editors of *Good Housekeeping* thought it prudent to note that since Macmillan already had more demands upon him than he could possibly meet, they could not undertake to put potential patients into touch with him. And when, several months later, the book he was promoting appeared, the *Sunday Express* ran a four-part series of extracts from it. This time, as one might expect, an editor's note stated that in view of Macmillan's heavy commitments he could not even interview any new patients for the present.

The Reluctant Healer was published in 1952 by Victor Gollancz, and revealed how little Macmillan fit any of the standard images of a healer. Playing upon the theme in his title he offered a version of himself and his profession that intrigued and impressed many of the reviewers. He had been a young idealistic seminarian looking forward to ordination in the Episcopal Church when he was singled out for a life of healing, a life totally alien to his background and training. Without going into much detail, Macmillan made it nonetheless clear that everything in his heritage had caused him to shrink from practices he always associated with charlatanism—fortune-telling carried on behind beaded curtains or seances conducted in darkened rooms—practices emanating, in his eyes, from western New York, the acknowledged birthplace of a suspect American spiritualism. He himself had been born and raised in the eastern half of the state, where New York blended into New England, and where by contrast George Santayana's "genteel tradition" prevailed. Indeed, Macmillan took considerable pains to point out how thoroughly unsuited he was—by orientation as well as inclination—to the life and career of a healer, remarking that his spectacular success had forced him into what he described as "bondage to a career [he] had never wanted" because, in his own words, he lacked the "moral courage to endure failure."

As presented by Macmillan, his was a success story par excellence—if not vintage American. During the seven years covered by *The Reluctant Healer* the young seminarian, long on social credentials but short of funds and far from happy as a theology student who was looking for God Himself rather than His Word, turned into the spitting image of a Harley Street specialist, with elegant rooms in Great Cumberland Place and a country house in Kent. He would not have looked out of place in a novel by Henry James. In fact, he might have stepped out of *The Wings of the Dove* as a latter-day Sir Luke Strett. Macmillan's reputation was international. Patients came to him from all over the world, from Europe, from South Africa and India, from the United States. They came because of his high percentage of cures, and they kept his waiting-lists as well as his treatment-rooms full. He charged the standard high fees of a Harley Street establishment and ran both his practice and his life as though he were not only a full-fledged member of the medical fraternity but a high priest as well. Everything having to do with practical or business matters was taken care of for him. He signed his name on the checks made out by his secretary without noticing to whom they were drawn or in what amounts and was reverently led from room to room and patient to patient, all his attention focused on the signals his intuitions were sending, which told him what to do and whether indeed the person placed before him could be treated at all.

But the war declared in 1939 put an effective end to his fairy-tale existence, to the "green pastures and the cup running over," in Macmillan's borrowed and charged words. If he had known, he said, what lay in store for him during the next eleven years he would have cried out with Samuel: "Lord I am not ready."

That story—what happened to him between 1939 and 1950—he did not want to tell yet, for it had to do with penury and loss of status. In *The Reluctant Healer* the emphasis was on his rising star, the establishment of his remarkable career: those were the years he wanted and needed to recall. And he decided to make his next book another attempt to account for the phenomenon of healing itself rather than a continuation of his own story. This volume, *Heaven and You,* published in 1953 by Hodder and Stoughton, is a companion to his earlier *This Is My Heaven,* a reworking of the same materials: the mysterious effects on certain people of the touch of a few individuals who are themselves unable to explain what they do. Speaking as one of those rare individuals, mindful of his difficult task, Macmillan modestly disclaimed any knowledge of "the pathology of disease or how to heal": he could write of healing, he said, only by reporting what he was able to see through the magnifying glass thrust into his hands, a glass that had come into being for him as "a particular manifestation of God's action upon humanity." He was convinced, in other words, that his powers could only be accounted for by giving them a divine source, with which as a healer he cooperated, while his patients were accomplishing the essential shift of focus from illness to health. For the most part, then, Macmillan simply described the healing process, which took place, so far as he could tell, under certain sets of conditions rather than others, and it was these conditions—largely psychological—that seemed to him to determine the success or failure of the treatment.

As a matter of fact, descriptions of results were pretty much all that anyone could provide in the way of information about William Macmillan's healing. Even his novelist-friend Dorothy Richardson was at a loss. As Macmillan indicated in *The Reluctant Healer,* they had met at the beginning of his career in the mid-thirties, and she promptly introduced him to her own closest friend, who was successfully treated by him and then stayed on for a time to run his establishment. But despite her ties with him, Dorothy Richardson herself never claimed to understand Macmillan. She was fond of reporting his spectacular cures and naming the famous doctors in each case who had been consulted before "Mac" but could do nothing, yet she did not pretend to know what took place, not even when he treated *her* for severe nervous strain. And from her letters we can just make out the man she saw, in all the unresolved contradictions that intrigued her. His own record, however, permits us to go much further—to recover a voice and a style as well as the elements of an extraordinary life.

The record Macmillan finally left behind is in four parts: a quartet of books. The last and most important one—the one in which he returned to autobiography, taking up the story of his early life and carrying it through the period of the war—he did not quite finish before he died. Published by Faber, posthumously, as *Prelude to Healing,* it provides us with the principal means by which to get at the configuration of a remarkable life. But his own words tell a rather different tale than he intended, one that has more to do with seeking than with finding, and with a special kind of creativity that comes under no general heading. The full story of Macmillan's life will probably never be known, but even so, a whole story emerges from the four separate parts of his own labored narrative. As Yeats would have it, "there is always a living face behind the mask."

1

William Macmillan was born in Cambridge, New York, on 7 June 1904 to parents with equally strong family traditions and claims upon their descendants. The Macmillans had come to America from Scotland after the 1745 Rebellion, in time to side with the rebellious colonies over here and to be rewarded for their support with a gift of choice land, part of an immense parcel that once belonged to the Duke of Argyll. Located in upper New York State, at the foothills of the Adirondacks and close to the Vermont border, this stretch of country boasted wooded hillsides, numerous small lakes, and valleys full of rich farm soil. Most of the inhabitants had emigrated from the Scottish Highlands. The community they founded was prosperous and self-contained, admirably suited to the Macmillans, who settled down with their bit of farmland on the outskirts of Cambridge, chief among the villages and hamlets carved out of the Duke of Argyll's extensive estates.

Attached to the traditions they brought with them from the old country, the Macmillans also developed their own in the altered circumstances of the new world. They kept their ornate crest, with its sacred family motto, "I aim to succour the unfortunate," and they reared their sons with the understanding that one of them must always look after the family farm, one was obliged to be a clergyman (Presbyterian, of course), and the third son a doctor. So it was—with a minor variation here and there—down to the twentieth century. William's father, Joseph Macmillan, was the doctor in his generation, and an uncle William never knew was the clergyman, but his other uncle had declined to be the family's farmer and became an inventor instead, perhaps because the family farm had been allowed to run down. It was being looked after at this time by the lone female Macmillan, who had also decided that in spite of her family's disapproval the sensible thing for her to do was to marry her foreman.

Young William did not fail to take in the fact that the fortunes of the Macmillan family had begun to decline by the time he arrived on the scene. Scottish thrift notwithstanding, as he later commented ruefully, his inheritance amounted to "a vast cemetery plot, with a magnificent view, the upkeep of which [was] paid for in perpetuity." He absorbed quite as thoroughly the unhappy fact that the family itself was in danger of dying out. He was the last male in direct line. This made him the sole inheritor, too, of the family tradition for its sons, and it is tempting to see the healer William Macmillan became an ingenious combination of all three professions, proving, no doubt, that one son could be as dutiful as three.

The maternal tradition made somewhat different demands upon him, no less clearly spelled out. He knew very well that one of his mother's ancestors (Roger Sherman) had signed the Declaration of Independence, that another was Sara Delano, and that her family (the Smarts) went back—like the Macmillans—to pre-Revolutionary days. But they had a more scholarly bent. The story told to him was that the first Smart to arrive on this side of the Atlantic came not as a refugee from the 1745 Rebellion but as an emissary of classical learning—brought over from Edinburgh to organize the Latin and Greek departments in one of our southern universities. What puzzled his descendant was the two-sided legacy handed down by the learned Smarts: "Scholarship combined with luxury was the accepted standard of life," yet no one seems to have earned his living, and no one talked about the origins of the large fortune that by the end of the nineteenth century was considerably diminished. William Macmillan's mother never solved this mystery for him, even though (or perhaps because) she was the main source of his knowledge of the Smart family. The relationship between this mother and son resembled the son's relationship with God later on: it was at the center of his life, but all the avenues of communication were indirect.

His parents had met in 1902 when Joseph Macmillan was home on a spring holiday from his medical practice in New York City. Sara Smart had just returned to Cambridge from the continent, to look after her aged and ailing parents. While Macmillan was still in town, her father needed emergency medical treatment. Everyone advised her to call in the brilliant young surgeon who happened to be temporarily available; and after making his diagnosis Joseph Macmillan decided to stay on to see the old man out of a long and varied life, and to marry his only daughter.

The marriage, however, would be short-lived indeed. When his own only child was barely a year old the doctor developed a cancer of the throat. His wife, convinced he could be cured under sunny Italian skies, where she had spent such happy days before their marriage, took him and their infant to Florence. Although his condition improved during their stay, he was by no means cured; and he died in 1907, the year after their return, when his son was three and a half.

Sara Macmillan remained in Cambridge for ten years, living for the most part in makeshift circumstances, still growing up herself even as her son developed into a self-conscious inarticulate boy, uncertain of his role or place. He saw that his mother would have much preferred to live in other surroundings. She was always going off on visits to more sophisticated Smart relatives, sometimes taking him along, but more often leaving him among the Macmillans in Cambridge, whom he began to see as country folk by comparison. In his child's way he summed up the differences by noting that when they visited the Smarts, they were waited on by servants, but when they visited the Macmillans, they were expected to help dry the dishes.

Two of the Smarts—a brother and sister who lived together—eventually made Sara an offer hard for her to resist. She was asked to come as a companion-housekeeper for their declining years, to be spent (they hoped) in their large house on lower Fifth Avenue in New York and their summer home in Litchfield, Connecticut. Already too old, in their view, even to contemplate adding a child to their household, the proposal they made to Sara did not include her son. So Sara's son found himself, nearing thirteen, faced with his first real decision. He could stay in Cambridge and continue at the local school, living with a widowed Macmillan cousin, who had a child of her own, or go to boarding school.

He chose boarding school; and he and his mother spent a last memorable summer's day together in New York. With the aged cousins still in Litchfield, Sara could bring her son for the night to the Fifth Avenue house—the "crystal mausoleum," as he described it years later. The next day, after a shopping expedition and lunch at the Waldorf, they took the train out to Tarrytown and boarding school in the land of Rip Van Winkle's long sleep. Arriving just at the dinner hour and not wishing to face an unknown headmaster and his wife over an evening meal, Sara fed her son—as he vividly recalled—in the dirty, fly-ridden station café, and then—as he put it long afterward—emerged victorious in the emotional contest between them. Instead of comforting her child, who must have suspected he was being deserted, Sara Macmillan broke down first, and the teen-aged boy was obliged to minister to his mother. He remembered it as one of the typical occasions when, in his own words, she had "beaten" him again.

This was how things stood between them for years. In his mother's New York life there was no space for him. In Litchfield, however, where the Fifth Avenue entourage took up annual summer residence, his existence could at least be acknowledged and some accommodation made for him. He boarded with a village family. When he wanted to see his mother, he had to enter the house through a side door and proceed up the stairs that led directly to her suite. He was never to ring the bell or to use the front or back doors. Free to come whenever he wished, he also understood that his mother would seldom be available. Every morning, however, they met on the village green to do Sara's daily marketing together. And he was expected to make friends with the local children whose families were socially acceptable.

So it was that Litchfield supplanted Cambridge as the important place in his emotional life. He would boast of it as a storehouse of American culture and history, describing it, with pride, as "unique" rather than typical—like Cambridge—of thousands of villages scattered over the eastern seaboard. Indeed, full of houses that were architectural gems, Litchfield was still beautifully preserved in the period toward the end of the Great War, when Sara Macmillan's son spent his precious summers here, needing all the solace he could find. In spite of his anomalous domestic arrangement, he was glad he "belonged" to one of the chief families of Litchfield, where once upon a time *Uncle Tom's Cabin* had been written, and now, every afternoon, his mother and Cousin A. L. sallied forth in an open victoria, with the family coachman perched on his box.

2

After the war Sara Macmillan was moved to call on her family for special help when her son came down with a serious case of influenza in the great epidemic. To keep him out of school for a year—which is what she wanted to do—he had to be lodged with assorted relations in Syracuse and elsewhere. As a result, he fell further and further behind in an already haphazard education. Yet once he had fully recovered his mother decided that instead of sending him back to Tarrytown he ought to be enrolled in a school with a higher scholastic standing. She had in mind nearby Choate, where the best Litchfield boys tended to go. And here, in due course, her ungainly son, known to his schoolmates by now as Mac, struggled—ill-prepared and incoherent—through the next three years, unable to satisfy anyone, least of all himself.

He was to say that he "lived in a state of perpetual astonishment" at Choate. He might just as well have said the same thing of the ten succeeding years, the decade in which he labored, uncertainly and artlessly, to fulfill the expectations of his mother's family. His only success at Choate was in "creative writing," which led him to the drama workshop at the University of North Carolina in Chapel Hill. After a year there, he was admitted to Yale's drama school, where he began to learn—among other things—that to provide for his mother in the style to which her family was accustomed he would have to find a way other than writing to make a living. Oddly enough, he had this pointed out to him by Thornton Wilder, who was writing *The Bridge of San Luis Rey* in the Yale dormitory room next to his. But no one gave him comparable advice when, not long afterward, without a degree or any sort of specialized training, he ventured into the world to look for a job. On the strength of his own limited experience he would decide that the staid businessmen who interviewed him found especially unattractive the combination of his background and lack of qualifications. Choate boys, he was convinced, either had important fathers who got them jobs or they did not have to work at all, and it followed that no one believed he would stick to ordinary employment. Chances are, however, that a young business aspirant who confessed to not knowing the difference between a stock and a bond would have inspired little confidence under any circumstances.

At the same time, the form of employment suited to this hypersensitive young man is hard to imagine. With his solemn face and restless hands, his large stature and dazed look, he might well have been an American Pontifex. Samuel Butler comes inevitably to mind in the mixture of worldliness and inexperience, the total bewilderment about sex, that this earnest, awkward boy revealed. As an adolescent at his first summer camp, for instance, he had not had the faintest notion what he was being accused of when, tormented by mosquito bites and too shy to scratch his genitals openly, he waited until the lights went out and he was in his bunk under blankets. Later, the student at Yale reacted with equal astonishment when one of his friends was accused of molesting the man seated next to him in a New Haven movie-house: he had never even heard of homosexuality.

In fact, as a result of the New Haven episode, Macmillan became intrigued—he said—by the "psychological approach" to the problems of the world, and thought he would like to work for a social service agency. Finding a temporary position in New York that required him to collect data in Harlem for a compulsory insurance law, he proceeded as though a Butlerian script had been written for him. He was given a sheaf of forms to be filled in with the answers to questions that struck him at once as "of a very personal nature indeed." Moreover, the people he was supposed to interrogate lived in conditions "sordid beyond description" and resented his questions. Aware that he had no authority to force them to answer, he decided that the solution was to try to persuade them that the scheme was for their own protection. But the only way to achieve this, he felt, was to make them *like* him—"an exhausting process," as he soon discovered to his great chagrin. Yet he claimed he was disappointed when he could not convince the director of the agency that he had a vocation for social work.

Macmillan's was a curious apprenticeship indeed. He moved through the twenties from one temporary job to another, disliking each in turn but hating even more the successive positions his mother took during this time, after both her aged cousins had died. It was one thing for her to live with relatives and merge her life with theirs, quite another—in his eyes—to absorb herself just as completely in the lives of strangers, which also meant that there continued to be no place for her son. But so long as he had no resources of his own, he could exert no influence over her. And nothing seemed to work for him—neither an attempt at the Diplomatic Service (through another Smart cousin) nor an engagement to wed the sister of a Choate schoolmate. Twice during these years, at decisive moments, he fell seriously ill, as though this were the only way he could extricate himself from situations everyone else, including his mother, looked upon with favor. Long afterward, for example, he would comment wryly, about the young woman he nearly married, that she and his mother were entirely right for each other.

One summer, as the decade of the twenties was drawing to a close along with another of his short-lived jobs, and New York grew hot and dusty, he decided to go abroad again with money saved from his earnings. His first trip, while still a student at Yale, had been to England, his second to France during the brief diplomatic phase, both made possible by a small inheritance. This time he booked passage on a cargo boat—the mode of foreign travel elected by numerous young literary men of the period. Macmillan's destination was neither Berlin nor Paris but a small village on the coast of Normandy where friends of his mother were staying and who helped him find cheap lodgings in a kind of bistro. The only guest, he had his meals served in the garden and could reach the sea simply by walking across the road. In this "primitive and peaceful" setting that struck him as both a refuge and (with sufficient reason) something of a last resort, he sat day after day chain-smoking the cigarettes that had become habitual. He had brought a few books with him, one of them *Twelve Tests of Character* by the popular clergyman Harry Emerson Fosdick. When Macmillan began to read him in his Normandy retreat, Fosdick had already been acknowledged as Modernist leader in the Fundamentalist controversies of the twenties. Pastor of the Park Avenue Baptist Church since 1926, he and his congregation were getting ready to move into the impressive new structure on Riverside Drive that for many years would be synonymous with this influential practical theologian. But the book and the man might have had no more than a passing effect on Macmillan if he had not been able to put certain feelings into words, in conversations with one of his mother's friends. An ardent Catholic whose religious life was vitally real to her, she was also witty and intelligent, and she encouraged Mac to talk. Convinced he would have been too self-conscious to do so had she been Protestant or his own age, he interpreted her presence there, her availability, as a sign and a message. He began to wonder if God had any connection with the missing center of his own life: Was there a divine intent he ought to be unraveling, and some humble capacity in which God wanted him to serve?

Seeking the answer to this question during the next few years, he believed he was being led from event to event, as though a divine plan were unfolding. The Episcopal service into which he wandered, for example, on a morning walk down Fifth Avenue shortly after his return from Normandy, struck him as yet another omen; and when the sympathetic clergyman, listening to his tale of self-doubt and woe, asked him whether he had thought of the priesthood, Macmillan took this as a clear instruction from above. Surely, in a theological seminary, he would be able to find out God's intent with regard to him. But it did not occur to him to tell any of the Episcopal clergymen he proceeded to confer with— whether Dean or Bishop—that he had never even been confirmed in their church.

There were multiple misunderstandings in the serio-comic drama that ensued. The last act began in the summer of 1931, a year after the fateful service in the Fifth Avenue church. The agreement he thought he had reached with the dean of Cambridge

Theological Seminary in Massachusetts had turned out to be nothing of the kind. Both sides had failed, it would seem, to ask the right questions. Falling back in disappointment and exasperation on familiar ground, Macmillan had arranged to enter Berkeley Theological Seminary instead, in New Haven. He was scheduled to begin his studies in the fall, and having convinced himself that a seminary would be like a monastery of a closed Order, he felt that unless he made a supreme effort to shed his embarrassing worldliness he would not be spiritually ready. What better way to begin to do this, he reasoned, than to steep himself all summer in the writings of the mystics. There was a course in them, he reported to his mother, at the University of Toulouse that very summer; and conveniently nearby was Lourdes, where he could attend the famous services for the pilgrims who came there to be healed.

Except for the advanced commercialism at Lourdes, which surprised him, the summer met his personal requirements. But when he arrived at Berkeley in the fall, what proved even more desirable than "kissing the leper" at Lourdes was becoming a full-fledged member of the community—a Postulant—through the customary channels of confirmation and sponsorship. In this respect, despite Macmillan's mistaken belief to the contrary, Berkeley's entrance requirements were no different than those at Cambridge—or at any other seminary, for that matter. But Macmillan seemed determined to feel he had not been allowed to ease himself into a religious life. Prepared for disillusionment, misinterpreting nearly everything said to him, he found Berkeley wanting on every score.

The seminary had moved just a few years earlier (in 1928) from Middletown to New Haven, and its financial circumstances were precarious. The new relationship with Yale, moreover, was neither a strong nor happy one as yet. Looking back from the vantage point of time, Macmillan admitted that the seminary buildings might have seemed less shabby had they not been surrounded by the contrasting Gothic presence of Yale, whose student fraternity houses adjoined Berkeley's nondescript buildings. As a result, the seminarians—in the words of one who, despite his commitment to an unworldly life, was chronically sensitive to such things—felt like hungry children from the slums gazing upon the opulence of their betters.

In fact, the entire operation struck him as inept and low-class. He criticized the dean himself, the unchallenging courses, the other students. There were not many of these—under two dozen—and

most were younger than his own twenty-eight years. They tended
to come from simple homes in small towns, with boys' clubs and
Sunday schools the "boundaries"—as Mac put it—"of their theological and social aspirations." Small wonder that he became, for
the others, the snob who thought he was still at Choate or Yale.
Nor did he endear himself to the dean (who had his own problems)
by playing a prominent part in the dismissal of a fellow-student
found suffering from an active case of venereal disease.

Although he returned to Berkeley for a second year, during
which the future of the seminary itself was in doubt and rumors of
all sorts were rife, he welcomed the suggestion that he finish his
studies abroad, accompanied as it was by the offer on Berkeley's
part to share the expenses of a final year in England.

In June 1933 he set sail for the old world, guardedly optimistic
that under beneficent Anglican skies his accumulated uncertainties
would dissolve. But ordination was not to be the answer to the
pressing question of God's purpose and his own life's work. As the
real answer gradually dawned on him during his first few months
in London, he was frightened, repelled, dismayed—and absolutely
exhilarated.

3

William Macmillan told the story of the emergence of his healing
powers several times: how at a dinner party in London a man seated
opposite him leaned across the table and uttered the shocking
words, "You are a healer"; how he was persuaded, after dinner, to
exercise his gift on the hostess, who was suffering from painfully
congested sinuses; and how his startling successes—that evening
and on subsequent occasions in other people's houses—revolutionized his existence. In his own suggestive words, "like lava ex-
ploding from a volcano, the healing power burst its bonds—and
added an almost overwhelming problem to my life." It also created
a new and powerful being whose resemblance to the ineffectual son
of Sara Smart virtually disappeared, who gladly learned to follow
his own internal laws and to act in accordance with them rather
than seeking the approval of a bishop or a dean.

So that when he wrote to New Haven for advice about his new-
found powers and was told, in horrified tones, to return at once,
the response made it easier to do what he wished—to break with
Berkeley altogether. He did not communicate at all, however, with

his mother in New York, for there were elements in this strange situation of his that made him uneasy: he had been told of his healing powers by a medium, who had instructed him in the laying-on of hands and the ritual of passes, which he could not bring himself to describe but which he feared were indispensable—and involved just the kind of physical contact that made him slightly ill.

Nevertheless Macmillan's early successes convinced the friends he had made in London religious circles that his gift for healing was a powerful one. Among them were Dick Sheppard, the popular vicar of St. Martin-in-the-Fields, and Maud Royden, the well-known preacher and women's suffragist, who claimed relief from a chronic case of rheumatoid arthritis at Mac's hands. Both of them argued that a gift such as his carried with it an overriding moral obligation and should not be suppressed for any reason (private or public). When he refused to heal, however, without some form of legal sanction, they drew up a petition to the Home Office, collecting the necessary signatures and testimonials. And as soon as his license to practice as a psychotherapist came through, he treated his first patients—in the vestry of Maud Royden's church in Eccleston Square. In no time at all, he was able to rent a maisonette in St. John's Wood. Here, in 1934, his practice officially began. While the world at large stumbled toward another great war, William Macmillan stepped onto a tightrope of a career.

Afraid from the start of doing harm, he never lost sight of the dreadful possibilities and never fully understood what was taking place in any single moment. In due course, he would offer theories about healing, but once the patients began to flock to St. John's Wood his main concern was the actual exercise of this gift that seemed to reside in his hands. They were said to radiate intense heat and to soothe even while rubbing raw or sensitive skin. Yet in the early days of his practice he understood so little of anatomy and disease that his patients had to explain their own illnesses to him before he knew where to apply his hands. Familiar with their own bodies and all their symptoms as only people with long-standing, life-threatening conditions can be, they were able to tell him what he needed to know. But at first, appalled to discover the extent of his ignorance, he tried to learn as much as he could about the human body and medical science as well as about the strange phenomenon of healing.

These courses of self-instruction did not take him very far. But in his unsystematic fashion he looked into theosophy and psychical research, inquired about psychoanalysis, experimented with meditation and vegetarianism, and came out on the side of what he called a "normal life" (English style) and a peculiarly American brand of self-reliance. While the Power continued to flow through him and suffering people claimed to feel its effects, he learned important things about them and himself. The results were better, for instance, when he approached each case as though it were unlike any other, instead of trying to generalize from experience. So he kept no records or case histories and relied increasingly on intuition to tell him what to do—first, whether to treat at all, and then, whether to continue if the patient's responses were not favorable enough.

Experience also made it plain to him that the simple, rapid "cures" (of congested sinuses or a painful bunion or a bad burn) effected in the early days of his healing were not typical. Nor was immediate improvement all that common. An average course of treatment tended to take three weeks, and some difficult cases required even longer. Since, moreover, an essential part of his treatment came to involve teaching or persuading the patient to relax, it was clear that he needed considerable space and comfortable surroundings for himself as well as for them. No one would quarrel, he said, with the insistence on first-class equipment for a medical specialist or surgeon. And it followed as incontrovertibly that he, William Macmillan, was himself a finely honed instrument requiring special care not only every day, as a matter of course, but also at periodic intervals, in the form of luxurious holidays abroad.

Gradually, then, Macmillan's professional life took on the character that suited the social class to which he felt he belonged. From the small maisonette in St. John's Wood—already criticized as too plush by friends who worried about his worldly tastes—he decided to move into larger quarters in the Harley Street area, the heart of London's medical establishment. An address here was the measure of success for a medical man, and Macmillan reasoned that since he had been singled out for the profession of healing it must also be his responsibility to present healing to the world in such a way as would put it on a footing with the best in medicine.

With his first quarters in the West End—in Devonshire Place—Macmillan began to achieve this goal. Here—and in country houses he rented as summer living quarters for those patients who could not make daily trips for treatment—he had some of his most spectacular successes, recorded for us by his friend Dorothy Richardson as well as in his own books: the woman, for example, whose progressive muscular atrophy was reversed by Macmillan

after all her doctors had given up hope and who recovered sufficiently to manage his affairs for him in the late 1930's; the paralyzed
businessman with the disabling violent temper; and the children
suffering from polio or tuberculosis whom he took in hand and
seemed to help. Here, too, he charged the same fees as his medical
confrères, never accepting a patient without the consent of the
doctor in charge, using the available medical means—including
x rays—to monitor a patient's condition during treatment. His
work, he would insist, was as far removed from faith healing as he
could make it.

He would also say that he viewed healing primarily as a challenge to "the smugness of orthodoxy," religious or medical. There
is little doubt that his most striking successes flew in the face of
established medical authorities. Dorothy Richardson periodically
registered amazement, for example, that "Mac ha[d] taken another
child out of an iron lung." But it remains true that for the most
part he took on cases considered hopeless, those referred to him by
a medical doctor who had already exhausted the conventional
methods of treatment. In other words, he treated only patients
who were desperately ill, who had no other option and knew it,
and perhaps by this means he gained for himself an important psychological advantage. Such patients certainly provided him with
plenty of evidence that "the unconscious [was] deeply involved in
the experience of healing," and from them, no doubt, he learned
how to read so well the extent to which individuals could be
taught to cooperate with their own recuperative forces.

His own nature, however, remained more of a mystery to him
than anyone else's, and he was always trying to peer into it. Sometimes he saw himself as William James's hypothetical white crow,
secretly wondering what color he really was in other people's eyes.
Sometimes he felt like "a healing machine," with nothing inside,
or a switchboard operator, or even a prehistoric mammal who
ought to be exhibited in a glass case. And twice he had the extraordinary experience of his person giving off a strong smell of per-
fume in the open air. A mystery indeed. But more and more celebrated in a world once so resistant to all his youthful efforts. And
wealthy enough—after the move to Devonshire Place—to bring
his mother to England. They lived together at first in a maisonette
off Sloane Street, where Macmillan expected her to fit into his
busy life. He did not seem to realize that this would be as difficult
for her to do as it had been for him years before. There had been

no place for him then; there was no place for her now, no matter what elaborate and costly arrangements he made. Their situations were exactly reversed, as though the fantasy of a neglected and impotent boy had come into being at last.

He would say, nevertheless, that the lavish country house in Kent was bought for her when it seemed to him there was not enough for her to do in Sloane Street. But she did not throw herself into the decorating and furnishing of it, leaving most of this to her son's efficient staff, the staff that was also in charge of every aspect of Macmillan's regimented daily life. Divided now between the house in Kent, where a small number of patients were installed, and the new splendid treatment rooms in Great Cumberland Place, it was a life essentially closed to everyone, to himself, it would seem, no less than to his mother. For all his developed insight into the psychological workings of the desperately ill, he remained to the end of his life baffled by his own make-up, as all his efforts to explain himself in book after book reveal to us.

4

Convinced when the Second World War began that some record of his healing should be set down for keeping, and unable to persuade any of his friends (Dorothy Richardson among them) to write about him, Macmillan began his first book on a holiday in Cornwall early in 1940. He was visiting Dorothy Richardson and her husband, who for many years had been spending their winters in one or other of the villages surrounding Padstow. Here, on the southwest coast of England, where fears of invasion and Nazi brutality were rampant and where, as a result, plans were being laid not only for defense but also for self-destruction, Macmillan occupied himself with a treatise on healing that Dorothy Richardson had agreed to edit for him. It was not destined to be published until 1948.

Right now, as an alien in a country at war, his activities and movements were already restricted. He knew he would have to give up his two large establishments and move into more economical quarters. Yet he did not want to return to the States, sure that he would feel even more of an alien there than in England. But for reasons that remain unclear, after they had settled into a small cottage near Aldershot, he and his mother sailed for New York in the spring of 1941. Macmillan seemed to think he was undertaking a "good-will mission" on behalf of Britain that would keep him in the States for no more than a few months, while he described to American audiences the actualities of the desperate war being fought by their English cousins. As things turned out he did not get back to England until the beginning of 1946. The years in between were apparently spent moving from one state to another, seeking opportunities for healing where the laws permitted, finding instead a country even more unfamiliar than he had feared and less receptive to him than ever. Once again he was unregarded and unvalued—and the shock of the re-experience vibrates through the account he could not bring himself to set down until long afterward. The facts about these years may never be known but the feelings are plain. So is the conclusion to be drawn—that as of old Macmillan had not the faintest inkling of how to deal with the world of ordinary phenomena. The America pictured by him in his last book bears a remarkable resemblance to Franz Kafka's. Allowing himself to be misled, treated now as a dancing dog, now as a charlatan or thief, Macmillan felt like a helpless child thrown to a pack of adult wolves—and he behaved, it would seem, just like the innocent seminarian of the early '30s, determined, above all, to ignore the sphere of operations known as "reality."

By the time he was able to return "home" to England he had almost forgotten the tenor of his life there, and he nearly wept when his London shirtmaker presented him on arrival with the cashmere dressing-gown he had brought in for cleaning in 1941. His friends were on hand as well, to help him treat again, first in rooms in a private hotel near Guildford and then in a large country house overlooking the Thames valley. With the wheels of his practice turning again, he was able to send for his mother in the spring of 1946. Outwardly all seemed well. His old life began to emerge. But there were signs that the American experience had taken its toll.

In the country house was a young girl being treated for polio, whose psychological state worried Macmillan. She woke up night after night, often screaming with fear. When nothing he did or said resulted in improvement he suggested to her father that they try hypnosis by a London specialist. The girl's father refused, and Macmillan decided to act on his own by calling in a diagnostician. The doctor was already in the house having coffee with Macmillan before seeing the girl, when one of the maids came down to report that she had fainted. They rushed upstairs, and as the doctor touched her she died. Because the doctor was present, Macmillan did not have to face a charge of manslaughter. But he saw the death as a failure, and he heard in it an obscure warning.

A few months later, in October 1947, his mother died of a cerebral hemorrhage. She had time only to telephone him in his own neighboring flat; when he arrived she was dead. Convinced he ought to have intuited that something was radically wrong, he viewed the two deaths as failures; and they had a curious effect upon him. They precipitated a shift from the practice of healing to the explanation and justification of it, as though the idea of writing down his experiences, of formulating a philosophy, of coming to terms—in the language of discourse rather than feeling—with the mysterious anomalies of his life, had taken sudden possession of him. By 1951, the year of his interview in *Good Housekeeping,* when by all appearances he had become the "reluctant healer" in a sense that he never intended his title to convey, he was in the midst of the series of accounts of himself and of healing that had become for him supremely important. But these, far from representing his most creative accomplishment, allow us to glimpse instead the emotional underside of his life, the energies that drove him to healing, and to recognize what Macmillan suggests throughout in the faintest of outlines—his willed achievement of control, the literal taking of his life into his own hands by a young man who discovered unwittingly how to tap his private source of power. Dorothy Richardson testified to the emergence from those restless hands of "a strong magnetic current." Who can tell whence it came and how therapeutic it actually was? Or what part was played in the whole strange affair by Macmillan's imperative need for success, if not the sheer force that powerlessness will sometimes exert?

Toward the end of his healing career Macmillan could be heard constantly berating people for not using their own energies to treat themselves, for allowing disease or illness to take control, for giving up their autonomy. Yet he does not seem to have grasped the origin in his own life-history of this prescription for well-being, that is, the skillful exploitation of his unusual gift. So that in 1951, when he expressed uncertainty about his future as a healer, he may have been more knowing than he cared to admit. Already embarked on his several writing projects, he had begun to realize that these books and nothing else would carry his legacy even though words were not his creative medium. But while attempting to translate psychic force into narrative exposition and building upon the circumstances of the two deaths that had shaken him, he him-self died, just as suddenly, early in 1955, in the process of finishing the book that said more about him than any of the others. It con-tained the last part of his story, which happened also to be the first, underlying the whole—the account of his early years in all their veiled frustrations, the life with Sara Smart Macmillan, who could only attend to him sporadically. This is the "prelude to healing" that nevertheless constitutes the heart of the matter: the unsatisfied need and the fired ambition. His conscious intent was to bring an inspirational story full circle and put to rest—at the same time— the old emotional conflicts that had energized him but which he was still reluctant to acknowledge. He wanted to be the dutiful son until the very end. But his unconscious feelings, as always, were far stronger than the intention behind the words.

SOURCES AND ACKNOWLEDGMENTS

Dorling, Jane. "A Man with the Gift of Grace." *Good Housekeeping,* (December 1951): 46–47, 118, 120, 122.

Macmillan, William J. *This Is My Heaven: Two Treatises on Healing and Other Es-sential Matters,* introd. Paul Brunton. London: John M. Watkins, 1948.

———. *The Reluctant Healer.* London: Victor Gollancz, 1952.

———. *Heaven And You.* London: Hodder and Stoughton, 1953.

———. *Prelude to Healing.* London: Faber & Faber, 1957.

The Sunday Express (London), 24, 31 August, 7, 14 September 1952.

Dorothy Richardson to Peggy Kirkaldy. 15 August 1939. Yale.

DR to PK. 9 January 1940. Yale.

DR to Winifred Bryher. 19 March 1940. Yale.

DR to WB. 17 April 1940. Yale.

DR to PK. 30 May 1940. Yale.

DR to WB. 3 June 1940. Yale.

DR to PK. 5 February 1946. Yale.

DR to PK. [June] 1946. Yale.

DR to PK. 3 July 1946. Yale.

DR to WB. 11 January 1948. Yale.

DR to PK. 1 September 1948.

DR to P. Beaumont Wadsworth. 16 October 1949. New York Public Library.

DR to Rose Odle. 31 October 1949. Yale.

DR to Bernice Elliott. 2 July 1950. Yale.

DR to Ruth and Ferner Suckow. 22 April 1951. Yale.

DR to Henry Savage. 17 August 1952. Yale.

DR to PBW. 3 September 1952. NYPL.

I am grateful to Dorothy Richardson's friends (in particular, Pauline Marrian, the late Col. Edward Hickey, and the late Norah Hickey) for their memories and impressions of William Macmillan as well as for information about him, and to Newland Smith, librarian of Seabury Western in Evanston, Illinois, for informa-tion about Berkeley Theological Seminary.

"I REACH BEYOND THE LABORATORY-BRAIN":* MEN, DOLPHINS, AND BIOGRAPHY

Gavan Daws

THIS ESSAY discusses an episode in the lives of three men and two animals: three men of strongly marked personality and their relationship with two animals of equally powerful individuality. Each man in his own way had much of his life invested in the animals, and the animals had lived most of their life in association with humans. Each man in his own way was concerned with the question of what sort of a life of their own the animals might have, or should have—life in a biological and behavioral sense, but beyond this individual life experienced in terms that a human being would understand as resembling the terms on which his own life was lived. The event that involved them all together was for all five, humans and animals, the genuine stuff of biography. With the event, their lives broke apart and re-formed. All five were permanently marked by the event, branded by it. It was *the* event of their lives.

The two animals were dolphins, mature female Atlantic bottlenoses, species *Tursiops truncatus montagu*. At the time of the event they were in captivity, and had been for several years, in separate concrete tanks, 50 feet in diameter and 5 feet deep, at a university research laboratory at Kewalo Basin in Honolulu, Hawaii. They were the only experimental subjects there. They had been given Hawaiian names: Puka and Keakiko (Kea for short).

The director of the laboratory and the designer of the research carried out on the two dolphins was Louis M. Herman, professor of comparative psychology at the University of Hawaii. Herman

---

*These words, quoted by Leon Edel on the last page of his life of Henry James, are from James's late essay, "Is There Life After Death?"

was a behavioral scientist who had, so to speak, enjoyed a great deal of positive reinforcement for his work at Kewalo. He was a full professor with tenure. He spoke at professional conferences. He published in refereed journals. He was editing a collection of papers on cetacean behavior.† His work was funded by the National Science Foundation. Herman had made a mature professional life, a career, out of the experiments he conducted on Kea and Puka, and he expected to go on extending his research into the cognitive characteristics of the bottlenose dolphin for the life span of his two subjects.

Steven Sipman and Kenneth Le Vasseur came to Kewalo as students of Louis Herman, earning undergraduate academic credit for running experimental sessions. They stayed on at the laboratory, living on the premises. They became as absorbed as Herman in the nature of the dolphin, but in a different way. In time their experience with Kea and Puka convinced them that it was wrong on principle to use dolphins as research subjects in tanks, and they ceased to take part in the experiments, working from then on only as maintenance men, feeding the dolphins and cleaning their tanks. Eventually they arrived at the fixed conviction that it was altogether wrong to keep dolphins in captivity. After discussing alternative courses of action, they decided they had no choice but to liberate the captives. On the night of 29 May 1977, they lifted Puka and Kea from their tanks and turned them loose in the ocean.

The furor that followed this event was remarkable. All the principal characters became instantly celebrated or notorious: Puka and Kea as the dolphins who were taken from their tanks, Herman as the scientist who lost his dolphins, Sipman and Le Vasseur as the men who put the dolphins in the Pacific.

If ever a man found himself in a mid-life crisis, it was Louis Herman. In the decade of his forties he had had three dolphins under his sole control. They represented his research capital, his professional reason for being. Some years earlier, the first of the three had been found dead in its tank at Kewalo. One night it was alive, the next morning it was dead. Now the other two were gone. One night they were in their tanks, the next morning they had disappeared. Herman felt grievously harmed—betrayed and irreparably damaged by Le Vasseur and Sipman and what they had done to him.

---

†*Cetaceans are dolphins and whales.

Going back before the event, a sharp antagonism of style and substance could be observed between the life of Herman and the life of Sipman and Le Vasseur. It is by no means the whole story of the three, but it is a place to start. Herman was a middle-aged scientist from the East Coast, upwardly mobile professionally, who saw nothing wrong with doing research work on dolphins under contract to the United States Navy and reporting results in the form of classified documents. Sipman and Le Vasseur were separated from Herman by almost a generation—at the time of the event they were twenty-six and Herman was forty-seven—and by all the differences in attitude that separate the classic Depression baby from the classic child of the sixties. Each of the two for his own reasons was antimilitary, especially over military use of dolphins. Beyond that, it would be as hard to imagine either Sipman or Le Vasseur settling down to a conventional middle-class job with good prospects for the right young man as it would be to imagine Louis Herman in his mid-twenties opting against hard work toward professional advancement, respectability, and a comfortable assured income, in favor of hanging around dolphins indefinitely, with a makeshift roof over the head, very little spending money, no professional goal, and apparently nothing much else in view.

There were great individual differences between Sipman and Le Vasseur, but a police witness's description would have made them sound like two of a kind numerous in Hawaii: mid-twenties, tallish, with the kind of permanent tan, streaky hair, chronically reddened eyes, and the chest and shoulder development of those who spend endless hours in the water. Le Vasseur was a swimmer and competition diver; Sipman as a high school student and later a college graduate put surfing ahead of most things in life. And both of them were hairy. Louis Herman had a beard of his own, but it was the beard of the controlled scientist, close-cropped. By contrast, Sipman's beard was not so much cultivated as allowed to flourish with occasional tending. Le Vasseur for his part went back and forth among beard-and-mustache, mustache alone, and clean-shavenness. In fact Le Vasseur was sensitive on the subject of hair, and this had to do with his upbringing. He was what is called a military brat, one of five children of a career army officer who during the increasingly hairy sixties imposed on all his sons the shortest of back-and-sides barbering, "whitewalls." Le Vasseur had difficulty remembering all the places he lived as a child; the family went through more than twenty-five military postings in the

United States and Europe. Later, his father did two tours of duty in Vietnam, helping design helicopter strategy and working on a computer system for integrating sensor information on the Ho Chi Minh trail.

Le Vasseur himself always had innumerable computerlike programs running in his head. The impression he was likely to give was that his energetic, even hyperactive body could not keep up with his racing mind. He generated a staggering output of spoken words delivered at top speed, but the faster he talked the faster yet the leaping synapses in his brain kept firing, so that there was always—urgently—more to be said. Not surprisingly, Le Vasseur often found himself in the position of telling people more than they wanted to know. He was well known at Kewalo for appearing out of nowhere, zeroing in on targets of opportunity—fellow students, research associates, visitors, the man delivering the frozen fish—and firing off huge bursts of animated and highly complicated technical prose about his great intellectual project, the use of neural coding theory to solve the problem of interspecies communication with dolphins. "I was just thinking—" he would begin, and suddenly it would be five, ten, thirty minutes later. He would buttonhole Herman in the same way, with suggestions for improving the design of the research: "Lou, why don't we. . . ." Herman had a doctorate in psychology. Le Vasseur had done no graduate work. These considerations did not abash Le Vasseur; he thought of himself as a serious cetologist, a good citizen of the republic of scientific learning.

Le Vasseur was also an inventor. One of his projects, completed just before the release of Puka and Kea, was a specially designed kayak for quietly and unobtrusively keeping company with schools of dolphins in the wild and observing their behavior. But even this did not make for the optimum dolphin–man interface, as Le Vasseur termed it, and so he had invented—his pride and joy—a dolphin suit. It was meant to turn a human into an artificial marine mammal, increasing the human's speed in the water so that he could keep up with cruising or playing dolphins. A streamlined helmet that had eye seals with curved lenses, nostril blocks and a snorkel "blowhole," hand paddles that formed fins, and a shaped lower body that ended in a large propulsive fluke—the idea was worked out in detail in fifteen technical drawings and seventeen claims covering the eight pages of packed text that made up United States Patent 3,934,390, awarded to Le Vasseur on 27 January 1976, several months after he started work at Kewalo.

"That's my only redeeming feature," Le Vasseur used to say, "my inventions."[1] If he could not think of himself as a scientist, he did not know quite how to think of himself. He knew he was often hard to understand, that his noise-to-signal ratio might be off-putting, that his highspeed bursts of information-heavy communication tended to make some people flinch or even duck for cover. And, as he would acknowledge with some emotion, he distrusted emotions, at least his own; they always seemed to get him into trouble. Even where Puka and Kea were concerned he did not want to rely on emotion to tell him what was happening.

> Like, the dolphins want me to do something, right? Now, Steve would say, "Yes, the dolphins want me to do this." And I would say, "What do you have to back that up?" "Well, the dolphin wants me to." Whereas I would say, "The dolphin has solicited me three times; she's soliciting me, doing this and that and the other thing, and that's how I can tell." I have reasons for virtually everything I do. And that's because I can't trust my emotions. I've got to have reasons instead.

Accordingly, Le Vasseur talked of control, of working things out ahead of time, of having detailed plans for doing things, of his whole life being one big experiment. "Do what you set out to do, and have the discipline to follow through on that sort of effort. Like any type of research." In short, he said, he was a scientist running endless tests—on himself, on other people, on the world. He was not at all against research on dolphins—just against research in captivity. And it is in these terms that he described the release of the dolphins. "This is a fight within science, not a fight against science. I don't want to be regarded as weird."

Sipman was less worried about being regarded as weird. He did not think he was, but he certainly thought the world he lived in was weird enough, and so he had to be ready for the thought that the world in return was likely to think that *he* was weird. Many a California dreamer of the late sixties has passed through the seventies into the eighties in the same frame of mind, actively disconnected from society and very aware of the disconnection. Sipman grew up in the tract housing of the San Fernando Valley and suffered through high school in the last bitter days before the terminal collapse of dress and hair codes (he grew a mustache especially for graduation and then decided at the last moment not to go to the ceremony). He surfed every beach within a day's drive of Los Angeles, and he had a moral tale to tell about coming home with black globules of the great Santa Barbara oil spill stuck all over his board, in his hair, between his toes. And he had other peculiarly Southern California surfer's stories about scary hot-dogging off Camp Pendleton under sporadic small arms fire from returned Vietnam veterans undergoing Marine debriefings and reorientations, still disoriented and generally enraged, using these obviously draft-evading surfers as last targets of opportunity. As yet another part of his continuing California education, at a community college in Los Angeles, Sipman encountered Eastern philosophy, taught by an ex-Jesuit whose attractive wife was a practicing (nonmalevolent) witch. Much attracted to the idea of flow as an organizing principle of life, Sipman came to Hawaii for the surf, taking a semester of work at a time at the university as a precaution against the draft and getting excellent grades, keeping himself alive by running a gardening service in Honolulu on much the same principles as he applied to his beard. Very good at making things grow and keeping them alive, reluctant to spray and prune and give "whitewall" cuts to lawns, he limited his customers to those with a positive attitude to natural plant shapes and natural luxuriance of growth in their Hawaiian gardens.

The difference in general velocity and mode of progress through the world as between Herman, Le Vasseur, and Sipman was notable. Herman, as it happened, was a swimmer too; he regularly did his training miles with a local club. He took his work along in the same disciplined way, as slowly as necessary to make sure his results were sound, as fast as he could against the need to publish and get his grants renewed. Le Vasseur, far too speedy for most humans, invented a suit that was meant to make him as speedy as a dolphin, enabling him to pursue the dolphin in the wild and get valuable scientific information, then return so that he could process the information at even higher speed. Sipman was more of a floater, a meditator. Kick back, he would say, lay back, go with the flow; if the dolphin wants to come, he will. For Sipman, all research should begin with play, and he was content that it should be the dolphin who decided what the game would be, the human who would learn from the dolphin. And the game would always be the master game of understanding the whole dolphin and the whole human in the whole ocean of life.

If Le Vasseur had his own version of scientific reasons for everything he did, Sipman's reasons were differently articulated. He had a story about his first close encounter with a dolphin, and it was obviously a tale with great value for him as something to meditate on:

> It was my last semester in high school. We were out at Malibu Point. It was an overcast day and we were the only ones there, sitting around this driftwood fire, and we looked out and saw a fin and thought it must be a shark. It was cutting back and forth right inside where the waves were. So we all threw stones, and I grabbed a stick and waded in, because it was only knee-deep to waist-deep water—and it wasn't a shark, it was a dolphin, whistling, just whistling away, and he came right up to me and started sort of leaning against my leg, whistling away, just pressing against me. . . . And I thought, what's with this dolphin, is it sick or something? It was following me in to shore, so I swam out and tried to pick it up past the waves and have it swim away in the right direction. But it insisted on coming back to shore. We kept trying to take it out and it kept coming back. So eventually—it was a small enough dolphin that we could pick it up, and we put it in the lagoon because where it swam in on the rocks it was getting smashed around and cut up.
>
> So we put it inside the lagoon and we were putting water on it and wondering what was wrong with it, and then we ran down to the lifeguard station, and he called Marineland. And they responded that once a dolphin comes ashore there's nothing you can do—they die. You know, that's all there was to it. We were pretty upset and there wasn't . . . there wasn't anybody to come down and do anything.
>
> So a friend and I just stayed with this dolphin all day. It wouldn't swim round, it would just stay right on the shore. Wherever it went it would just beach itself. We just sat there while it whistled and whistled all day, and we just, you know, sprinkled water on it to keep it from overheating. So no one came down to do anything about it. And eventually it got dark, and the dolphin died.
>
> We came back that weekend and the body was all puffed up from the sun, and the birds were pecking away at it. People were throwing rocks at it, kids were poking it with sticks, and I just never forgot that.

> I felt sorry that there was nothing I could do and that there was nothing anybody else was willing to do. I thought somebody would at least come down and make a gesture. . . . And Marineland said there was nothing that could be done. . . . Nowadays there's a different attitude to that, with animals that are stranded there are various things they can do. . . . Probably it was better that they didn't come, because if they came they may have taken the dolphin and put it in a tank, and it would have lived with the dolphins in captivity

and that might have been worse. Or it might have been better, I
don't know.

You know, it was weird, or at least it *seemed* weird that it came to
where we were. It could have gone anywhere on any beach up and
down the coast. But we were the only ones on the beach and it came
to where we were and sought us out. It wasn't just looking for a
beach, it was looking for company, it was looking for comfort.

Now I don't want you to think that was my road to Damascus or
anything like that. But it's something I remember.

When it came time for Sipman and Le Vasseur to justify their
release of Puka and Kea, they were more than willing to describe
the dolphins in words which made the animals sound human in
terms of awareness, intelligence, sociability, and capacity for suffering. They were doing more than indulging in anthropomorphic
thinking. They wanted to personify the dolphins in a more demanding sense, to bring dolphins within the human community
of rights, duties, and moral obligations. In the view of Le Vasseur
and Sipman, no more than humans should dolphins be forcibly
captured, taken from their free state and imprisoned, as at Kewalo,
for no crime, in isolation, unable to communicate or have physical
contact with others of their kind, in featureless concrete tanks like
water-filled cells, doing repetitive labor at the command of others
who were in absolute control of their working hours and food sup-
ply. This was a life sentence against which there was no appeal,
hard labor on rationed food in solitary confinement until death.
Sipman in particular was absolutist about it all. He would concede
that conditions for captive dolphins in some oceanaria might be
better than at the Kewalo laboratory—more swimming space in
company with other dolphins, less demanding work regimes—but
to Sipman this was no more than the difference between, say, a
Mexican jail and an American jail. Prisons were prisons. Dolphins
should be free just as humans should be free. So he and Le Vasseur
freed Puka and Kea.

The attempt to personify the dolphins was carried further, into
the legal arena. When the state of Hawaii required the releasers of
Kea and Puka to answer for their act in court, the defense they put
forward was one that would have applied to the rescue of human
beings in imminent danger of harm.

On the other side, Louis Herman and several of his assistants
were equally ready to use language that sounded as if they valued

the life (and death) of dolphins in human terms. At Kewalo, they said, the dolphins had been treated better than children. The researchers spoke the language of bereavement: losing a dolphin was like losing a member of the family. Soon after the event, Herman published a "requiem for two dolphins," in which he described the taking of Puka and Kea as a personal loss. He thanked at length all those who had offered help and comfort. And he addressed the two departed dolphins directly: "For the both of you, I regret that your trust in humans will likely soon lead to your deaths, for that is what my heart and my long experience with dolphins tells me."[2] In a later published work, he envisioned a "tragic picture of the emotional distress of Kea and Puka at their end."[3] What Le Vasseur and Sipman had done was described as kidnapping, abduction, even murder (not that Le Vasseur and Sipman killed the dolphins with their own hands). The assumption here was that on re-entering the ocean Puka and Kea would die or be killed by sharks.

So for Herman and those who thought like him, the taking of Puka and Kea to the open ocean was not only a personal blow, not only a crime against science and against the state, but also a crime against the dolphins. Which was to say that dolphins were— like humans—beings capable of having human crimes committed against them and suffering from these crimes like humans. Thus for Le Vasseur and Sipman to have taken Kea and Puka (against their will?) from the laboratory to the ocean was a crime against the dolphins.

Yet if the dolphins could suffer in such circumstances in a human way, would they not have suffered comparably in a human way when they were first taken from the ocean (against their will?) into captivity? How was capture by humans different in principle from release by humans? And if taking dolphins from tanks was abduction, what was the proper word for keeping dolphins in captivity, in isolation (against their will?) prospectively for life?

Herman preferred not to engage these questions, speaking only about the benefits of research.

What does freedom mean? What we should talk about is what we can learn from these animals. What can they do to help our own life? How does their physiology enable them to dive? If man is to make his way about undersea, what can he learn about the dolphin's echo-location system? In vision, myopia in dolphins can be overcome in interesting ways. The dolphin's brain is as large as ours and very complex. Wouldn't you like to know why? Shall we try to learn from two animals—two dolphins? You see the absurdity of taking all that away from us, and from dolphins. To turn that into an issue of freedom just dilutes and diminishes the truth of what it meant for them to be in that setting, to them and to us.[4]

At any given moment there are literally millions of experimental animals captive in laboratories worldwide, from the most lowly species up to man's closest evolutionary neighbors, undergoing the widest possible variety of testing with the widest range of scientific results, including death by the most extravagant variety of lethal agents. Yet this goes mostly without remark. What is it about the dolphin in particular that arouses such intense and highly charged interest, emotion, and involvement on the part of human beings? The answer comes to center upon the large and complex dolphin brain referred to by Louis Herman. Anyone, scientist or layman, who spends much time with dolphins, either in the wild or in captivity, comes to appreciate them as alert and engaging, with an exceptionally sharp awareness of the world about them and a surprising interest in human beings. The dolphin's range of behavior is a function of the dolphin brain, which is indisputably one of the most remarkable phenomena of the animal kingdom. The imposingly big human brain is what has made man king of the earth and conscious of his sovereignty. It tends, then, to come as a surprise to humans to learn that the brain of the Atlantic bottlenose dolphin is considerably bigger than man's, averaging something like 1600 cubic centimeters as against the average human brain of about 1400.

Scientific argument rages over the significance (or lack of significance) of brain size as an index of other attributes such as intelligence (however intelligence might be measured and compared across species boundaries). But certain things are worth noting about the cetacean brain in relation to the human brain. The "humanness" of the human brain resides in the quantity and quality of neocortical material, its regionalization, lamination, fissurization, and cellular interconnectivity. As for the neocortex of the cetacean brain, it has an enormous surface area; it is regionally differentiated; and, in the words of Peter Morgane, compiler of a dolphin brain atlas, it is luxuriant and highly convoluted in appearance.[5] This is to say (without certainty but with plausibility, at least) that the size and structure of the dolphin brain suggest the possibility that there exists, alongside man, another formidable intelligence on earth.

Scientists such as Louis Herman are cautious indeed about what they put on paper concerning the significance of the dolphin brain. For them, not brain size or structure but behavior is the measure of "intelligence" in a species; behavior is what is tested in laboratory tanks; and not nearly enough behavioral tests have been carried out (though Herman is determined they will be: one of the behaviors of behavioral scientists is the repeated carrying out of behavioral tests). Bidding his reluctant farewell to the dolphins of Kewalo, Herman wrote: "Know, somehow . . . that others of your kind will be with humans as you were to help us in our understanding of all the marvels of your biology and your life. By your abduction, that understanding has been delayed; but the search for understanding will begin again and will always continue."[6]

Others have been prepared, without benefit of exhaustive behavioral research, to postulate the existence of a cetacean intelligence that is nonhuman, that does not speak in words as we do, that is nonhanded, nonartifact-producing, nonterrestrial, nondry: "mind in the waters," in the classic phrase. Among present-day thinkers it is John Lilly who has been most willing—eager—to credit dolphins and other cetaceans with an intelligence not only equal to man's but superior, including even a superior ethical sense and a religious life. Lilly, a scientist by training, is as well the leading poetic thinker and fantasist of cetology. When he lets his own mind swim free to play with the idea of mind in the waters, he likes to meditate upon the biggest brain on earth, that of the largest cetacean, the sperm whale. "Often," Lilly writes, "I have asked myself what would a brain six times the size of mine think about?"[7] Surely with a biocomputer of this capacity the sperm whale need use only a small part of his brain for "survival computations"—feeding, hunting, reproduction, and so on. Perhaps, Lilly suggests, the sperm whale can rerun past experiences in three-dimensional sound-color-taste-emotion. Building on the age-old knowledge that cetaceans respond to human music (the Greeks remarked on this characteristic of dolphins), Lilly fantasizes a full symphony orchestra playing to a sperm whale, thus displaying one of the most attractive of our complicated acoustic products to the acoustically oriented brain of the underwater mind. Lilly goes on to suggest that with the storage capacity of this great cetacean biocomputer, very likely the whale could recreate a symphony in his

mind at will. (Humpback whales among themselves "sing" complex "songs" of from eight to thirty minutes in duration, which
they repeat with variations, so that by the end of a year the song is
changed.) Lilly goes further, suggesting that the sperm whale, gi-
gantically weightless in water, washed by the tides of the world,
is capable of transcendental states and religious experiences quite
beyond the present capacities of humans. Here Lilly is with the
Byzantine philosopher who intuitively identified the cetacean as
the mind of God in the waters.

In the course of his own lengthy spiritual odyssey, which began
in earnest with his decision in 1968 to abandon research on captive
dolphins, Lilly found himself conducting seminars at Esalen, the
center of the human potential movement of the late sixties, in the
Big Sur country of California. In one of his workshops there he
undertook to give human seekers the experience of being a dolphin.[8] He did not use a dolphin suit of the kind Kenneth Le Vasseur
designed. Nor did he play the kind of party game that was tried at
an oceanarium in Hawaii some years ago, using a special helmet
designed to give blind humans a sonar picture so that they could
"see" with their sense of hearing, as dolphins do. Lilly taught dol-
phinhood by teaching dolphin respiration (very different from
human breathing), dolphin mutual dependence, dolphin playfulness, and dolphin lovingness, all of which Lilly considered to be
freighted with the most important of messages for humans. The
least species-bound of his students, so he reported, were able to
hyperventilate and reach new states of consciousness while floating
in the water, and were gratefully able to surrender their fears and
constraints, their very bourgeois selves, to the supportive minis-
trations of their fellow-human apprentice-cetaceans bobbing bare-
skinned in the Esalen hot spring baths.

This attempt to alter human consciousness in order to approximate cetacean consciousness is of course a tentative and faltering
one, however daring it may sound in terms of conventional Western human ways of experiencing reality. Perhaps such a leap out of
ourselves can never be made, even momentarily. There is a stupen-
dous philosophical problem to be considered: how can a consciousness of a given type and structure conceivably encompass
another consciousness of quite different type and structure? The
thoughtful student of animal behavior Donald Griffin states the
issue with fine brevity: perhaps human mental experiences "are so
closely bound up with our species-specific neurophysiological

mechanisms that we are not capable of understanding any [animal] mental, as distinct from neurophysiological processes, even if such exist. In this view, should other species have feelings, hopes, plans, or concepts of any sort—even very simple ones—they would take a form so different from our own thoughts that we should not recognize them."[9]

Certainly the sea world in which cetacean consciousness evolved over a period of forty million years is radically different from the land world of humans. Water, not air. Buoyancy, not gravity. Hearing as the dominant sense, not sight. And a distribution and processing of sensory information so unfamiliar to humans that we have no way of bringing it together to make it spell consciousness, at least in our spelling: oceanic change of temperature, light, color, barometric pressure, chemical and nutritive composition, acidity and salinity of water, and—on a cosmic scale—the pull of sun, moon, and stars, the turning of the earth, acting on the massive ocean currents and the running of the tides.

Lacking properly operationalized definitions of cetacean states of consciousness of the kind that would satisfy behaviorists, some human beings attempt empathy. Joan McIntyre was once the most forceful of the full-time whale-savers of California, a founding figure of Project Jonah, a terrestrial mammal who wanted desperately to know what it was like to be a marine mammal. "I imagine myself in the water," she wrote, "in a world of shifting currents and cycling days and nights, where the moon's pull on my body is as clear in my consciousness as the call of my infant beside me. Living there, where the world moves, shifts, changes around me minute by minute—but is recognizable by my kind over thousands of years—I float and breathe and think, and let the water smash down on me and the sun silver my eyes."[10]

This kind of empathy goes very far back in history. A special relation between dolphin and man, amounting to a deep identification, existed in the time of the ancient Greeks. "Like thoughts with man have the attendants of the gods of the looming sea," wrote Oppian, "wherefor they also practice love of their offspring and are very friendly to one another."

Among themselves dolphins gesture incessantly. With their bodies they communicate aggressiveness and defensiveness, dominance and submission, acknowledgment of status, fear, confidence, affection—and sexual appetite. And in all these ways, including the last, the dolphin gestures as well to humans. In ancient

Greek art Eros rides the dolphin, and there are Greek stories of love until death between dolphins and humans, mostly young boys. In fact the dolphin is all things sexual. The classicist Charles Doria writes: "The dolphin is a good embodiment of the triadic hermaphrodite. Its bland, round, apparently self-contained body shows no obvious sexual differences; its genital organs are kept snugly withdrawn in a pouch below the belly until needed. Yet her billowing curves and graceful swells that recall the waves of the sea and statues of pre-Greek wom(b)an goddesses earned her the name *delphys*. His blunt snub nose, strong snout, flashing speed, the smooth, bulging head white with water, and generally cylindrical shape lends him a phallic character. . . . So, in a sense, all the hermaphrodite is realized in the dolphin."[11]

Joan McIntyre, striving toward cetacean consciousness, perceived this while swimming with two dolphins, a male named Liberty and a female named Florida.

> The dolphins spin out of the water in the shimmering light of the growing moon. Swimming with them I lose track of what belongs to who. Is it Liberty, is it Florida. Am I being touched by male or female. Is it flukes or fins. Liberty uses his penis like a hook. Takes me behind the knees and tows me toward the rubber boat. I dip below the surface, stroke his—her—pink underbody. They twine around me, strong and powerful. It is a little scarey, this androgynous mixing below the surface. A dolphin floats by. . . . Is it he, is it her. I don't care. I only care that I cannot release myself to them. Cannot let go into the churning gentle maelstrom of the contact of our bodies.[12]

A powerful attraction is being described here, and an equally powerful troubled nearness to sexual surrender. This is not really surprising. Dolphins and humans are highly evolved creatures, big-brained mammals with as much freedom as exists anywhere in creation to indulge in sexual play.

A classic story of modern-day work with dolphins is how one of John Lilly's animals, named Peter, carried out a successful courtship of a young woman named Margaret Howe. Lilly's idea was to have human and dolphin live day-round for weeks in a social situation to promote learning. So at Lilly's Communication Research Institute in the Virgin Islands Peter and Margaret shared quarters that were part wet, part dry: a seawater pool for the dolphin connecting with a simple living space for the human. Margaret was teaching Peter, and not until some weeks passed did she become aware that Peter was conducting his own course of instruction.

The two of them played a game, a simple amusement, in which they would toss a ball back and forth over a distance of some feet in the pool. Gradually Peter began tossing the ball a shorter distance, so that Margaret had to come closer to him to pick it up. Then it became a matter of Margaret not having to throw the ball at all but just put it in Peter's mouth, with Peter lying very still, trancelike, until Margaret cautiously took the ball out again. Bottlenose dolphins have eighty-six teeth in a powerful set of jaws, and it was not a negligible thing for Margaret to be able to trust her hand in Peter's mouth on relatively short acquaintance. But she managed it. Then—gradually again—Peter would roll the ball farther and farther back in his mouth so that Margaret would have to reach in to retrieve it. Now Peter changed the game. Holding the ball forward in his mouth, he would gently sink into the water and run the tip of his mouth up and down Margaret's legs. Then the ball went farther back into his mouth, and now it was his teeth that were rubbing gently up and down. Then he dropped the ball altogether, and at this point what was really happening became clear to Margaret: "Peter is courting me . . . or something very similar," she wrote in her journal.

> I began to take an active part in the play. After several minutes of Peter "stroking" me gently with his teeth, I compliment him vocally, soothingly, and rub him as he turns to be stroked. Several minutes of this and Peter is back stroking me.
>
> Two things about all this stand out in my mind. One is the overall way Peter was able to woo me, to teach me that *I could play this game.* I had many fears. . . . Peter obviously realized them and found ways, and *props* (the ball after all was a very convenient tool) to reassure me. Peter has worked long for this contact . . . he has been most persistent and patient. Second is the mood in general of the play. This is obviously a sexy business . . . all it really involves is physical contact. The mood is very gentle . . . still . . . hushed . . . all movements are slow . . . tone is very quiet . . . only slight murmurings from me. Peter is constantly, but ever so slowly, weaving his body around . . . eyes near closed. He does not usually get an erection during this, but does present his tummy and genital area for stroking. . . . I feel extremely flattered at Peter's patience in all this . . . and am delighted to be so obviously "wooed" by this dolphin.

All this took weeks, and when more weeks still had passed, Peter led Margaret further. In his sexual excitement he used to become rough and turbulent, and Margaret would withdraw. Now he remained gentle, even with an erection.

> He no longer tries to run me down and knock me off my feet, rather he slides very smoothly along my legs, and I can very easily rub his penis with either my hand or my foot. Peter accepts either and again seems to reach some sort of orgasm and relaxes . . . it is a very precious sort of thing. Peter is completely involved, and I involve myself to the extent of putting as much love into the tone, touch, and mood as possible. . . .

Looking back, Margaret remembered that she started out afraid of Peter's mouthful of teeth and afraid of his sex.

> It had taken Peter about two months to teach me, and me about two months to learn, that I am free to involve myself completely with both. It is strange that for the one, *I* must trust completely . . . Peter could bite me in two. *So he has taught me that I can trust him.* And in the other, he is putting complete trust in me by letting me handle his most delicate parts . . . *thus he shows me that he has trust in me.* Peter has established mutual trust. Could I have devised such a plan?[13]

There is at least one male human who has consummated a sexual relationship with a female dolphin captive in a mainland American oceanarium. By his account it was a powerful experience, and also by his account it was as powerfully willed by his dolphin partner as by himself. And at Kewalo, among the rich folklore of the student workers at the lab, accumulated over the years, telling of things that will never be written down in scholarly articles or included in applications for renewals of Louis Herman's grants, there is the shadowy story of a young man who is said to have coupled with Kea. No one is explicit, no one volunteers details, no name is given for the human. Perhaps he does not exist; but even if he does not, it has evidently been necessary to invent him.

If humans and cetaceans are ever to know each other more than empathetically, more than behaviorally, more than physically, if the barrier between highly self-aware species of vastly different sorts is ever to be crossed, so that individuals on either side can describe their own and each others' individual lives, then presumably it will be language that will do it: communication back and

forth between two sets of minds that have things to discuss and
ways of discussing in common. Then the fundamental question
posed by the anthropologist-psychologist-biologist Gregory Bateson about humans and cetaceans who inhabit the same earth will
be susceptible of an answer: "If it be so that human language with
its identification of things and the identification of purposes and all
the rest of it leads to an epistemology in which the sensible thing is
to eat the environment—and eat up the environment—then how
do dolphins structure their universe?"[14]

In the 1960s John Lilly tried to teach dolphins to speak English.
(That was the formal subject matter of Peter's lessons with Margaret Howe.) It was a great adventure; Lilly was sure that he and his
dolphins were developing a common understanding about language. Of course, the dolphin's physical apparatus for noisemaking
is so different from the human's that it was very difficult indeed for
the dolphin even to approximate sounds in English: he had to
abandon his natural underwater clicking and whistling, and make
sounds in air laboriously formed by blasting an air jet out of
his spiracle, the blowhole on top of his head, using the spiracle
muscles to shape the flow of air into sound, in imitation—understanding imitation—of his trainer. Lilly got as far as questions
and answers—human questions and dolphin answers—on simple
fetch-and-carry subjects. But even at that elementary level he ran
into a great deal of skepticism within the scientific community,
amounting to a downright refusal on the part of a good many scientists to believe a word of what he said he was accomplishing.
William Evans, who spent most of his career doing research on
marine mammals for the military at the Naval Undersea Center at
San Diego, listened to tapes of Peter, and could detect nothing hu-
manoid in the dolphin's utterances. "So I listened again. Then I had
a lot of sherry and listened again. . . . Still nothing. I find Dr
Lilly's work very interesting. I like Dr Seuss too."[15]

Other scientists tried to break down dolphin underwater sounds
into their smallest components and establish whether these mini-
mum units represented (in human terms) words or the building
blocks of words. There was a great argument about the findings.
Dolphins communicate using highspeed clicks and whistles, out-
pourings of sound over a frequency range too broad for humans to
pick up at its extremes with the unaided ear, delivered at speeds
involving thousands of separately uttered sounds a minute. One
interpretation of data suggested that dolphins made a limited num-

ber of sounds, repeated in varying frequencies, which would seem to make the dolphin, though highly vocal, no more genuinely communicative than a whole range of animals not highly regarded for their intelligence—chickens, for example—and certainly not endowed with language as defined by human standards. By contrast, another interpretation yielded the hypothesis that dolphins, computer-fashion, emitted "bits" of sound information that could be combined and recombined endlessly, like the letters of a human alphabet or the phonemes of a human spoken language. And if this was so, it was at least theoretically possible that dolphins might be composing and reciting the works of undersea Homers. Yet another theory, untested but interesting, is that dolphin communication includes a rebroadcasting of information received by bouncing sound off objects underwater with the dolphin's natural sonar apparatus. Thus, for example, a dolphin might not be *saying* SHARK, but rather transmitting to other dolphins a sonar image of a shark, drawing sound pictures. Le Vasseur was enraptured by this idea (as were others, including John Lilly), and was all for designing a helmet for his dolphin suit incorporating miniaturized computer and TV equipment, so that a human could receive dolphin transmissions in the same mode as they were sent out, translated instantaneously into pictures that humans could understand. Another theory about sounds was of more interest to Sipman: the idea that the dolphin's sonar operates—as it does—much like an audio x-ray, so that dolphins sonaring each other are actually getting back instantaneous information on each other's internal condition—pulse rate, breathing rate, agitation of internal organs, state of sexual arousal, in other words a perfect readout of internal individual truth, unimpeded communication of physical and psychological states, the ultimate, surely, in empathy.

It is still not known whether dolphin communication might amount to a language in the human definition. And here we are at what is strongly held to be a Rubicon in the relations between the life of humans and the life of other animals.

Language has come to be the most jealously guarded of human attributes, the thing by which humans most stringently distinguish themselves from animals. If animals were capable of language—and even more if we could talk to them and they could talk to us—then we would be in for some agonizing reappraisals of what it is to be animal and what it is to be human.

The general assumption that our species is unique, and uniquely superior, has suffered a number of blows in the years since Darwin set out his views on the evolutionary continuity of man with other forms of animal life. In the redefinition of humanity that followed, the ability to learn from past experience was advanced as a unique human attribute, then tool-using, then tool-making, and a number of other criteria.[16] But in all these important matters of nature and culture, evidence piles up that as between animal behavior and human behavior there are differences of degree but not kind. If the notion of the unique superiority of humans as a species is to be preserved, then more and more depends on the uniqueness of language as an exclusively human attribute. But as Donald Griffin observes, if we consider the recent history of the study of communication among animals, it is clear that far more complex behavior has been found than any scientist would have dared to predict as recently as thirty years ago.

One response has been to reshape the definition of language again and again—to keep the animals out. Another response has been to take a mode of communication accepted among humans as language and to try to teach it to animals and see if they then use it as humans use language, productively, reflexively, creatively.

The most interesting work along these lines has been with close phylogenetic relatives of man among the primates: chimpanzees (and more recently gorillas and orangutans).[17] The first attempts to create conversation with chimpanzees were made on the same basis as Lilly had used with his dolphins: the hope was to teach the animals to speak English. But it was discovered that the vocal equipment of the chimpanzee did not permit it to acquire spoken language of our kind. Then a brilliant intuition opened up a whole new area of accomplishment. Chimpanzees were introduced to American Sign Language, a hand language of the human deaf and dumb. This shift from lungs, larynx, and tongue to the hand was an inspired one, and it made all the difference. Chimpanzees and humans now talk back and forth, using signs. Chimpanzees use names for themselves and the humans they know. They recognize pictures and mirror-images of themselves. They express needs. They indicate strong preferences. They comment on their environment. They remember. They plan ahead. They ask questions. They abstract. They join word-signs together to express new meanings. They invent new signs. They make jokes. They lie.

They cast ethnic slurs (chimpanzee to laboratory animal of inferior species: "Dirty macaque"). They enunciate political programs (chimpanzee as trainer locks it in cage at end of working day: "You in, me out"). They are learning to follow the story lines of narratives presented to them in pictures. A gorilla is reported to be playing in sign language with rhymes and puns, and to have a tested IQ of 90. And primates raised with humans who use sign language identity themselves with humans.

This picture of the "language"-using primate emerges from a jungle of anecdote, laboratory lore, and carefully reported scientific experiment, in varying proportions. It is a recent picture, adumbrated in the 1970s; and as the 1980s opened a massive scientific counteroffensive was mounted against the claim that it adds up to a true linguistic capacity.[18] But that there is two-way communication seems indisputable, and it also seems indisputable that this communication is opening up the individual lives of animals to human understanding in ways that even the most scrupulous behavioral experiments in the laboratory and the most meticulous ethological studies in the wild do not and by their nature cannot.

Here is the chimpanzee Nim conversing with one of his human teachers, Mary:

> Nim: (looking at a magazine) *Toothbrush there, me toothbrush.*
> Mary: *Later brush teeth.*
> Nim: *Sleep toothbrush.*
> Mary: *Later . . . now sit relax.*
> Nim: (seeing a picture of a tomato) *There eat. Red me eat.*
> Mary: *There more eat! What that?*
> Nim: *Berry, give me, eat berry.*
> Mary: *Good eat. You have berry in house.*
> Nim: *Come . . . There.*
> Mary: *What there?* (Nim leads Mary into house.)
> Nim: (at refrigerator) *Give eat there, Mary, me eat.*
> Mary: *What eat?*
> Nim: *Give me berry.*
> Mary: (later) *See rain outside?*
> Nim: *Afraid. Hug.*
> Mary: *You afraid noise?*
> Nim: *Mary, afraid. Hug.*
> Mary: *What you think about now?*
> Nim: *Play.*
> Mary: *What play?*
> Nim: *Pull, jump.*

Mary: (later) *You tired now?*
Nim: *Tired. Sleep, brush teeth. Hug.*[19]

What Nim is saying with his signing hands may still not satisfy those who maintain that language proper is species-specific to humans. But Nim is communicating *something,* indeed a great deal; and what comes out of it is that he has a genuine interior life. And all this with a brain only a quarter the size of the human brain.

Behind interspecies conversation of this kind looms the question of Kafka: If we succeed in eliciting something like language from something like a chimpanzee, have we taught an animal to talk, or have we released a human being? No wonder humans discussing nonhuman intelligence are by and large more comfortable talking about computer brains than about animal minds. And the discomfort induced by the contemplation of the cetacean brain—larger than the human brain—is palpable.

The record of Nim's conversation with Mary is still a long way from Boswell and Johnson. It is of great related interest, though, to find that the limits of vocabulary in primates have not been reached; and, further, that some chimpanzees, having been taught American Sign Language in captivity, are going on to teach signing to the young of the next generation (which is to say that chimpanzees are transmitting elements of a verbal culture). The astronomer Carl Sagan, who has an interest in "alien" intelligence on earth as well as in space, picks up this fact and plays with its possibilities as John Lilly plays with the computational possibilities of the sperm whale brain. "It does not appear to me out of the question," writes Sagan, "that, after a few generations in such a verbal chimpanzee community, there might emerge the natural history and mental life of a chimpanzee . . . (with perhaps an "as told to" after the by-line)."[20]

Language studies with dolphins pose the same tremendous conceptual difficulties as language studies with primates, and enormously difficult problems of technique as well, because of the phylogenetic distance between dolphins and humans, expressed (to take just one example) in the dolphins' lack of hands for signing. Difficult as it might be to get a dolphin to receive and understand linguistic signals—gestural, acoustic, or visual—directed at it by humans, it would be far more difficult to arrange for a dolphin to signal back comprehensibly.

For these reasons, among others, not much work has been done in this field. But in what has been done, one of the most industrious researchers has been Louis Herman at Kewalo.

One of the reasons, in fact, why the release of Puka and Kea caused such an uproar was that Kea was the subject of language experiments at Kewalo. These had been not long begun. Kea had a working vocabulary of three nouns referring to objects, and three action verbs, and she would fetch and carry in response to commands delivered to her by electronically generated tones. She was also learning the names of two trainers.

Herman, never one to overstate a scientific case, took the view that nothing in dolphin language studies so far suggested that dolphins possessed a natural language as did humans. His own work did demonstrate, however, that dolphins were capable of learning elements of an imposed language in a laboratory situation. He came to see the possibility that they could acquire a rich receptive vocabulary and comprehend complex instructions within the imposed language. And, despite the technical problems, he saw the possibility that dolphins might be able to acquire a productive vocabulary—that is to say, an ability to talk back. And at that point, the interior life of a genuinely big-brained animal would begin to become accessible to humans.

If language is *the* human attribute, then Kea was undergoing preliminary testing for "human potentiality," so to speak. The results, if encouraging, would represent a landmark in the entire history of laboratory work with animals—and, of course, would be the crowning achievement of Herman's scientific life, the triumphant justification of long-term captivity in isolation for his experimental subjects.

But at the Kewalo laboratory were two humans who had been "dolphinized," and they let the dolphins go. Le Vasseur and Sipman were not direct disciples of John Lilly, but certainly they acted in the spirit of a manifesto Lilly published in 1976 on the subject of rights for cetaceans.[21] Lilly argued that cetaceans should have rights as individuals, that they should not be exploited or owned by humans, and that they should have the freedom of the seas: all this on the basis of the attributes flowing from the existence of the remarkable cetacean brain. Le Vasseur and Sipman saw such propositions as self-evident truths, and acted accordingly.

In doing so, they defined themselves for life: as the men who released the dolphins. They also put themselves at risk with the law; and as matters turned out, this too would define them for the rest of their lives. They were taken to court for releasing the dolphins. Their attempt at legal personification of dolphins failed.[22] The ruling at law was that dolphins had the legal status not of persons but of property. The charge was grand theft; the jury decided they were guilty; Sipman and Le Vasseur are thus convicted felons.

Kea and Puka were regarded by Le Vasseur and Sipman as having rights and interests deserving of equal consideration with the rights of humans.[23] The dolphins, at least after they were taken from Kewalo, were regarded by Herman and his assistants as having humanlike reactions to stress and being capable of grievous personal injury, as humans are. In the view of the law, dolphins were things merely.

Whether Puka and Kea survived in the ocean is a matter of debate, debated fiercely still. It is a life-and-death matter that cannot be settled one way or another. The old verdict from Scottish jurisprudence applies: not proven. The thought of death in the ocean for Puka and Kea induced deep emotional distress in Herman and his assistants. Not so for Le Vasseur and particularly for Sipman. Le Vasseur was confident of the dolphins' ability to survive. And Sipman took the position that even if they died, they died free, and freedom was the important thing, the absolute. A minute of freedom was worth more than a lifetime lived in captivity; the really horrifying prospect was the thought of life captivity in Herman's tanks.

For Herman, tanks empty of dolphins brought a curious access of professional and personal renown, more than he had ever had while the tanks were occupied. He became a scientific celebrity; he was interviewed for mass-circulation magazines; *National Geographic* photographed him standing in the drained, empty concrete tank at Kewalo.

By the same token, tanks empty of dolphins meant professional clinical death for Herman—a cessation of vital functions. He moved at once to have two more dolphins captured from the wild, as Kea and Puka had been captured, and they were brought to the tanks at Kewalo to be habituated to life in captivity.

Herman got his National Science Foundation grant renewed. Language experiments were begun again. In the wake of the loss of the dolphins, Herman and his wife, childless into their middle years, had a baby. In 1980 Herman published his first book, an edited collection of papers on the mechanisms and functions of cetacean behavior, and dedicated it to Kea and Puka.

NOTES

1. Quotations, unless otherwise identified, are from interviews.
2. For Herman's "requiem," see *Honolulu Advertiser,* 8 June 1977. For related material, see *Honolulu Advertiser,* 30 May 1977, 3 June 1977; *Honolulu Star-Bulletin,* 20 December 1979, 20 January 1980, 30 July 1980.
3. Louis M. Herman, ed., *Cetacean Behavior: Mechanisms and Functions* (New York: John Wiley & Sons, 1980), 415n.
4. Arthur Lubow, "Riot in Fish Tank II," *New Times* (14 October 1977), 46.
5. Peter Morgane, "The Whale Brain: The Anatomical Basis of Intelligence," *Mind in the Waters,* ed. Joan McIntyre (New York: Charles Scribner's Sons, 1974), 84–93.
6. *Honolulu Advertiser,* 8 June 1977.
7. John C. Lilly, *Lilly on Dolphins* (New York, Anchor Press, 1975), 217 ff.
8. Interviews.
9. Donald R. Griffin, *The Question of Animal Awareness: Evolutionary Continuity of Mental Experience* (New York: Rockefeller University Press, 1976), 98.
10. Joan McIntyre, "Mind Play," *Mind in the Waters,* 95.
11. Charles Doria, "The Dolphin Ride," *Mind in the Waters,* 42–43.
12. Joan McIntyre, "Mashta," *Co-Evolution Quarterly* (Spring, 1974), 52.
13. Margaret Howe's notes are quoted in Lilly, *Lilly on Dolphins,* 173–182.
14. Gregory Bateson, "Observations of a Cetacean Community," *Mind in the Waters,* 163.
15. *Wall Street Journal,* 9 May 1972.
16. For a short discussion, centering on primate behavior, see Gordon G. Gallup, Jr., et al., "A Mirror for the Mind of Man, or Will the Chimpanzee Create an Identity Crisis for *Homo Sapiens?*" *Journal of Human Evolution* 6(1977), 303–313.
17. The literature is vast. Two useful accounts in nontechnical language are: Eugene Linden, *Apes, Men, and Language* (New York: Pelican Books, 1976); Adrian J. Desmond, *The Ape's Reflexion* (New York: Dial Press, 1979).
18. A brief nontechnical account of the issues in dispute is Beryl Lieff Benderly, "The Great Debate: Can Gorillas and Chimps Use Language or Not?" *Science* 80 (July–August, 1980), 61–65. See also Thomas Seboek and Donna Jean Umiker-Seboek, eds., *Speaking of Apes: A Critical Anthology of Two-Way Communication with Man* (New York: Plenum, 1980). For an informal account of a highly acrimonious conference on the subject, see *New Yorker,* 26 May 1980, 28–30.
19. Herbert S. Terrace, *Nim* (London: Eyre Methuen, 1980), 124. Mary is Mary Wambach. Nim's last name is Chimpsky. He was named after Noam Chomsky, the linguist adamant about the proposition that language is innate in human beings and in human beings alone, a product of the "deep structure" of the human brain and no other brain—species-specific. Project Nim was meant to discredit Chomsky's theories; but Terrace emerged instead skeptical about the linguistic capacities of chimpanzees. His "revisionist" book was one of the first manifestations of the "counteroffensive." By 1985, however, Terrace and some others were coming again to think language possible in chimpanzees on the basis of the accomplishments of a pygmy chimpanzee named Kanzi at the Yerkes Primate Center in Georgia.

20. Carl Sagan, *The Dragons of Eden: Speculations on the Evolution of Human Intelligence* (New York: Ballantine Books, 1977), 126.

21. John C. Lilly, "The Rights of Cetaceans under Human Laws," *Oceans* 9 (March, 1976), 66–68. Lilly later—in a great about-face—went back to working with captive dolphins. At the time of the Kewalo case, he published an article condemning Le Vasseur and Sipman for "illegal and revolutionary behavior" in having released dolphins not "theirs," and arguing in favor of research on dolphins in captivity as being for the ultimate benefit of dolphins in the wild. *Honolulu Advertiser,* 30 January 1978.

22. Le Vasseur's trial, in which the theory was first advanced, is discussed in Gavan Daws, "'Animal Liberation' as Crime: The Hawaii Dolphin Case," *Ethics and Animals,* eds. Harlan B. Miller and William H. Williams (Clifton, New Jersey: Humana Press, 1983), 361–371.

23. Discussion of the relations between human and animal rights and/or interests may be sampled in Peter Singer, *Animal Liberation: A New Ethics for Our Treatment of Animals* (New York: Avon Books, 1977); Stephen R. L. Clark, *The Moral Status of Animals* (Oxford: Clarendon Press, 1977); Mary Midgley, *Beast and Man: The Roots of Human Nature* (Ithaca: Cornell University Press, 1978); Mary Midgley, *Animals and Why They Matter* (Athens, Georgia: University of Georgia Press, 1974); John Passmore, *Man's Responsiblity for Nature: Ecological Problems and Western Traditions* (London: Duckworth, 1974); R. G. Frey, *Interests and Rights: The Case Against Animals* (Oxford: Clarendon Press, 1980); Tom Regan, *The Case for Animal Rights* (Berkeley: University of California Press, 1983). The literature, at book length and in scholarly and activist periodicals, is growing at a rapid rate.

V
OPERA VITAE

THE WRITINGS OF LEON EDEL

WILLIAM LASKOWSKI, JR.
(assisted by Vivian Cadbury)

THIS BIBLIOGRAPHY of Leon Edel's writings does not include his extensive earlier critical journalism and reportage on the arts written for newspapers: it confines itself to his writings in the field of biography, literary psychology, and literary criticism, as well as his book reviews in the familiar media. It lists most of his work from the time he began at twenty-two to appear in various journals in Canada. Those interested in his fugitive writings would have to pursue them through what he calls his juvenilia in *The McGill Fortnightly Review* (1925–1927); his cultural reportage from Europe mostly in the metropolitan daily, *The Montreal Star,* from 1928 to 1932—letters on theatre, music, literature in Paris, as well as some travelogues of his journeys to other parts of Europe; his subsequent writings as theatre, music, and cinema critic for the *Montreal Herald* during the Depression, from 1932 to 1934. From 1940 to 1942 he was on the cable desk of the Canadian Press in New York but he also reviewed various plays in New York as a "second nighter." These appeared in many Canadian newspapers. Finally, on his return from the war, during 1946–1948, he did some reviewing for the book page of the newspaper *PM,* with which he was affiliated in other capacities.

1929
1. "Montparnasse Letter." *The Canadian Mercury* 1:42.
2. "Montparnasse Letter." *The Canadian Mercury* 1:66.
3. "Montmartre Letter." *The Canadian Mercury* 1:121.

1930

4. "The New Writers—James Joyce." *Canadian Forum* 10: 329–330.
5. "The Eternal Footman Snickers." Short story. *Canadian Forum* 11: 96, 98.
6. "A Note on Translations of H. James in France." *Revue Anglo-Américaine* 7: 539–540.
7. "Letters of Henry James." Review of *Letters to A. C. Benson and Auguste Monod by Henry James,* ed. E. F. Benson. *Canadian Forum* 11: 112.
8. Letter to the editor on James's letters to Benson and Monod. *Times Literary Supplement* 2 October: 782.

1931

9. *Henry James: Les Années Dramatiques.* Paris: Jouve et Cie. Reprint Folcroft, Pennsylvania: Folcroft Press, 1969; Norwood, Pennsylvania: Norwood Editions, 1978.
10. *The Prefaces of Henry James.* Paris: Jouve et Cie. Xerographic reprint, Ann Arbor, Michigan: University Microfilms, 1970. Folcroft, Pennsylvania: Folcroft Press, 1970; Norwood, Pennsylvania: Norwood Editions, 1977. These volumes, LE's dissertations for the French State Degree of Doctor of Letters, were printed in two editions. The first was a limited edition of ninety copies, bound in brownish-green wrappers. On the cover of *Les Années Dramatiques* the words "Thèse Principale pour le Doctorat ès Lettres" were printed below the title. Under *The Prefaces of Henry James* the subtitle was "Thèse Complémentaire pour le Doctorat ès Lettres." The trade edition, 300 copies bound in white wrappers, carried the titles lettered in red without allusion to the theses.
11. "A Paris Letter." *Canadian Forum* 11: 460. An account of the reading at Adrienne Monnier's bookshop of the French translation of "Anna Livia Plurabelle" from James Joyce's *Work in Progress,* later known as *Finnegans Wake.*

1932

12. "Canadian Writers of Today—Abraham M. Klein." *Canadian Forum* 12: 300–302.

13. "An Amazing Family." Review of *The Three Jameses* by C. Hartley Grattan, and *Theatre and Friendship*, ed. Elizabeth Robins. *Saturday Review of Literature* 12 November: 236.

1933

14. "Canadian Writers of the Past—Alan Macdermott." LE invented a writer with a Jamesian past. *Canadian Forum* 13: 221–222.

15. "The Exile of Henry James." *University of Toronto Quarterly* 2: 520–532.

15a. "Films and Propaganda." *The Alarm Clock* (publication of the McGill Labor Club) 2 (November): 9.

16. Review of *Are We All Met?* by Whitford J. Kane. *Canadian Forum* 13: 155.

17. Review of *Poetry Year Book* of the Canadian Authors' Association, *Poems* by Laurence Dakin, and *The Wind in the Field* by Leo Cox. *Canadian Forum* 13: 155–156.

18. "Tempest in a Tea-Cup." Review of *The Shakespearian Tempest* by G. Wilson Knight, and *Elizabethan Stage Conditions* by M. C. Bradbrook. *Canadian Forum* 13: 272–273.

19. "Friendly Correspondence." Review of *Letters of Mrs. Gaskell to Charles Eliot Norton*, ed. Jane Whitehill. *Canadian Forum* 13: 314.

1934

20. "Europe from the Cable Desk." *Canadian Forum* 15: 57–58.

21. "Freedom of the Birds." Review of *Icaro* by Lauro de Bosis, ed. Ruth Draper, and *The Tragedy of Man* by Imre Murdoch. *Canadian Forum* 14: 232–233.

22. "Sir Richard Steele Lives Again." Review of *Sir Richard Steele* by Willard Connolly. *McGill News* 15 (December): 42.

1935

23. "Sean O'Casey." Toronto *Saturday Night* 9 March: 13.

1936

24. "New York Letter." *New Frontier* 1: 25–26.

1937

25. "Eugene O'Neill: The Face and the Mask." *University of Toronto Quarterly* 7: 18–34.

1938

26. "Two Volumes of Memoirs." Review of *Memoirs of Julian Haw-
    thorne,* and *Three Rousing Cheers* by Elizabeth Jordan. *McGill
    News* 19 (Autumn): 31–32.
27. "Novelized 'Life.'" Review of *Fanny Kemble: A Passionate Vic-
    torian* by Margaret Armstrong. *McGill News* 20 (Winter):
    35–36.

1939

28. "The McGill Fortnightly Review: A Casual Reminiscence."
    McGill News 21 (Autumn): 1, 19–22, 61.
29. "James Joyce and His New Work." Review of *Finnegans Wake.*
    University of Toronto Quarterly 9: 66–81.
30. "Henry James Discoveries." Letter to "Bibliographical Notes."
    Times Literary Supplement 29 July: 460.

1940

31. "Editing the War News." *McGill News* 22 (Winter): 11–12, 24.

1941

32. "Henry James: The War Chapter, 1914–1916." *University of
    Toronto Quarterly* 10: 125–138.
33. "Poetry and the Jewish Tradition." Review of *Hath Not a Jew* by
    A. M. Klein. *Poetry* 58: 51–53.
34. "The Poet as Journalist." Review of *New Poems,* ed. Oscar
    Williams. *Poetry* 58: 215–219.
35. "A Henry James Essay." Letter to the editor on the first appear-
    ance of James's appeal for the American Volunteer Motor
    Ambulance Brigade. *Times Literary Supplement* 24 May:
    251, 253.

1943

36. "Henry James and the Poets." *Poetry* 62: 328–334.
37. "Propaganda for Poetry." Review of *A Treasury of Great Poems,*
    ed. Louis Untermeyer. *Poetry* 62: 45–48.

1944

38. "The Question of Canadian Identity." *Canadian Accent: A Col-
    lection of Stories and Poems,* ed. Ralph Gustafson. Harmonds-
    worth: Penguin. 68–71.

1947

39. *James Joyce: The Last Journey.* New York: Gotham Book Mart. Reprint Brooklyn, New York: Haskell House, 1977. See also item 43.
40. Introduction. *The Other House* by Henry James. Norfolk, Connecticut: New Directions; London: Hart-Davis, 1948. vii–xxi.
41. "Portrait of a Professor: G. W. Latham." *McGill News* 28 (Summer): 8–10.
42. "The Major Phase of Henry James." Review of *Henry James: The Major Phase* by F. O. Matthiessen. *University of Toronto Quarterly* 16: 424–428.

1948

43. "The Last Days of James Joyce." *Story Magazine* 32: 139–147. Revised version of item 39.
44. "The James Revival." *Atlantic Monthly* September: 96–98.
45. Review of *The Legend of the Master* by Simon Nowell-Smith. *New England Quarterly* 21: 544–547.

1949

46. Editor. *The Complete Plays of Henry James.* Philadelphia: Lippincott; London: Hart-Davis; Toronto: Longmans. Introductory essay, "Henry James: The Dramatic Years," 19–69, and prefaces to the nineteen plays and scenarios. Micropaque reprint New York: Readex Microprints, 1979.
47. Foreword. *Henry James: The Scenic Art,* ed. Allan Wade. London: Hart-Davis; New Brunswick, New Jersey: Rutgers University Press. v–viii.
48. "Henry James and *The Outcry*." *University of Toronto Quarterly* 18: 340–346.
49. "The Text of Henry James's Unpublished Plays." *Harvard Library Bulletin* 3: 395–406.
50. Review of *Henry James and the Expanding Horizon* by Osborn Andreas. *American Literature* 21: 362–364.
51. "Henry James Reprints." Letter to the editor. *Times Literary Supplement* 12 March: 169.
52. Letter to the editor about G. W. Johnson and American writing. *New York Times Book Review* 15 May: 25.

1950

53. Editor. *The Ghostly Tales of Henry James.* [Title page errone-
    ously gives year of publication as 1949.] New Brunswick,
    New Jersey: Rutgers University Press; Toronto: Smithers.
    Introduction, v–viii, and headnotes to the eighteen tales,
    with the exception of "The Turn of the Screw," which has
    the equivalent of a full-length preface. See also items 212
    and 326.

54. "James and Joyce: The Future of the Novel." *Tomorrow* 9 (Au-
    gust): 53–56. Published separately as *The Future of the Novel,
    James and Joyce.* New York: Garrett.

55. Program note on the play *Disengaged* by Henry James, produced
    by the Idler Players at Radcliffe College. May 4, 5, and 6:
    2, 5.

56. Review of *The Crooked Corridor* by Elizabeth Stevenson, *Henry
    James and the Expanding Horizon* by Osborn Andreas, and
    Henry James and Robert Louis Stevenson, ed. Janet Adam Smith.
    New England Quarterly 23: 245–249.

57. Review of *Recollections of Logan Pearsall Smith,* ed. Robert
    Gathorne-Hardy. *Tomorrow* 9 (July): 58–59.

58. Review of *Berlioz and the Romantic Century* by Jacques Barzun.
    Tomorrow 10 (September): 55–56.

59. "Tales That James Forgot." Review of *Eight Uncollected Tales of
    Henry James,* ed. Edna Kenton. *New York Times Book Review*
    10 September: 5.

60. Letter to the editor about a review of Henry James. *New York
    Times Book Review* 13 August: 23.

61. Letter to the editors on Marius Bewley's views of Henry James.
    Scrutiny 17: 53–55.

1951

62. "The Architecture of James's New York Edition." *New England
    Quarterly* 24: 169–178.

63. "Hugh Walpole and Henry James: The Fantasy of 'The Killer
    and the Slain.'" *American Imago* 8: 351–369.

64. "Notes on the Use of Psychological Tools in Literary Scholar-
    ship." *Literature and Psychology* 1 (4): 1–3.

65. "A Further Note on 'An Error in *The Ambassadors.*'" *American
    Literature* 23: 128–130.

66. "He Introduced Us to Omar Khayyam." Review of *Thomas*

Sergeant Perry: A Biography and Letters to Perry from William, Henry, and Garth Wilkinson James by Virginia Harlow. *New York Times Book Review* 4 February: 3.

67. "Mr. James, Disentangled." Review of *Henry James* by F. W. Dupee. *New York Times Book Review* 8 April : 5.

68. "Battler Against Shams." Review of *The Philosophy of Henry James Sr.* by Frederic Young. *New York Times Book Review* 22 July: 6, 20.

69. "A Rounded Picture." Review of *Henry James* by F. W. Dupee. *The Hopkins Review* 4: 58–60.

70. "The Versatile James." Review of *The Portable Henry James,* ed. Morton Dauwen Zabel. *Nation* 10 November: 406–408.

71. "Two Innocents at Home." Review of *Turn West, Turn East: Mark Twain and Henry James* by Henry Seidel Canby. *New York Times Book Review* 11 November: 8.

72. Review of *Thomas Sergeant Perry* by Virgina Harlow. *American Literature* 23: 373–376.

73. Review of *Living Ideas in America* by Henry Steele Commager. *Book Find News* nos. 112–113.

1952

74. "*The Aspern Papers:* Great-Aunt Wyckoff and Juliana Bordereau." *Modern Language Notes* 67: 392–395.

75. Letter to the editor on Henry James's Order of Merit. *New York Times Magazine* 13 January: 4.

76. Letter to the editor about an error in *The Ambassadors.* (See item 65.) *American Literature* 24: 370–372.

1953

77. *Henry James: The Untried Years, 1843–1870.* The first volume of *The Life of Henry James.* Philadelphia: Lippincott; London: Hart-Davis; Toronto: Longmans.

78. Co-author, with E. K. Brown. *Willa Cather: A Critical Biography.* Completed by Leon Edel. New York: Knopf. Editor's Foreword (xvii–xxiv), Chapters 4 and 5 (74–124), Epilogue (320–341), and portions of Chapter 9 were written by LE. Reissued New York: Avon, 1980.

79. Editor. *Henry James: Selected Fiction.* New York: Everyman's Library-Dutton. Introduction, ix–xix, and notes. Reprinted New York: Dutton, 1964.

80. Editor. *The Sacred Fount* by Henry James. New York: Grove

Press. Introductory essay, v–xxxii. Reprinted in *Henry James's Major Novels: Essays in Criticism*. Ed. Lyall H. Powers. East Lansing: Michigan State University Press, 1973. 205–223.

81. Editor. "Henry James in Harley Street" by Harold L. Rypins. Edited and annotated by LE for the light it throws on "The Turn of the Screw." *American Literature* 24: 481–492.

82. "Willa Cather's Canada." A chapter from Brown's *Cather* (item 78) annotated by LE. *University of Toronto Quarterly* 22: 184–196.

83. "Jonathan Sturges." *Princeton University Library Bulletin* 15: 1–9.

84. Unsigned biographical note to a reprint of Henry James's review of *Middlemarch* by George Eliot. *Nineteenth-Century Fiction* 8: 161.

85. "The Gift Was Rubbing Off." Review of *Edith Wharton: A Study of Her Fiction* by Blake Nevius. *New York Times Book Review* 28 June: 7.

86. "A Fluid Portrait." Review of *Portrait of André Gide* by Justin O'Brien. *New Republic* 31 August: 18–19.

87. "The Call of the Wild." Review of *Rebels and Ancestors: The American Novel, 1890–1915* by Maxwell Geismar. *New York Times Book Review* 27 September: 7, 42.

88. "The Thing Remembered." Review of *Willa Cather: A Memoir* by Elizabeth Shepley Sergeant. *New York Times Book Review* 11 October: 5, 25.

89. "A Man of Convictions." Review of *Ideas and Places* by Cyril Connolly. *New Republic* 7 December: 16.

1954

90. "Willa Cather's *The Professor's House:* An Inquiry into the Use of Psychology in Literary Criticism." *Literature and Psychology* 4 (December): 66–79.

91. "Henry James and Vernon Lee." *PMLA* 69: 677–678.

92. "A Buried Life." Review of *The Ordeal of George Meredith* by Lionel Stevenson. *New Republic* 4 January: 19.

93. "Tolstoy's View of History." Review of *The Hedgehog and the Fox* by Isaiah Berlin. *Nation* 13 March: 223–224.

94. "A Critic's Memoirs." Review of *Scenes and Portraits* by Van Wyck Brooks. *New Republic* 22 March: 20.

95. "'Superstitious' Valuations." Unsigned review of *The Complex Fate* by Marius Bewley. *Nation* 10 April: 11.

96. "The Two Flauberts." Review of *Selected Letters of Flaubert,* ed. Francis Steegmuller; and *Bouvard et Pécuchet* and *The Dictionary of [Received] Accepted Ideas. Nation* 24 April: 361–362.

97. "A Backward Glance." Review of *Politics and Opinion in the 19th Century* by John Bowle. *Nation* 7 August: 118.

98. "The Smiling and Unsmiling Aspects." Review of *Howells and the Age of Realism* by Everett Carter. *New York Times Book Review* 14 November: 4.

99. "Miss Glasgow's Private World." Review of *The Woman Within* by Ellen Glasgow. *New Republic* 15 November: 20–21.

100. Review of *Three Men* by Jean Evans. *Book Find News* nos. 156–157.

101. Review of *The Thought and Character of William James* (abridged one-volume edition) by Ralph Barton Perry. *Book Find News* no. 162.

102. "Edna Kenton." Letter to the editor on her death. *New York Times Book Review* 18 April: 25.

1955

103. *The Psychological Novel, 1900–1950.* Philadelphia: Lippincott; London: Hart-Davis. Reprinted New York: Haskell House, 1966. See also items 172 and 225.

104. Editor. *The Selected Letters of Henry James.* New York: Farrar, Straus, and Cudahy; London: Hart-Davis, 1956. A Note on the Text, vii–viii. Acknowledgment, ix–x. Introduction, xiii–xxx. James Family and Other Correspondents, xxxi–xxxiv. Reprint Garden City: Anchor-Doubleday, 1960.

105. Discussion with Alfred Kazin and Lyman Bryson of William James's letters, originally broadcast by CBS radio 5 June 1955. *Invitation to Learning Reader.* Ed. Ralph Backlund. New York: Muschel. 5 (#18, "Self-Revelation"): 176–185.

106. Discussion with Maxwell Geismar and Lyman Bryson of *The Professor's House* by Willa Cather, originally broadcast by CBS radio 2 October 1955. *Invitation to Learning Reader.* Ed. Ralph Backlund. New York: Muschel. 5 (#20, "Reappraisals"): 397–402. Reprinted in *Invitation to Learning: English and American Novels.* Ed. George D. Crothers. New York: Basic Books, 1966. 282–289.

107. "Time and the Biographer." *New Republic* 21 February: 19–21.

108. "The Art of Evasion." Hemingway and the Nobel Prize. *Folio*

20: 18–20. Reprinted in *Hemingway: A Collection of Critical Essays*. Ed. Robert P. Weeks. Englewood Cliffs, New Jersey: Prentice-Hall, 1962. 169–171.

109. "Time and the Biographer: Leon Edel on Writing about Henry James." *Listener* 22 September: 461–462.

110. "The Choice So Freely Made." A reappraisal of James's *The Portrait of a Lady*. *New Republic* 26 September: 26–28.

111. "Henry James's Revisions of *The Ambassadors*." *Notes and Queries* ns 2 (1): 37–38.

112. "Mr. Allan Wade: Studies of an Edwardian Era." Obituary tribute. *Times* (London) 27 July: 12.

113. "No More Opinions . . . No More Politics." Review of *The Letters of W. B. Yeats,* ed. Allan Wade. *New Republic* 14 March: 21–22.

114. "The Fulgent Age of Flux." Review of *The Twenties* by Frederick J. Hoffman. *Saturday Review* 26 March: 17–18.

115. "With Vigor and Wit." Review of *The Lion and the Honeycomb* by R. P. Blackmur. *New York Times Book Review* 17 April: 4.

116. "The Mocking Madonna." Review of *The Moth and the Star* (Virginia Woolf) by Aileen Pippett. *Saturday Review* 23 September: 13–14.

117. "Crossing the Critics." Review of *Longfellow: A Full-Length Portrait* by Edward Wagenknecht. *Saturday Review* 5 November: 20, 39–40.

118. "Mind, No Biography." Review of *Thackeray: The Uses of Adversity* by Gordon N. Ray. *New Republic* 7 November: 17–18.

119. "Remembering at Middle Age." Review of *The Whispering Gallery* by John Lehmann. *New Republic* 21 November: 26–27.

120. "Full-Length Prophet." Review of *Henry Adams* by Elizabeth Stevenson. *Saturday Review* 10 December: 15–16.

121. "The Making of an American." Review of *The American Adam* by R. W. B. Lewis. *New York Times Book Review* 25 December: 4.

122. Letter to the editors about J. Korg's review of *The Psychological Novel*. *Nation* 27 August: 12.

1956

123. Editor. *The American Essays of Henry James*. New York: Vintage-Knopf. Introduction, v–xvii.

124. Editor. *The Future of the Novel: Essays on the Art of Fiction* by Henry James. New York: Vintage-Knopf. Introduction, [v]–xvi.

125. Editor. *The Portrait of a Lady* by Henry James. Boston: Riverside-Houghton Mifflin. Introduction, v–xx. See also item 219.

126. Various entries in *The Reader's Companion to World Literature*. Ed. Lillian Herlands Hornstein. New York: Holt, Rinehart and Winston. Contains entries on *The Ambassadors*, 16–17; T. S. Eliot, 145–147; William Faulkner, 162–163; Ernest Hemingway, 204–205; Henry James, 231–234; James Joyce, 238–240; *The Magic Mountain*, 264–265; Thomas Mann, 268–270; Marcel Proust, 368–371; the Stream-of-Consciousness Novel, 426; *The Waste Land*, 477–478; and Virginia Woolf, 484–485. See also item 362.

127. "Dorothy Richardson, Feminine Realist." ("Novelists of Influence—VII.") London *Times Educational Supplement* 1 June: 743.

128. "That One May Say This Was the Man. The Biographer Must Blow the Breath of Life Into Inert Bits of the Past." *New York Times Book Review* 24 June: 1.

129. "'A Tragedy of Error': James's First Story." Reprint with a prefatory note of the anonymous story published in the February 1864 *Continental Monthly* [5 (2): 204–216]. *New England Quarterly* 29: 291–295.

130. "Rousseau in Our Time." Review of *Jean-Jacques Rousseau* by F. C. Green. *Nation* 14 January: 36–37.

131. Review of *Transatlantic Migration: The Contemporary American Novel in France* by Thelma M. Smith and Ward L. Miner. *American Literature* 28: 99–101.

132. "Art and the Critic." Review of *Critical Approaches to Literature* by David Daiches. *New York Times Book Review* 15 April: 3.

133. "The Art of Remembering." Review of *The Flowers of the Forest* by David Garnett. *New Republic* 24 September: 20–21.

134. "In the Days of Poe and Melville." Review of *The Raven and the Whale* by Perry Miller. *New Republic* 4 June: 22.

135. "The Measurement of an Era." Review of *The Energies of Art* by Jacques Barzun. *Saturday Review* 6 October: 25.

136. "A Tragedy of Arrested Adolescence." Review of *With Love*

from Gracie by Grace Hegger Lewis. *New Republic* 15 October: 29.

137. "Nebraskan Abroad." Review of *Willa Cather in Europe,* ed. George N. Kates. *New York Times Book Review* 21 October: 6, 50.

138. "The Critic en Pantouffles." Review of *A Gathering of Fugitives* by Lionel Trilling. *New Republic* 19 November: 25–26.

139. ". . . Am I Then in a Pocket of the Past?" Review of *A Piece of My Mind* by Edmund Wilson. *New Republic* 17 December: 25–26.

1957

140. *Literary Biography: The Alexander Lectures 1955–1956.* Toronto: Toronto University Press; London: Hart-Davis. See also items 173, 358, and 479.

141. Co-author, with Dan H. Laurence. *A Bibliography of Henry James.* London: Hart-Davis. The Soho Bibliographies no. 8. Fair Lawn, New Jersey: Essential Books, 1958. See also items 192 and 445.

142. Editor. *The House of Fiction: Essays on the Novel* by Henry James. London: Hart-Davis. Introduction, 9–19. Reprint London: Mercury Books, 1962; Westport, Connecticut: Greenwood Press, 1973 and 1976.

143. Co-editor, with Ilse D. Lind. *Henry James: Parisian Sketches.* (James's letters to the *New York Tribune* 1875–1876.) New York: New York University Press. London: Hart-Davis, 1958. Introduction, v–xxxvii. Reprinted New York: Collier, 1961. Reprint Westport, Connecticut: Greenwood Press, 1978.

144. Preface. *We'll to the Woods No More* by Édouard Dujardin. New York: New Directions. vii–xxvii.

145. "James Joyce and the Academician." *A James Joyce Miscellany.* New York: The James Joyce Society. 44–48. Reprinted as the Preface to *Claybook for James Joyce* by Louis Gillet. Trans. George Markow-Totevy. New York: Abelard-Schumann, 1958. 7–11.

146. Discussion with Alfred Kazin and Lyman Bryson of *The American Scene* by Henry James, originally broadcast by CBS radio 27 May 1956. *Invitation to Learning Reader.* Ed. Ralph Backlund. New York: Muschel. 6 (#22–23, "The 'Other' Book & Strange Landscapes"): 145–154.

147. "Autobiography in Fiction: An Unpublished Review by Henry James." *Harvard Library Bulletin* 11: 245–257.

148. "The Literary Convictions of Henry James." *Modern Fiction Studies* 3: 3–10.

149. Prefatory Note to "A Pre-Freudian Reading of 'The Turn of the Screw'" by Harold C. Goddard. *Nineteenth-Century Fiction* 12: 1–3.

150. "A Novelist With a Painter's Eye." Review of *Henry James: The Painter's Eye,* ed. John L. Sweeney. *New York Times Book Review* 24 February: 16.

151. "Genesis of a Justice." Review of *Justice Holmes: The Shaping Years* by Mark De Wolfe Howe. *New Republic* 8 April: 19.

152. "The Isolation of James Joyce." Review of *Letters of James Joyce,* ed. Stuart Gilbert. *New Republic* 10 June: 16–17.

153. Review of *On Poetry and Poets* by T. S. Eliot. *Playbill* 7 October: 48.

154. "Looking into the Artist's Deeper Self." Review of *Art and Psychoanalysis,* ed. William Phillips. *New York Times Book Review* 27 October: 6.

155. "Plutarch's Art." Review of *The Nature of Biography* by John A. Garraty. *Saturday Review* 16 November: 21–22.

156. "Throttling the Voice of Passion." Review of *Byron: A Biography* by Leslie A. Marchand. *New Republic* 2 December: 17–18.

157. Review of *Louis Jouvet* by Bettina L. Knapp, and *Scandal and Parade* by Jean Cocteau. *Playbill* 2 December: 55.

158. Review of *Old Vic Drama* by Audrey Williamson. *Playbill* 2 December: 55.

159. Review note of *Early Stories of Willa Cather,* ed. Mildred Bennett. *Saturday Review* 8 June: 18.

160. "Henry James's Ancestry." Letter to the editor. *Times Literary Supplement* 8 March: 145.

161. "The American Henry James." Letter to the editor on Quentin Anderson's study. *Times Literary Supplement* 19 July: 441.

1958

162. Co-editor, with Lyall H. Powers. "Henry James and the *Bazar* Letters." *Bulletin of the New York Public Library* 62: 75–103. Prefatory essay 75–82. Reprinted by the library as a pamphlet (with "Novel-Writing and Novel-Reading" by W. D. Howells). New York: New York Public Library, 1962.

163. Co-editor, with Gordon N. Ray. *Henry James and H. G. Wells: A Record of Their Friendship, Their Debate on the Art of Fiction, and Their Quarrel.* Urbana: University of Illinois Press; London: Hart-Davis. Introduction, 9–41. Photocopy reprint Ann Arbor, Michigan: University Microfilms, 1971. Reprint Westport, Connecticut: Greenwood Press, 1979.

164. "Dorothy Richardson, 1882 [1873]–1957." *Modern Fiction Studies* 4: 165–168.

165. "Time and *The Ambassadors.*" *Modern Language Notes* 73: 177–179.

166. Review of *The American Henry James* by Quentin Anderson. *American Literature* 29: 493–495.

167. "Postal Portrait." Review of *Letters of Ellen Glasgow,* ed. Blair Rouse. *Saturday Review* 18 January: 17.

168. "Short Turns With a Man of Many Parts." Review of *A Henry Adams Reader,* ed. Elizabeth Stevenson. *New York Times Book Review* 23 February: 43.

169. Review of *My Brother's Keeper* by Stanislaus Joyce. *Book Find News* nos. 220–221: 3–4.

170. Review of *Versions of Melodrama: Fiction and Drama of Henry James, 1865–1897* by Leo B. Levy. *American Literature* 30: 251–252.

171. "Cosmopolitan American." Review of *The Image of Europe in Henry James* by Christof Wegelin. *New York Times Book Review* 17 August: 4.

1959

172. *The Modern Psychological Novel.* New York: Grove Press. Revised version of item 103.

173. *Literary Biography.* Garden City: Anchor-Doubleday Books. Reprint, with additional material (see item 174), of item 140.

174. Co-editor, with Thomas H. Johnson, Sherman Paul, and Claude Simpson. *Masters of American Literature.* Gen. ed. Gordon N. Ray. 2 vols. Boston: Houghton Mifflin. The Hawthorne section in vol. I (571–723) and the James (397–610), O'Neill (689–753), Eliot (781–849) and Faulkner (850–931) in vol. II are edited by LE. A shorter edition in one volume appeared in 1959. The T. S. Eliot essay (781–789) in revised form was used in item 173.

175. New Introduction to *The Sacred Fount* by Henry James. London: Hart-Davis. 5–15.

176. Special Introduction for the Japanese edition of item 172. See *Translated Writings* below.

177. Co-author, with Simon Nowell-Smith. "H. J." Letter to the editor of the *Times* (London) on the inclusion of Henry James as a character in Michael Redgrave's production of "The Aspern Papers." 18 August: 9.

1960

178. *Henry James.* University of Minnesota Pamphlets on American Writers no. 4. Minneapolis: University of Minnesota Press; London: Oxford University Press. Reprinted in *Six American Novelists of the Nineteenth Century.* Ed. Richard Foster. Minneapolis: University of Minnesota Press, 1968. 191–225. See also item 211.

179. *Willa Cather, The Paradox of Success.* A lecture delivered under the auspices of the Gertrude Clarke Wittall Poetry and Literature Fund in the Coolidge Auditorium, Library of Congress, 12 October 1959. Printed as a pamphlet, Washington, D.C.: Reference Department, Library of Congress. Reprinted in *Literary Lectures Presented at the Library of Congress.* Washington, D.C.: Library of Congress, 1973. 350–367. Reprinted in *Willa Cather and Her Critics.* Ed. James Schroeter. Ithaca, New York: Cornell University Press, 1967. 249–271.

180. Editor. *The Ambassadors* by Henry James. Boston: Riverside-Houghton Mifflin. Introduction, v–xvi.

181. Editor. *Guy Domville: A Play in Three Acts* by Henry James. Philadelphia: Lippincott. London: Hart-Davis, 1961. The introduction (13–121) reprints "Henry James: The Dramatic Years" from *The Complete Plays of Henry James* (item 46). Micropaque reprint of Hart-Davis ed. New York: Reader Microprint, 1979.

182. Editor. *The Tragic Muse* by Henry James. New York: Harper Torchbook. Introduction, vii–xvii.

183. Editor. *Roderick Hudson* by Henry James. New York: Harper Torchbook. London: Hart-Davis, 1961. Introduction, vii–xvii.

184. Editor. *Watch and Ward* by Henry James. New York: Grove Press; London: Hart-Davis. Introduction, 5–18.

185. Address by LE, as president of the American P. E. N., on the Congress theme, "Imaginative Literature in the Age of Science." Proceedings of the 30th P. E. N. Congress, *P. E. N.*

XXX Kongress des Internationalen P. E. N. Frankfurt Am Mein.
Darmstadt: Roetherdruck. 156–162.

186. "The Text of *The Ambassadors.*" *The Harvard Library Bulletin*
14: 453–460. Reprinted in *Twentieth Century Interpretations
of* The Ambassadors. Ed. Albert E. Stone Jr. Englewood
Cliffs, New Jersey: Prentice-Hall. 88–95.

187. "Who *Was* Gilbert Osmond?" *Modern Fiction Studies* 6: 164.

188. "He Kept His Audience Well Posted." Review of *The Selected
Letters of Charles Dickens,* ed. F. W. Dupee. *Saturday Review*
23 April: 48–49.

189. "A Bat for a Butterfly." Review of *The Landscape and the Looking Glass: Willa Cather's Search for Value* by John H. Randall.
Saturday Review 25 June: 25, 35.

190. "All Is Not Solitude." Review of *The Oxford Book of Canadian
Verse,* ed. A. J. M. Smith. *New York Times Book Review*
27 November: 5, 61.

191. Letter to the editor on Morton D. Zabel's *The Art of Ruth
Draper. New York Times Book Review* 3 July: 12.

1961

192. Co-author, with Dan H. Laurence. *A Bibliography of Henry
James*. 2nd. ed. London: Hart-Davis. Revised and augmented
version of item 141.

193. Co-editor, with Elizabeth Whitee and Madolyn Brown. *5
World Biographies.* An anthology. New York: Harcourt, Brace
& World. Includes preface [vi] and afterwords: to Plutarch's
Caesar, 52–57; to Vasari's *Michaelangelo,* 104–108; to E. Lud-
wig's *Napoleon,* 419–423; to E. Curie's *Madame Curie,* 710–
714; to V. Sheehan's *Gandhi,* 840–844.

194. Foreword. *Pulitzer Prize Reader,* compiled by Leo Hamalian
and Edmond Volpe. New York: Popular Classic Library.
13–14.

195. "Literature and Psychology." *Comparative Literature: Method
and Perspective.* Ed. Newton P. Stallknecht and Horst Frenz.
Carbondale: Southern Illinois University Press. 96–115. Revised edition by Southern Illinois University Press and London: Feffer & Simons, 1971. 122–144. Revised and included
in *Encyclopedia of World Literature in the 20th Century.* Gen. ed.
Wolfgang Fleischmann. 3 vols. New York: Ungar, 1967. 3:
123–131. In the German "Psychologie U. Literatur." *Lexicon
der Weltliteratur im 20. Jahrhundert.* 2 vols. Freiberg: Herder,

1960, 1961. 2: 698–704. In the Italian, *Dizionario della lettera-
tura mondiale del Novecento.*

196. "The Biographer and Psychoanalysis." *International Journal of
Psychoanalysis* 42: 458–466. Reprinted in abridged form in
New World Writing no. 18. Philadelphia: Lippincott. 50–64.
Also reprinted in *Biography as an Art.* Ed. James L. Clifford.
New York: Oxford University Press, 1962. 226–239.

197. "Criticism and Psychoanalysis: Notes on the Two Disciplines." *Chicago Review* 15 (2): 100–109.

198. "Henry James and the Short Story." *Story Magazine* 34 (November): 83–88.

199. "From a Worshipful Friend." Review of *The Last Days of
Shelley and Byron* (Trelawney's recollections), ed. J. E. Mor-
purgo. *New York Times Book Review* (II) 15 January: 12.

200. "The Enduring Fame of Henry James." Review of vols. I and
II of the Scribner reprint of the *New York Edition of Novels
and Tales* by Henry James. *New York Times Book Review*
3 September: 1, 16–17. Reprinted in *Opinions and Perspec-
tives.* Ed. Francis Brown. Boston: Houghton Mifflin, 1964.
102–109.

201. Review of *The Comic Sense of Henry James* by Richard Poirier.
American Literature 33: 87–88.

202. Obituary letter to the *Times* (London) on the late William
("Billy") James. 10 October: 14.

1962

203. *Henry James: The Conquest of London, 1870–1881.* The second
volume of *The Life of Henry James.* Philadelphia: Lippincott;
London: Hart-Davis.

204. *Henry James: The Middle Years, 1882–1895.* The third volume
of *The Life of Henry James.* Philadelphia: Lippincott; London:
Hart-Davis. Reprint Ann Arbor, Michigan: University
Microfilms International, 1980.

Editor. *The Complete Tales of Henry James.* Philadelphia: Lippincott; London: Hart-Davis. (See 205–208 below.)

205. Vol. 1. General Introduction, 7–16. Introduction 1864–1868,
17–22.

206. Vol. 2. Introduction 1868–1872, 7–11.

207. Vol. 3. Introduction 1873–1875, 7–10.

208. Vol. 4. Introduction 1876–1882, 7–11.

209. "How to Read *The Sound and the Fury.*" *Varieties of Literary*

Experience: Eighteen Essays in World Literature. Ed. Stanley
Burnshaw. New York: New York University Press. 241–257.
Reprinted in item 225, *The Modern Psychological Novel.*
162–176.

210. "Brooks as Biographer." Review of *Fenollosa and His Circle
with Other Essays in Biography* by Van Wyck Brooks. *New
Republic* 17 September: 23–24.

1963

211. *Henry James.* Revised edition of item 178. Minneapolis: Uni-
versity of Minnesota Press. Microfiche reprint Millwood,
New York: KTO Microfilms, 1971. Microfilm reprint St.
Paul, Minnesota: International Microfilm Press, 1971.

212. Editor. *The Ghostly Tales of Henry James.* New York: Universal
Library–Grosset & Dunlap. Reprint of item 53. New Introduction, [v]–viii. See also item 326.

Editor. *The Complete Tales of Henry James.* Philadelphia: Lippincott; London: Hart-Davis. (See 213–216 below.)

213. Vol. 5. Introduction 1883–1884, 7–11.

214. Vol. 6. Introduction 1884–1888, 7–12.

215. Vol. 7. Introduction 1888–1891, 7–13.

216. Vol. 8. Introduction 1891–1892, 7–12.

217. Editor. *Henry James: A Collection of Critical Essays.* Twentieth
Century Views. Englewood Cliffs, New Jersey: Prentice-
Hall. Introduction, 1–10.

218. Editor. *The American* by Henry James. New York: Signet-
New American Library. Afterword, 326–333.

219. Editor. *The Portrait of a Lady* by Henry James. Boston: Riverside-Houghton Mifflin. Revised version of item 125.

220. "Henry James Sr." Text of address "Fathers and Sons" on LE's
receiving honorary degree from Union College (of which
Henry James Sr. was an alumnus). *Union Worthies* no. 18.
Schenectady, New York: Union College. 12–20.

221. Passage on "Winterbourne and Marcher." *James's* Daisy Miller*: The Story, the Play, the Critics.* Ed. William Stafford. New
York: Scribner's Research Anthologies. 154.

222. "Critics in Conference." Unsigned report and commentary
on the Ninth Congress of the International Federation for
Modern Languages and Literature (FILLM), held at New
York University, 25 to 31 August 1963. *Times Literary Supplement* 27 September: 745.

223. "Miller: Milder than 'Tropics.'" Review of *Black Spring* by Henry Miller. *New York Herald Tribune Books* 14 April: 3, 11.

224. "Persuader." Review of *Henry Wikoff: A Biography* by Duncan Crow. *New Statesman* 13 December: 882–883.

1964

225. *The Modern Psychological Novel.* New York: Grosset Universal Library. Further revision, with additional chapters (including item 209) in "Part Two: Modes of Subjectivity," of items 103 and 172. Reprint Gloucester, Massachusetts: Peter Smith, 1972.

Editor. *The Complete Tales of Henry James.* Philadelphia: Lippincott; London: Hart-Davis. (See 226–229 below.)

226. Vol. 9. Introduction 1892–1898, 7–12.

227. Vol. 10. Introduction 1898–1899, 7–13.

228. Vol. 11. Introduction 1900–1903, 7–11.

229. Vol. 12. Introduction 1903–1910, 7–11.

230. Editor. *The Diary of Alice James.* New York: Dodd, Mead; London: Hart-Davis, 1965. Preface, v–x. "Portrait of Alice James," 1–21. Reprinted New York: Apollo-Dodd, Mead 1966. See also item 450.

231. Editor. *Henry James: French Poets and Novelists.* New York: Universal Library-Grosset & Dunlap. Introduction, vii–xi.

232. "Sex and the Novel." *New York Times Book Review* 1 November: 2.

233. "The Dangers of Versatility." Review of *The Collected Novels of Conrad Aiken. New York Herald Tribune Book Week* 19 January: 1, 8.

234. "The Source of His Singing." Review of *Notes on Some Figures Behind T. S. Eliot* by Herbert Howarth. *Saturday Review* 8 February: 35.

235. "Grand Old Man—Not What He Seems to Be." Review of *The Rector of Justin* by Louis Auchincloss. *Life* 17 July: 11, 18.

236. "Filling in the Map of the Poet's Mind." Review of *The Romantic Image* by Frank Kermode. *New York Herald Tribune Book Week* 19 April: 5, 15.

237. "Poetry of Gide, Joyce and Mann." Review of *Three Philosophical Novelists* by Joseph G. Brennan. *Saturday Review* 23 May: 47.

238. "Hostess with Most of the Great." Review of *Memoirs of Lady*

Ottoline Morrell: 1873–1915, ed. Robert Gathorne-Hardy. *Saturday Review* 20 June: 37, 40.

239. "Appreciating Pritchett." Review of *The Living Novel and Later Appreciations* by V. S. Pritchett. *New Republic* 8 August: 26, 28.

240. "The Solid Center of a Charmed Circle." Review of *Beginning Again* by Leonard Woolf. *New York Herald Tribune Book Week* 13 September: 3.

241. "Spirals of Reason and Fancy." Review of *Selected Letters* by Robert Frost, ed. Lawrance Thompson. *Saturday Review* 5 September: 23–24.

242. "Critic in Search of a Controversy." Review of *The Common Pursuit* by F. R. Leavis. *Saturday Review* 19 December: 40.

243. "John Addington Symonds." Letter to the editor about premature publication of Symonds's diaries. *Times Literary Supplement* 3 December: 1107.

1965

244. Editor. *The Henry James Reader.* New York: Scribner's. Foreword, vii–xiii, and headnotes. Reprinted in Scribner's Hudson River Editions and in Omnibus paperback series.

245. Editor. *Literary History and Literary Criticism.* ACTA of the Ninth Congress, International Federation for Modern Languages and Literature (FILLM), held at New York University, 25 to 31 August 1963. New York: New York University Press. Prefatory Note, vii–xi.

246. "Literary Criticism and Psychoanalysis." *Contemporary Psychoanalysis* 50: 151–163.

247. "Henry James and the *Nation.*" *Nation* (100th anniversary number) 20 September: 237–240.

248. "To a Young Critic." *New York Times Book Review* 13 June: 2. Reprinted in *Page Two.* Ed. Francis Brown. New York: Holt, Rinehart & Winston, 1969. 30–32.

249. "A Proud Papa Speaks Up." Comments on biography. *New York Herald Tribune Book Week* 21 March: 2.

250. Remarks on election to the National Institute of Arts and Letters in 1964. *Proceedings* of the American Academy-National Institute of Arts and Letters 2 ser. 15: 447–449.

251. Review of *Henry James and the Modern Reader* by D. W. Jefferson. *American Literature* 37: 215.

252. "Under Skies Always Shining." Review of *The Art of Autobiography* by Van Wyck Brooks. *New York Herald Tribune Book Week* 21 February: 1, 10–11.

253. "Biography and the Narrator." Review of *The Art of Biography* by Paul Murray Kendall. *New Republic* 6 March: 25–27.

254. "Rage Against the Night." Review of *Taken Care Of: The Autobiography of Edith Sitwell. Saturday Review* 29 May: 34.

255. "The Wolfe Tamer." Review of *The Letters of Maxwell E. Perkins*, ed. John Hall Wheelock. *New York Herald Tribune Book Week* 29 August: 18.

256. "A Good Soldier Himself." Review of *The Letters of Ford Madox Ford*, ed. Richard Ludwig. *Saturday Review* 4 September: 23–24.

257. "Literature's Longest Bus Ride." Review of *Miss MacIntosh, My Darling* by Marguerite Young. *Life* 17 September: 14.

258. "In the Twilight of the Gods." Review of *The Gentle Americans* by Helen Howe. *New York Herald Tribune Book Week* 3 October: 5.

259. "Literature and Life Style." Review of *Beyond Culture* by Lionel Trilling. *Saturday Review* 6 November: 37–38.

260. "Biography Is No Stepchild." Review of *Lives and Letters* by Richard Altick. *New York Times Book Review* 14 November: 5, 78.

261. Review of *Prometheus: The Life of Balzac* by André Maurois. *Bulletin of the Hudson Book Club* no. 162.

262. "Henry James Letters." Letter to the editor about the Gosse-James correspondence. *Times Literary Supplement* 17 June: 523.

263. Reply to a reader explaining why Guedella's *Bonnet and Shawl* is a "spoof." *New York Times Book Review* 12 December: 32.

1966

264. "The Age of the Archive." Delivered 11 October 1965, Paul Horgan presiding. *Monday Evening Papers* no. 7. Middletown, Connecticut: Center for Advanced Studies, Wesleyan University. 1–20.

265. "Hawthorne's Symbolism and Psychoanalysis." *Hidden Patterns*. Ed. Leonard and Eleanor Manheim. New York: Macmillan; London: Collier-Macmillan. 93–111.

266. "Biography: The Question of Form." (The writing of *Roger Fry: A Biography* by Virginia Woolf.) *Friendship's Garland:*

Essays Presented to Mario Praz on His Seventieth Birthday. Ed.
Vittorio Gabrieli. 2 vols. Roma: Edizioni di Storia e Lettera-
tura. 2: 343–360.

267. "Psychoanalysis and Literary Biography." *A Mirror for Modern Scholars.* Ed. Lester A. Beaurline. New York: Odyssey
Press. 103–124.

268. "Henry James, Edith Wharton and Newport." An address delivered at the opening of an exhibition at the Redwood Library and Athenaeum, Newport, Rhode Island, July and August. Pamphlet: Newport. 15–28.

269. "To the Poet of Prose." On the fiftieth anniversary of Henry
James's death. *New York Herald Tribune Book Week* 27 February: 6. Reprinted in *Modern Fiction Studies* 12: 3–6.

270. "I Fear the Crook When Quoting Greek." Review of *The Em-
bezzler* by Louis Auchincloss. *Life* 11 February: 10.

271. "Critic's Choice of Contemporaries." Review of *The Modern
Movement* by Cyril Connolly. *Saturday Review* 2 April: 35.

272. "Biographer's Borrowed Personality." Review of *James Boswell:
The Earlier Years* by Frederick A. Pottle. *Saturday Review*
30 April: 30–31.

273. "Life Without Father." Review of *The Diary of Anais Nin: 1931–
1934,* ed. Gunther Stuhlmann. *Saturday Review* 7 May: 91.

274. "From Notes to Novels." Review of *Told in Letters: Epistolary
Fiction before Richardson* by Robert Adams Day. *Saturday Review* 11 June: 70.

275. "A Hard Journey to Treasure Island." Review of *From Scotland
to Silverado,* ed. James Hart. *Saturday Review* 3 September: 34.

276. "The Price of Peace Was War." Review of *Diaries and Letters:
1930–1939* by Harold Nicolson. *Saturday Review* 3 December: 53–54.

277. Review of *Dante and His World* by Thomas Caldecott Chubb.
Bulletin of the Hudson Book Club. No. 170.

1967

278. *Henry James and the Cosmopolitan Imagination.* Inaugural address by LE as Henry James Professor of English and American Letters at New York University, 13 March 1967. Printed
as a pamphlet. See also item 285.

Editor. *The Bodley Head Henry James.* London: Bodley Head. (See
279–282 below.)

279. Vol. 1. *The Europeans, Washington Square.* Introduction, 7–11.

280. Vol. 2. *The Awkward Age*. Introduction, 7–13.
281. Vol. 3. *The Bostonians*. Introduction, 5–11.
282. Vol. 4. *The Spoils of Poynton*. Introduction, 17–23.
283. "Literature and Biography." *Relations of Literary Study*. Ed. James Thorpe. New York: Modern Language Association. 57–72.
284. "Season of Counterfeit." *The Arts and the Public*. Ed. James E. Miller and Paul D. Herring. Chicago: University of Chicago Press. 75–92.
285. "Henry James: The Americano-European Legend." Another form of item 278, delivered by LE as Visiting Centennial Professor at the University of Toronto (marking Canada's centenary). *University of Toronto Quarterly* 36: 321–334.
286. "Government and the Arts: A Glance Abroad—and Next Door." *Proceedings* of the American Academy-National Institute of Arts and Letters 2 ser. 17: 168–176.
287. "The Biographer and His Double." *Montreal Star* 8 May, Entertainment sec.: 2.
288. "Henry James Looked Ahead." *New York Times Book Review* 12 November: 2, 70–72. Also appears as "A Prophetic Vision of America: Henry James's *The American Scene*." Cincinnati: McGraw Hill, 1969. Code 75600. Lecture recorded at New York University for Sound Seminars.
289. "Portrait of the Artist as a Crab." Review of *Letters of James Joyce*, vols. II and III, ed. Richard Ellmann. *Saturday Review* 21 January: 38.
290. "A Small Dose of Joyce." Review of *A Shorter Finnegans Wake*, ed. Anthony Burgess. *New York Herald Tribune Book Week* 19 February: 12–13.
291. "Poet Prosing." Review of *The Letters of Henry Wadsworth Longfellow*, vols. I and II, ed. Andrew Hilen. *New York Herald Tribune Book Week* 30 April: 16.
292. "She Was an Edwardian Camera." Review of *Pilgrimage* (a reissue with a hitherto unpublished section) by Dorothy Richardson, and *Dorothy Richardson: An Adventure in Self-Discovery* by Horace Gregory. *Saturday Review* 12 August: 29–30.
293. "A Thorn for Triflers and Dictators." Review of *Downhill All the Way* by Leonard Woolf. *Saturday Review* 25 November: 55–56.
294. "High Polish." Review of *Tales of Manhattan* by Louis Auchincloss. *New York Herald Tribune Book Week* 9 April: 14.

295. "The New York Public Library." Letter to the editor. *Times Literary Supplement* 23 February: 147.
296. "Muffled Majesty." Letter to the editor about Dan Jacobson on James and Joyce. *Times Literary Supplement* 9 November: 1061.
297. "Muffled Majesty." Letter to the editor about D. Jacobson's response to item 296. *Times Literary Supplement* 23 November: 1109.

1968

298. Editor. *The American Scene* by Henry James. Bloomington, Indiana: Indiana University Press; London: Hart-Davis. Introduction, vii–xxiv.
299. Editor. *The Portrait of a Lady*. Vol. 5 of *The Bodley Head Henry James*. London: Bodley Head. Introduction, 5–12.
300. "Psychoanalysis and the Creative Arts." *Modern Psychoanalysis*. Ed. Judd Marmor. New York: Basic Books. 626–640 (Chapter 25).
301. "Henry James in Washington Square, Circa 1968." What James might say about the Picasso unveiled at New York University. *New York Times* 9 March: 28. Reprinted in *America at Random*. Ed. Herbert Mitgang. New York: Coward-McCann. 215–218.
302. "Journalism and Mischief." Transcript of a panel presided over by LE under the auspices of the Authors Guild. *American Scholar* 37: 627–641. Reprinted in *The Writer's World*. Ed. Elizabeth Janeway. New York: McGraw-Hill, 1969. 389–415.
303. "Upton Sinclair: 1878–1968." Commemorative tribute for the National Institute of Arts and Letters. *Proceedings* of the American Academy-National Institute of Arts and Letters 2 ser. 19: 121–122.
304. "Henry James's 'Last Dictation.'" *Times Literary Supplement* 2 May: 459–460. Reprinted as "The Deathbed Notes of Henry James." *Atlantic Monthly* June: 103–105.
305. "Henry James and Sir Sydney Waterlow: The Unpublished Diary of a British Diplomat." *Times Literary Supplement* 8 August: 844–845.
306. "Authentic Voice for History Makers." Review of *Lytton Strachey* by Michael Holroyd. *Saturday Review* 27 April: 32–33.
307. "His Last Words: Our Business Is to Wake Up." Review of

The Huxleys by Ronald W. Clark, *The Timeless Moment* by Laura Archer Huxley, and *Aldous Huxley* by John Atkins. *Chicago Tribune-Washington Post Book World* 14 July: 1, 3.

308. Review of *Henry James: A Reader's Guide* by S. Gorley Putt. *Nineteenth-Century Fiction* 22: 410–412.

309. "Moral Refinements." Letter to the editor. *Times Literary Supplement* 11 April: 373.

310. "Henry James's 'Last Dictation.'" Letter to the editor about H. Montgomery Hyde's comments about item 304. *Times Literary Supplement* 23 May: 529.

311. "James's Last Dictation." Letter to the editor about Hyde and item 304. *Times Literary Supplement* 6 June: 597.

312. "Sylvia Plath." Letter to the editor. *Times Literary Supplement* 7 November: 1251.

1969

313. *Henry James: The Treacherous Years, 1895–1901.* The fourth volume of *The Life of Henry James.* Philadelphia: Lippincott; London: Hart-Davis.

Editor. *The Bodley Head Henry James.* London: Bodley Head. (See 314–315 below.)

314. Vol. 6. *What Maisie Knew.* Introduction, 5–10.

315. Vol. 7. *The Wings of the Dove.* Introduction, 5–12.

316. "*The Ambassadors.*" *Landmarks of American Writing.* Ed. Hennig Cohen. New York: Basic Books. 182–193.

317. "Henry James." *Encyclopaedia Brittanica.* 14th ed. Vol. 12: 860–862.

318. "The Heartsease and Rue of Biography." Review of *Biography: The Craft and the Calling* by Catherine Drinker Bowen. *New York Herald Tribune Book Week* 9 February: 4–5.

319. "The Lady Was a Drifter." Review of *Diaries: 1915–1918* by Cynthia Asquith. *Saturday Review* 22 March: 58.

320. Review of *In My Own Time: Memoirs of a Literary Life* by John Lehmann. *Saturday Review* 12 July: 31, 34.

321. Review of *J. Ross Browne: Letters, Journals, Writings,* ed. Lina Browne. *Saturday Review* 19 July: 32.

322. Review of *George du Maurier* by Léonée Ormond. *Saturday Review* 1 November: 43.

323. Review of *Experiments in Form: Henry James's Novels 1896–1901* by Walter Isle. *American Literature* 40: 562–564.

324. "Henry James at Home." Letter to the editor about M. Bell's

criticism of the handling of the Dilke and Wilde cases in *The Life of Henry James* in her review of H. Montgomery Hyde's *Henry James at Home*. *New York Times Book Review* 23 November: 46.

1970

325. *Henry D. Thoreau.* University of Minnesota Pamphlets on American Writers No. 90. Minneapolis: University of Minnesota Press; London: Oxford University Press. Reprinted in *Six American Writers*. Ed. Sherman Paul. Minneapolis: University of Minnesota Press. 160–194. Reprinted in *Dictionary of American Writers*. New York: Scribner's, 1978.

326. Editor. *Stories of the Supernatural* by Henry James. Revised version of item 53, with a new preface and some new headnotes. New York: Taplinger, x–xiv. London: Barnes and Jenkins, 1971.

327. Editor. *Partial Portraits* by Henry James. Ann Arbor: University of Michigan Press. Introduction, v–xvii.

328. Editor. *The Ambassadors.* Vol. 8 of *The Bodley Head Henry James.* London: Bodley Head. Introduction, 5–10.

329. Introduction. *Memoirs of Montparnasse* by John Glassco. Toronto: Oxford University Press; New York: Viking. vii–xi.

330. Address of Presentation to Yasunari Kawataba of the Credentials of Honorary Membership in the Academy Institute [in Honolulu]. *Proceedings* of the American Academy-National Institute of Arts and Letters 2 ser. 20: 29–30.

331. "The Portrait of a Lady." *Studies in* The Portrait of a Lady. Ed. Lyall H. Powers. Charles E. Merrill Studies. Columbus, Ohio: Merrill. 94–105.

332. Review of *The Journey Not the Arrival Matters* by Leonard Woolf. *Saturday Review* 11 April: 34–35.

333. Review of *Memoirs 1885–1967* by André Maurois. *Saturday Review* 22 August: 49–50.

334. Review of *Passages of Thought: Psychological Representation in the American Novel* by Gordon O. Taylor. *American Literature* 42: 267–268.

335. Review of *The Negative Imagination* by Sallie Sears. *Nineteenth-Century Fiction* 25: 116–118.

1971

336. Editor. *The Golden Bowl*. Vol. 9 of *The Bodley Head Henry James*. London: Bodley Head. Introduction, 7–13.
337. "James Joyce." *Brief Lives*. Ed. Louis Kronenberger. Boston: Little Brown. 419–422.
338. "Willa Cather" and "Alice James." *Notable American Women: A Biographical Dictionary*. Ed. Edward T. James. Cambridge: Belknap-Harvard University Press. I: 305–308; and II: 267–268.
339. "The Novel as Poem." *Virginia Woolf: A Collection of Critical Essays*. Ed. Claire Sprague. Twentieth Century Views. Englewood Cliffs, New Jersey: Prentice-Hall. 63–69.
340. "The Mystery of Walden Pond." Inaugural Lecture of the Citizens Chair in English, University of Hawaii, 12 May 1971. Honolulu: University of Hawaii. 9–23.
341. "On the Use of Private Papers." Informal remarks at a dinner meeting of the Academy-Institute, 19 November 1970. *Proceedings* of the American Academy-National Institute of Arts and Letters. 2 ser. 21: 43–60.
342. "Victory for Henry James, Defeated Dramatist?" On the TV adaptation of *The Spoils of Poynton*. *New York Times* 4 April, sec. 2: 17, 24.
343. Review of *Letters of Thomas Mann*, translated and selected by Richard and Clara Winston. *Saturday Review* 27 February: 26–27.
344. Review of *William Dean Howells* by Kenneth S. Lynn. *Saturday Review* 21 August: 24.
345. "Robert Frost." Letter to the editor. *Times Literary Supplement* 21 May: 595.

1972

346. *Henry James: The Master, 1901–1916*. Fifth and final volume of *The Life of Henry James*. Philadelphia: Lippincott; London: Hart-Davis.
347. Editor. *The Princess Casamassima*. Vol. 10 of *The Bodley Head Henry James*. London: Bodley Head. Introduction, 5–12.
348. "A Young Man from the Provinces: Rudyard Kipling and Wolcott Balestier." *Rudyard Kipling: The Man, His Work and His World*. Ed. John Gross. London: Weidenfield & Nicolson. 64–70.

349. "From *Henry James: The Untried Years*." Excerpts from the chapter "An Obscure Hurt" in item 77. *Critics on Henry James*. Ed. J. Don Vann. Coral Gables, Florida: University of Miami Press. 79–82.

350. Memorial Tribute to Harold Morton Landon. *The Century Association Yearbook*. New York: The Association. 299–300.

351. "The Final Chord of the Quintet." On the completion of *The Life of Henry James*. *New York Times Book Review* 6 February: 2, 34–35.

352. "Biography Is . . . " *Today's Education* 61 (December): 16–19.

353. Review of *Anthony Trollope* by James Pope Hennessy. *Saturday Review* 8 July: 59–60.

354. Review of *Henry James: The Vision of France* by Jeanne Delbaere-Garant. *American Literature* 43: 662–663.

355. Review of *Henry James and the Naturalist Movement* by Lyall H. Powers. *Nineteenth Century Fiction* 26: 498–499.

356. "The Jameses." Discussion of Jacques Barzun on the William James letter describing Henry James as "frivolous." *Times Literary Supplement* 13 October: 1226–1227.

357. "The Jameses." Discussion of Lionel Trilling's response to item 356. *Times Literary Supplement* 3 November: 1342.

1973

358. *Literary Biography*. New edition of items 140 and 173. Bloomington, Indiana: Indiana University Press.

359. Editor. *The Devils and Canon Barham* by Edmund Wilson. Ten [Posthumous] Essays. New York: Farrar, Straus & Giroux; London: Macmillan. Foreword, xi–xiv.

360. "Towards a Theory of Literary Psychology." *Interpersonal Explorations in Psychiatry*. Ed. Earl G. Witenberg. New York: Basic Books. 343–354.

361. "Through a Revolving Door." The Franklin Lecture in Science and the Humanities. *Our Secular Cathedrals*. Ed. Taylor Littleton. University, Alabama: University of Alabama Press. 155–179.

362. Various entries in the revised version of *The Reader's Companion to World Literature* (item 126). Ed. Lillian Herlands Hornstein. Revised and updated by LE, L. Hornstein, and Horst Frenz. New York: Mentor-New American Library. Contains entries on *The Ambassadors*, 21; T. S. Eliot, 170–172; William Faulkner, 189–190; Ernest Hemingway, 238–239; Henry

James, 269–272; James Joyce, 277–279; *The Magic Mountain,*
309–310; Thomas Mann, 314–316; Marcel Proust, 433–436;
the Stream-of-Consciousness Novel, 499–500; *The Waste
Land,* 556–557; and Virginia Woolf, 566.

363. "The Future of Humanism." A revised and abridged version
of the address delivered at the eighteenth annual meeting of
the American Academy of Psychoanalysis. *Journal of the
American Academy of Psychoanalysis* 3: 5–20.

364. "The Biographer's Trip to the Past Is Déjà Vu With a Difference." On LE's travels related to his writing *The Life of Henry
James. New York Times* 21 January, sec. 10: 1, 13.

365. "Henry James Flopped as a Playwright, But His Novels Succeed as Dramas." *TV Guide* 24 March: 35, 37–38.

366. "Pilgrim's Way." Review of *Dorothy Richardson: The Genius
They Forgot* by John Rosenberg. *New Statesman* 8 July: 20, 22.

367. "Dorothea's Husbands." Letter to the editor. *Times Literary
Supplement* 11 May: 529.

1974

368. Editor. *Henry James Letters I: 1843–1875.* Cambridge, Massachusetts: Belknap-Harvard University Press; London: Macmillan. Introduction, xiii–xxxvi.

369. Editor. "Daisy Miller" and "The Turn of the Screw." Vol. 11
of *The Bodley Head Henry James.* London: Bodley Head. Introduction, 5–11.

370. Introduction. *Alphabet of the Imagination: Literary Essays* by
Harold Clarke Goddard. Atlantic Highlands, New Jersey:
Humanities Press. i–vi.

371. "Literature and Psychiatry." *American Handbook of Psychiatry
I: The Foundations of Psychiatry.* Ed. Silvano Arieti. New
York: Basic Books. 1024–1033.

372. "Homage to Willa Cather" and panel discussion. *The Art of
Willa Cather.* Ed. Bernice Slote and Virginia Faulkner. Lincoln: University of Nebraska Press. 185–204 and 227–235.

373. "Henry James." *Encyclopaedia of American Biography.* Ed. John
Garraty. New York: Harper & Row. 575–577.

374. "Novel and Camera." *Theory of the Novel: New Essays.* Ed. John
Halperin. New York: Oxford University Press. 177–188.

375. "Henry James as an Art Critic." *American Journal of Art* 6 (2):
4–14. In the definitive edition of *The Life of Henry James*

(item 399), this essay supplanted the chapter "The Art of
Seeing" in *Henry James: The Conquest of London*.
376. "On Being an Educator." *Honolulu Magazine* January: 46–47,
73, 76–77.
377. "Edmund Wilson." Letter to the editor. *Times Literary Supplement* 22 November: 1316.

1975

378. Editor. *The Twenties: From Notebooks and Diaries of the Period*
by Edmund Wilson. New York: Farrar, Straus & Giroux;
London: Macmillan. Editor's Foreword, xi–xvi; "A Portrait
of Edmund Wilson," xvii–xlvi; and extensive headnotes.
Reprinted New York: Bantam, 1976.
379. Editor. *Henry James Letters II: 1875–1883*. Cambridge, Massachusetts: Belknap-Harvard University Press. Introduction, xi–xiv. London: Macmillan, 1978.
380. Introduction. *The Shrouding: Poems* by Leo Kennedy. Ottawa:
The Golden Dog Press. xii–xviii.
381. "When McGill Modernized Canadian Literature." *The McGill
You Knew*. Ed. Edgar Andrew Collard. Don Mills, Ontario:
Longmans Canada. 112–122. (Chapter 12).
382. "Marginal *Keri* and Textual *Chetiv:* The Mystic Novel of
A. M. Klein." *The A. M. Klein Symposium*. Ed. Seymour
Mayne. Ottawa: University of Ottawa Press. 15–29.
383. "The Cult of Inexperience." Inaugural address at the inauguration of Fujio Matsuda as President of the University of Hawaii, 15 March 1975. Honolulu: University of Hawaii. 7–18.
384. "The Madness of Art." The Benjamin Rush Lecture delivered
to the American Psychiatric Association, Anaheim, California, at its 128th annual meeting. *The American Journal of Psychiatry* 132: 1005–1012.
385. "Five Masterpieces for the Centennial." On *Leaves of Grass,
Moby-Dick, Walden, Huckleberry Finn,* and *The Portrait of a
Lady*. *Impulse* (quarterly journal of the East-West Center,
Honolulu), Fall issue.
386. "Walden: The Myth and the Mystery." Abridged and revised
essay version of item 340. *American Scholar* 44: 272–281.
387. "Mirrorings of A. M. Klein." Review of *A. M. Klein: Collected Poems,* ed. Miriam Waddington. *Tamarack Review* 66
(June): 94–98.
388. "At Home in the House of Mirth." Review of *Edith Wharton:*

A Biography by R. W. B. Lewis. Washington Post Book World 31 August: 1.

389. "A Stone into the Mirror." Review of Edith Wharton: A Biography by R. W. B. Lewis. American Scholar 45: 826–830.

390. "Henry James." Letter to the editor on the deletion of a sentence from the English edition of Henry James: The Treacherous Years. Times Literary Supplement 23 May: 567.

391. "On Writing and Writers." Cassette sound recording. Los Angeles: Pacifica Foundation, Pacifica Tape Library.

1976

392. Henry James in the Abbey. Address at the unveiling of a plaque in memory of James in Westminster Abbey. Times Literary Supplement 18 June: 741. Reprinted as a book, Honolulu: Petronium Press. Limited Edition, 26 copies bound and 300 copies soft cover, numbered and signed by the author. Also reprinted in Henry James Review 1: 5–9.

393. Foreword. Who's Who in Henry James by Glenda Leeming. London: Hamish Hamilton. vi–viii.

394. "L. Austin Warren." Teacher and Critic: Essays by and about Austin Warren. Ed. Myron Simon and Harvey Gross. Los Angeles: Plantin Press. 131–134.

395. Reminiscence. The Lonely Hunter: A Biography of Carson McCullers by Virginia Spencer Carr. Garden City, New York: Doubleday. 438, 487.

396. "Angst in the Ibid and the Odyssey." Also known as "Shocking Truths about Peter Rabbit" in other newspapers; a cautionary review of the book on its seventy-fifth anniversary. New York Times 26 December, sec. 4: 9.

397. "The Group and the Salon." Review of Letters of Virginia Woolf I: 1888–1922, The Loving Friends by David Gadd, The Bloomsbury Group by S. P. Rosenbaum, Ottoline at Garsington by Robert Gathorne-Hardy, and Ottoline by Sandra Jobson Darroch. American Scholar 46: 116–124.

398. Reply to Christopher Lohmann and George Arms concerning errors in Henry James Letters I. Nineteenth-Century Fiction 31: 248–251.

1977

399. The Life of Henry James. Definitive edition. The original five volumes have been extensively revised, some chapters

rewritten, others dropped and new ones inserted. Vol. I: 1843–1889; vol. 2: 1890–1916. Harmondsworth: Peregrine-Penguin. Preface to the definitive edition, I: 11–16.

400. Foreword. *Letters on Literature and Politics: 1912–1972* by Edmund Wilson, ed. Elena Wilson. New York: Farrar, Straus, & Giroux; London: Routledge & Kegan Paul. [xiii].

401. Introduction. *Roderick Hudson* by Henry James. Boston: Houghton Mifflin. v–xii.

402. "The Poetics of Biography." Originally an address delivered to the English Association of Great Britain, at Christ's College, Cambridge, in 1973. *Contemporary Approaches to English Studies.* Ed. Hilda Schiff. London: Heinemann; New York: Barnes & Noble. 38–58.

403. Acceptance of the Gold Medal for Biography presented by Malcolm Cowley in behalf of the American Academy and Institute of Arts and Letters. *Proceedings* of the American Academy and Institute of Arts and Letters 2 ser. 27: 24–25.

404. "Thornton Niven Wilder, 1897–1975." Commemorative tribute of the American Academy. *Proceedings* of the American Academy and Institute of Arts and Letters 2 ser. 27: 59–64.

405. Memorial tribute to John Alfred Parsons Millet. *The Century Association Year-Book.* New York: The Association. 226–228.

406. Review of a facsimile edition of *The American* by Henry James, showing his paste-up and revisions for the New York Edition. *Analytical and Enumerative Bibliography* 1: 255–261.

1978

407. *The Life of Henry James.* Reissue of the original five volumes. New York: Discus-Avon. The chapter "A Passion on Olympus" in *The Master* (410–420) contains significant revisions.

408. Foreword. *Israel and the Dead Sea Scrolls* by Edmund Wilson. New York: Farrar, Straus & Giroux. vii–xii.

409. "Portrait of the Artist as an Old Man." *American Scholar* 47: 52–68. Reprinted in *Aging, Death and the Completion of Being.* Ed. David D. Van Tassel. Philadelphia: University of Pennsylvania Press, 1980. 193–214.

410. "Biography: A Manifesto." *Biography: An Interdisciplinary Quarterly* 1 (1): 1–3.

411. "The Worldly Muse of A. J. M. Smith." *University of Toronto Quarterly* 47: 200–213.

412. "The Two Libraries of Henry James." *University of Chicago Library Society Bulletin* 3: 2–8.
413. "From My Journals." *Hawaii Review* 8 (Fall): 6–12.
414. "The Figure under the Carpet." Review of *Conan Doyle* by Ronald Pearsall, and *Rex Stout* by John MacAleer. *American Scholar* 47: 418–421.
415. "Callaghan Cinema." Review of *Close to the Sun Again* by Morley Callaghan. *Canadian Literature* 77: 100–103.

1979

416. *Bloomsbury: A House of Lions.* Philadelphia: Lippincott; London: Hogarth Press. Reprinted New York: Avon, 1980; Harmondsworth: Penguin, 1981.
417. Editor. *The Europeans: A Facsimile of the Manuscript* by Henry James. New York: Howard Fertig. Introduction, vii–xv.
418. Introduction. *Five Legs; Communion: Two Novels* by Graeme Gibson. Toronto: Anansi. 7–15.
419. "The American Artist and His Complex Fate." *American Studies Down Under.* Ed. Norman Harper and Elaine Berry. Proceedings of the sixth and seventh Biennial Conferences of the Australian and New Zealand American Studies Association. Victoria, Australia: Anzasa Press-La Trobe University. 188–203.
420. "The Figure under the Carpet." Keynote lecture at the biography symposium held in the National Portrait Gallery, Washington, 13–14 November 1978. *Telling Lives.* Ed. Marc Pachter. Washington, D.C.: National Portrait Gallery/New Republic Books. 17–34. Reprinted Philadelphia: University of Pennsylvania Press, 1981. A shorter version appeared as "Leon Edel: the Art of Biography: The Figure under the Carpet." *New Republic* 10 February: 25–29.
421. Memorial Tribute to Raleigh Parkin. *The Century Association Year-Book.* New York: The Association. 277–279.
422. "An Interview with Leon Edel on the James Family" by James William Anderson. *Psychohistory Reveiw* 8: 15–22.
423. "Revision of a Chapter from *The Life of Henry James.*" *Psychohistory Review* 8: 23–25.
424. "Triumphs and Symptoms." Review of *The Letters of Virginia Woolf IV,* ed. Nigel Nicolson and Joanne Trautmann. *New York Times Book Review* 25 March: 9.

425. "Polyglot Ping-Pong." Review of *The Nabokov-Wilson Letters*, ed. Simon Karlinsky. *New Republic* 26 May: 33–35.
426. "The Important One." Review of *E. M. Forster: A Life* by P. N. Furbank. *American Scholar* 48: 416–418.
427. "Narcissists Need Not Apply." Review of *Dubin's Lives* by Bernard Malamud. *American Scholar* 49: 130–132.

1980

428. Editor. *Henry James Letters III: 1893–1895*. Cambridge, Massachusetts: Belknap-Harvard University Press; London: Macmillan. Introduction, xiii–xx.
429. Editor. *The Thirties: From Notebooks and Diaries of the Period* by Edmund Wilson. New York: Farrar, Straus & Giroux; London: Macmillan. Editor's Foreword, [xi]–xiii; "Edmund Wilson in the Thirties," xv–xxix. Also published as "Edmund Wilson in the 1930s." *New Republic* 3 May: 29–33.
430. "The Genius and the Injustice Collector. A Memoir of James Joyce." *American Scholar* 49: 467–487.
431. Review of *The Life of Katherine Mansfield* by Anthony Alpers. *New Republic* 1 March: 34–35.
432. "Of Willie's Bondage." Review of *Maugham* by Ted Morgan. *Saturday Review* 15 March: 36–38.
433. Review of *In Pursuit of Coleridge* by Kathleen Coburn. *English Studies in Canada* 6: 252–254.

1981

434. Introduction. *English Hours* by Henry James. Oxford: Oxford University Press. vii–xvi. Also published as "The Three Travellers in English Hours." *Henry James Review* 2: 167–171.
435. "Principia Biographica: Notes for a Preface." *From Smollett to James: Studies in the Novel and Other Essays Presented to Edgar Johnson*. Charlottesville: University of Virginia Press. 1–10.
436. "Biography and the Science of Man." An expanded version of item 435. *New Directions in Biography*. Honolulu: University Press of Hawaii. 1–11.
437. "Literature and Journalism: The Visible Boundaries." *The Callaghan Symposium*. Ed. David Staines. Ottawa: University of Ottawa Press. 7–22.
438. "Happy Birthday to Waller [Barrett]." Tributes on his eightieth birthday. Chapbook. Charlottesville, Virginia (1 June). [17–19].

439. "Chronology of Henry James." *The Portrait of a Lady* by Henry James. Oxford: World Classics-Oxford University Press. xxii–xxiv.
440. "The Nature of Literary Psychology." *Journal of the American Psychoanalytic Association* 29: 447–467.
441. "Henry James Criticizes a Sonnet." Prefatory note to a Henry James letter. *Antaeus 1970–1980* 40/41 (Winter/Spring): 531.
442. "Critical Crotchets." Review of *Lectures on Russian Literature* by Vladimir Nabokov. *New Republic* 23 December: 35–36.
443. "The Very Young Thoreau." Review of *Journal: Vol. 1, 1837–1844* by Henry David Thoreau. *New York Times Book Review* 20 December: 3, 13.

1982

444. *The Stuff of Sleep and Dreams; Experiments in Literary Psychology.* New York: Harper & Row; London: Chatto & Windus. Contains collected essays in literary psychology, including five new essays: "Journey to Vienna" (autobiography), "Stuff of Sleep and Dreams" (Dickens and Coleridge), "Abulia and the Journey to Lausanne" (T. S. Eliot), "Wystan Auden and the Scissors Man," and "Psychopathology of Shem" (Joyce). The other papers are revised and updated versions and sections of these items: "The Nature of Psychological Evidence," items 440, 414, and 360; "The Mystery of Walden Pond," items 325, 340, and 386; "James Joyce," items 430, 39, 152, 289, and 54; "The Madness of Art," item 384; "Portrait of the Artist as an Old Man," item 409; "The Madness of Virginia Woolf," item 416; "Wystan Auden and the Scissors Man," item 402; "A Cave of One's Own," Ch. IV of item 173; "The Critic as Wound-Dresser," Introduction to item 378; "The James Family," item 220, Introduction to item 450, and Introduction to item 326; "The Killer and the Slain," item 63; and "Kipling's American Double," item 348. Reprinted New York: Discus-Avon, 1983.
445. Co-author, with Dan H. Laurence. *A Bibliography of Henry James.* Oxford: Clarendon Press, the Soho Bibliographies 8. 3rd ed. of items 141 and 192, revised with the assistance of James Rambeau. Foreword, 22.
446. Introduction. *Exile's Return* by Malcolm Cowley. New York: The Limited Editions Club. xi–xx. (Title page gives year as 1981, but publication occurred in 1982.)

447. Introduction. *The Outcry* by Henry James. New York: Howard Fertig, v–xiv.
448. Introduction. "The First Hundred Years." *Representative Essays: A Century Celebration, 1882–1982.* Honolulu: The Social Science Association of Hawaii. 1–4.
449. Foreword. *Like One That Dreamed: A Portrait of A. M. Klein* by Usher Kaplan. Toronto: McGraw-Hill Ryerson Limited. 7–12.
450. "Portrait of Alice James." Revised Introduction to reprint of item 230, *The Diary of Alice James.* New York: Penguin-Viking. 1–21.
451. "Symbolic Statement: A Psychological View." *The Symbolist Movement in the Literature of European Languages.* Ed. Anna Balakian. Budapest: Akadémia Kiadó. 661–668.
452. "The Question of Exile." *Asian and Western Writers in Dialogue: New Cultural Identities.* Ed. Guy Amirthanayagam. London: Macmillan. 48–54.
453. "The 'I' in A. J. M. Smith." *Canadian Poetry* 11 (Fall/Winter— Smith Memorial Number): 86–92.
454. "John Glassco (1909–1981) and his Erotic Muse." *Canadian Literature* 93 (Summer): 108–117.
455. "How I Came to Henry James." *Henry James Review* 3 (Spring issue dedicated to LE on his seventy-fifth birthday): 160–164.
456. "Shaping and Telling: The Biographer at Work." Lecture delivered by LE as Distinguished Visiting Humanist at Louisiana State University, Baton Rouge, 29 April 1982. *Henry James Review* 3: 165–175.
457. "Biographer and Subject: Lytton Strachey and Van Wyck Brooks." *Prose Studies* 5: 281–293.
458. "Arthur and Jeannie: In Memoriam." Memorial tribute to the Canadian poet Arthur J. M. Smith (1902–1980) and his wife Jeannie Robbins Smith (1904–1977), read at Michigan State University memorial, 11 April 1981. *Tamarack Review* 83–84 (Winter): 102–105.
459. Presentation to Francis Steegmuller of the Gold Medal for Biography on behalf of the American Academy and Institute of Arts and Letters. *Proceedings* of the American Academy and Institute of Arts and Letters 2 ser. 33: 36–39.
460. "Criticism's Double Agent." Essay-review of *A Mingled Yarn: The Life of R. P. Blackmur* by Russell Fraser. *Grand Street* 1 (2): 143–150.

461. "City Lights." Review of *Whitman: A Life* by Justin Kaplan. *American Scholar* 51: 138–141.

462. "Democratic Vistas." Review of *Visions from San Francisco Bay* by Czeslaw Milosz. *New York Times Book Review* 17 October: 24.

463. "Journals of a Narcissist." Review of *The Book of Concord: Thoreau's Life as a Writer* by William Howarth. *New Republic* 18 October: 16, 35–36.

464. "Well Versed." Review of *The New Oxford Book of Canadian Verse in English,* edited and introduced by Margaret Atwood. *Saturday Night* 97: 61–62.

465. Review of *Psychiatrist of America: The Life of Harry Stack Sullivan* by Helen Swick Perry. *Academy Forum* (American Academy of Psychoanalysis) 26 (Winter): 23–24.

466. "T. S. Eliot and Roger Vittoz." Letter to the editor. *Times Literary Supplement* 17 December: 1394.

1983

467. Editor. *The Forties: From Notebooks and Diaries of the Period* by Edmund Wilson. New York: Farrar, Straus & Giroux. Editor's Foreword, ix–xi; "Edmund Wilson at Middle Age: 'The Bit Between My Teeth,'" xii–xxvi. Introduction also published in *Grand Street* 1.4 (1982): 99–109.

468. Co-editor, with Adeline R. Tintner. "The Library of Henry James, from Inventory, Catalogues, and Library Lists." LE's Introduction, 158–160. *Henry James Review* 4: 158–190.

469. Introduction. *A Little Tour in France* by Henry James. New York: Farrar, Straus & Giroux. ix–xix. Reprinted Penguin.

470. "The Young Warrior in the Twenties." *On F. R. Scott.* Ed. Sandra Djwa and R. St. J. Macdonald. Kingston and Montreal: McGill-Queen's University Press. 6–16.

471. Review of *Alice James: A Biography* by Jean Strouse. *Academy Forum* (of the American Academy of Psychoanalysis) 27 (Spring): 12–13.

472. "The Pleasures of Proust." Review of *Marcel Proust: Selected Letters,* ed. Philip Kolb. *Washington Post Book World* 5 June: 1, 6–7.

473. "The Man in the Woman." Review of *Willa: The Life of Willa Cather* by Phyllis C. Robinson. *New Republic* 14 November: 34–36.

474. "Bloomsbury and La Dolce Vita." Review of *Vita: The Life of*

Vita Sackville-West by Victoria Glendinning. *Washington Post Book World* 27 November: 1, 14.

475. Review of *Lytton Strachey* (1880–1932) *biographie et critique d'un critique et biographer* (2 vols.) by Gabriel Merle. *Études Anglaises* 36: 487–488.

476. "Journals and Notebooks." Letter to the editor about R. W. B. Lewis's review of item 467. *New York Times Book Review* 10 July: 37.

477. "DeRussy Precious." Letter to the editor protesting proposals to sell potential parkland Fort DeRussy in Honolulu. Honolulu *Advertiser* 10 October.

478. Reply to a letter to the editors about item 473. *New Republic* 12 December: 4.

1984

479. *Writing Lives: Principia Biographica.* New York/London: Norton. Revised and rewritten version of items 140, 173, and 358, *Literary Biography.* The following chapters are revised and updated versions and sections of these items: "Introduction," item 410; "The New Biography," items 435 and 436; "Dilemmas," Chapter I of item 173; "Boswell," various sections of item 173, and item 272; "Subject," Chapter I of item 173 and item 457; "Transference," item 457; "Archives," item 264; "Quest," Chapter II of item 173; "Criticism," Chapter III of item 173; "Psychoanalysis," items 440, 360, and 196; "Myth," item 420, pp. 25–28 and 47–65 of item 444, and item 261; "Narratives," Chapter V of item 173 ("Time") and item 266; "Writing the Quintet," item 351; and "Journeys," item 364.

480. Editor. *Henry James Letters IV: 1895–1916.* Cambridge, Massachusetts/London: Belknap-Harvard University Press. Introduction, xii–xxxi.

481. Editor. With the assistance of Mark Wilson. *Literary Criticism: Essays on Literature, American Writers, English Writers* by Henry James. New York: Library of America. Chronology (by LE), 1415–1429; Note on the Texts, 1430–1443; Notes, 1445–1453.

482. Editor. With the assistance of Mark Wilson. *Literary Criticism: French Writers, Other European Writers, Prefaces to the New York Edition* by Henry James. New York: Library of Amer-

ica. Chronology (by LE), 1343–1357; Note on the Texts, 1359–1370; Notes, 1371–1381.

483. "Walter Berry and the Novelists: Proust, James, and Edith Wharton." *Nineteenth-Century Fiction* 38 (4—special issue dedicated to Blake Nevius): 514–528.

484. "The Klein-Joyce Enigma." *Journal of Canadian Studies* 19 (2—issue devoted to "A. M. Klein's Montreal"): 27–33.

485. "The Biographer and Transference." *Biography* 7: 283–291.

486. "Why the Dramatic Arts Embrace Henry James." *New York Times* 4 March, sec. 2: 1, 23.

487. "My Good Green Place." *New York Times Magazine* 18 March: 85, 117–122.

488. "The Artist Ages." Excerpt from an address delivered at the centenary of the Montefiore Medical Center, Rockefeller University, 25 October. *New York Times* 28 October: E24.

489. "Some Memories of Octavia Wilberforce." *Charlestown Newsletter* (of the Charlestown Trust, Richmond, Surrey), 8 (August): 14–17.

490. "I Wish I'd Been There"—"Thoreau's Walden." Reply to question put to authors and scholars: "What is the one scene or incident in American history you would like to have witnessed—and why?" *American Heritage* 36 (December): 31.

491. "Simenon's Own Case." Review of *Intimate Memoirs* by Georges Simenon. *Washington Post Book World* 8 July: 1–2.

492. Review of *The Diary of Virginia Woolf V: 1936–1941,* ed. Anne Olivier Bell, and *The Letters of Vita Sackville-West to Virginia Woolf,* ed. Louise DeSalvo and Mitchell Leaska. *Washington Post Book World* 9 December: 1, 11.

493. "The Beautiful and the Damned." Review of *Invented Lives: F. Scott and Zelda Fitzgerald* by James Mellow. *New Republic* 3 December: 37–38.

1985

494. *Henry James. A Life.* One-volume abridgement by Catherine Carver of *The Life of Henry James.* The edition, based on item 399, is minutely revised by LE, with several new chapters and rewrites of some of the old, and a number of new passages inserted. Revisions indicated in the notes to the volume. New York: Harper & Row.

495. Introduction. "Biographical Background of Fitzgerald's Ru-

baéiyaét" by Robert B. Martin, Inaugural Address of the Citizens Chair. Honolulu: University of Hawaii. 3–5.

496. "The Artist in Old Age." *The Hastings Center Report* 15 (2): 38–43.

497. "Biography and the Sexual Revolution." *New York Times Book Review* 24 November: 13–14.

498. "Myth and Media: The Fractured Imagination." *Black Warrior Review* 2 (Spring): 25–33.

499. "The Art of Biography I." First interview in this periodical on biography, conducted by Jeanne McCulloch. *Paris Review* 98: 156–207.

500. "Edmund Wilson in the Fifties: *La Douceur de la Vie.*" Excerpt from introduction to item 505. *Paris Review* 98: 208–217.

501. "Letters between Two Masters." Review of *The Letters of Flaubert and Turgenev*, ed. Barbara Beaumont. *New Criterion* 4 (December): 69–74.

502. "Correcting Wrongs." Letter to the editor on a recall election in Honolulu. *Honolulu Advertiser* 22 October: A-11.

1986

503. Foreword. *The Museum World of Henry James* by Adeline R. Tintner. Ann Arbor, Michigan: UMI Research Press. xvii–xxi.

504. Introduction. *My Friend, My Father* by Stanley Burnshaw. New York: Oxford University Press. vii–xii.

505. "Stalking the Literary Past." Review of *Footsteps: Adventures of a Romantic Biographer* by Richard Holmes. *Washington Post Book World* 5 January: 5.

Forthcoming

506. Editor. *The Fifties* by Edmund Wilson. To be published by Farrar, Straus & Giroux.

507. Co-editor, with Lyall H. Powers. *The Complete Notebooks of Henry James*. To be published by Oxford University Press.

508. "The Lost and Found Generation." Keynote address to the European American Studies Association meeting, Rome, spring 1984. To appear in the *Proceedings*.

509. "Memories of the Montreal Group." E. J. Pratt Lecture delivered at Memorial University of Newfoundland, Canada, 1984. To appear as a publication of this university.

510. "Phoenix and Sepulchre: Henry James in Venice." Message to a conference on James held in Venice, November 1985. To be published in the *Proceedings*.
511. "The Imagination in Action." In *Proceedings* of the Conference on Creativity and Science, Windward Community College, Oahu, Hawaii, 23–24 March 1985. A revised version of this paper is scheduled to appear in a festschrift for Professor Betty Flower of the University of Pennsylvania.

Undated Items

512. "Leon Edel Discussing Henry James." Cassette sound recording.
513. "The Art of Biography." Cassette sound recording. Los Angeles: Pacifica Foundation, Pacifica Tape Library.

Translated Writings

Arabic

The Psychological Novel. Item 103. Trans. Mahmoud As-Samrah. Beirut, Lebanon, 1960.
Literary Biography. Item 358. Trans. Sidki Hattab. Cairo: Moassaset El Halaby, 1973.

Bengali

Henry James. Item 178. Calcutta: Asia Publishing Company, 1965.

French

Journal d'Alice James. Item 230. Traduit de l'Américain par Marie Tadié. Introduction et notes de Léon Edel. Paris: Edition des Femmes.

German

"Literatur und Biographie." Item 283. Trans. Marianne Burneleit. *Interdisziplinare Perspektiven der Literatur*. Ed. Helmut Jensen. Stuttgart: Ferdinand Enke Verlag, 1977. 72–89.

Japanese

The Modern Psychological Novel. Item 172. With a special introduction by the author for the Japanese edition. Translation rights by Hyoron Sha through Orion Shoji. Tokyo: 1959.

Korean
Henry James. Item 178. English Literary Society of Korea, 1965.
   English and Korean texts.

Portuguese
Henry James. Item 178. Trans. Alex Severino. *Escritores Norte
   Americanos*. Sao Paolo, Brazil: Livraria Martins Editora,
   1963.

Spanish
Henry James. Item 178. *Tres Escritores Nortamericanos*. V. 2. Trans.
   Angela Figuera. Madrid: Editorial Gredos, 1961. 55–96.
"El Ultimo Accorde del Quinteto." Item 351. Trans. Aida Far-
   jardo. *Sin Nombre* (San Juan, Puerto Rico) 3.2 (1972): 84–90.

Urdu
Henry James. Item 178. [Undated. Translator not named.] [p. 2] has
   statement: "This is an authorized Urdu translation of *Henry
   James* by Leon Edel. Copyright 1960 by Leon Edel. Pub-
   lished by the University of Minnesota Press, Minneapolis.
   First Urdu Edition. Printed in Pakistan."

INDEX

Biography (*continued*)
  chronological approach to, 76
  Edel's achievements in, 3–4
  Edel's technique/approach in,
    25–33, 37–40, 66–68, 105
  flashback an innovation in, 33
  "new biography," 3, 40, 56, 61, 69,
    70n6
  psychology and fiction employed
    in, 3, 65–66, 68, 84, 88
  scholarly uses of, 25–30
  Strachey's influence on, 65–66
  truth vs. art in, 59–62, 69, 91, 105
  Virginia Woolf's essays on, 59,
    61–62
  writings by Edel on (excluding re-
    views of individual biographies),
    203 (no. 107), 204 (no. 109), 205
    (no. 128), 206 (no. 140), 207
    (nos. 147, 155), 208 (no. 173),
    210 (no. 193), 211 (no. 196), 214
    (no. 249), 215 (nos. 252, 253,
    260, 266), 216 (no. 267), 217
    (nos. 283, 287), 219 (no. 318),
    222 (nos. 352, 358), 223 (no.
    364), 226 (nos. 402, 403, 410),
    227 (no. 420), 228 (no. 436),
    230 (nos. 456, 457, 459), 232
    (no. 479), 233 (nos. 485, 495),
    234 (nos. 497, 499, 505), 235
    (no. 513)
Blake, William
  influence on Ginsberg of, 118, 123
Bloomsbury
  biographies, 11–12, 16, 17, 32–33,
    65–71
  Edel's writings on, 32–33, 66–68,
    225 (no. 397), 227 (no. 416), 231
    (no. 474)
Boon incident, 23
Bosanquet, Theodora, *Henry James at
  Work,* 5
Boswell, James, 21, 22, 216 (no. 272),
  232 (no. 479)
Brown, John
  Emerson inspired by, 89
Buddhism
  Beat interest in, 116, 117, 118, 123
Burne-Jones, (Edward), 29
Burroughs, William, 106–107, 108,
  109, 116, 117, 118, 119, 120, 121,
  122, 123
  his interest in crime, 111, 112

  his use of drugs, 107, 108, 110, 112,
    113–114
  kills his wife, 113
  life of, 110–114
  literary style of, 114
  Works:
    "The Autobiography of a Wolf," 111
    Junkie, 113
    Naked Lunch, 109, 113, 122
Butler, John S.
  Katherine Prince correspondence
    with, 139–140

Cameron, Elizabeth, 98–99
Capote, Truman
  on Beats, 122
Cargill, Oscar, 39, 121
Carlyle, (Thomas), 80
  on the "unconscious," 82
Carr, Lucien, 120
Carrington (friend of Strachey), 67
Cassady, Neal, 115–116
Cetaceans. *See* Dolphins and whales
Cherokee Indians, 89
Child-rearing
  adult (parental) dereliction in, 37,
    41–44, 47–48, 50–52
  American vs. European, 45–46, 56
  Awkward Age a comprehensive
    statement on, 44, 54–56
  French way of, 44–47
  Henry James Sr. on, 45
  Henry James's own, 37–38, 40,
    45–46
  James's (unstated) theory of, 36–37,
    40–41, 56
  Maisie indicts neglect of, 47–48,
    50–52
Chimpanzees
  and language controversy, 185–187,
    190n16–17
Chomsky, Noam, 190n19
Cold War
  and Beat Generation, 108–109
Coleridge, (Samuel Taylor), 80
Communication Research Institute,
  Virgin Islands, 180
Consciousness/Awareness
  in cetaceans, 178–179, 180, (190n9)
  in James's adolescents, 53–56
  See also Unconscious
Cooper, James Fenimore, Home as
  Found, 27

Notes on Contributors

Gay Wilson Allen is Emeritus Professor of English at New York University. He has published biographies of Walt Whitman, William James, and Ralph Waldo Emerson. His *Waldo Emerson* received the *Los Angeles Times* award for best biography of the year and the Lowell Prize of the Modern Language Association.

Gavan Daws is Research Professor of Pacific History in the Institute of Advanced Studies, Australian National University. Author of several books about Hawaii and the Pacific, including biographical studies, he is a fellow of the Australian Academy of Humanities. He also makes documentary films and has written for the stage.

Howard Fertig is a graduate of New York University. He has been an assistant editor of *Commentary*, literary secretary to Norman Mailer, an editor at Alfred A. Knopf, Inc., and chief editor of the paperback division of Grosset and Dunlap, Inc. Since 1966 he has been editor-in-chief and president of Howard Fertig, Inc., a publishing house in New York City.

Gloria G. Fromm is Professor of English at the University of Illinois at Chicago and author of *Dorothy Richardson: A Biography*, published in 1977. Her essays on such modern literary figures as Proust and Joyce, Wells, Bennett, Virginia Woolf, Rose Macaulay and Jean Rhys have appeared in *Kenyon Review, Novel, The New Criterion* and other journals. She is currently editing Dorothy Richardson's letters.

Sir Rupert Hart-Davis (knighted 1967), born 1907, was educated at Eton and Oxford. In publishing from 1929 (director of Jonathan Cape 1933–40), he started his own firm in 1946 and retired in 1964. He has published *Hugh Walpole*, a biography, *The Arms of Time*, a memoir, edited *The Letters of Oscar Wilde*, and works by George Moore, Max Beerbohm, Siegfried Sassoon, William Plomer and Arthur Ransome.

William Laskowski Jr., a candidate for the Ph.D. in English literature at the University of Illinois at Chicago, is writing his dissertation on George Orwell and English prose traditions.

Harvena Richter teaches creative writing at the University of New Mexico, has published a book on Virginia Woolf (dedicated to Leon Edel), two novels, short fiction, poetry, and criticism. She has just completed a book for Princeton University Press on her father's writing notebooks (Conrad Richter).

Muriel G. Shine, Professor of English at Pace University, New York, has particular interest in nineteenth-century English and American literature. Her book, *The*

Fictional Children of Henry James, is a study of childhood and adolescence in the novels and tales of Henry James.

Jean Strouse is the author of *Alice James, A Biography* (Houghton Mifflin, 1980) and is currently writing a life of J. Pierpont Morgan. Her work as a literary critic and freelance writer has appeared in *The New Yorker, The New York Review of Books, The New York Times, Newsweek,* and other publications.

Adeline Tintner, author of *The Museum World of Henry James* and more than 200 articles about art and literature, is on the editorial boards of the *Henry James Review* and the *Journal of Pre-Raphaelite Studies.* She is also a founding member of the Society for the Study of Narrative Literature.

John Tytell is Professor of English at Queens College. He is the author of *Naked Angels: The Lives and Literature of the Beat Generation* (McGraw Hill, 1976), which is being re-released by Grove Press in 1986. His screenplay, "Kerouac's America," was produced in 1984. His work has appeared in *The American Scholar, Partisan Review,* and *Vanity Fair,* and he is now completing a biography of Ezra Pound.

Viola Hopkins Winner is the author of *Henry James and the Visual Arts* (1970), originally a dissertation of which Leon Edel was adviser, and an editor of *The Letters of Henry Adams* (1982–86). Her work in progress is a book-length study of Henry Adams in Washington.